The Economy and the Vote

Economic Conditions and Elections in Fifteen Countries

WOUTER VAN DER BRUG

University of Amsterdam

CEES VAN DER EIJK

University of Nottingham

MARK FRANKLIN

European University Institute, Florence

CAMBRIDGE
UNIVERSITY PRESS

CAMBRIDGE UNIVERSITY PRESS
Cambridge, New York, Melbourne, Madrid, Cape Town, Singapore, São Paulo

Cambridge University Press
32 Avenue of the Americas, New York, NY 10013-2473, USA

www.cambridge.org
Information on this title: www.cambridge.org/9780521863742

First published 2007

Printed in the United States of America

A catalog record for this publication is available from the British Library.

Library of Congress Cataloging in Publication Data
Brug, Wouter van der.
The economy and the vote : economic conditions and elections in fifteen countries /
Wouter van der Brug, Cees van der Eijk, Mark Franklin.
p.   cm.
Includes bibliographical references and index.
ISBN-13: 978-0-521-86374-2 (hardback)
ISBN-10: 0-521-86374-0 (hardback)
ISBN-13: 978-0-521-68233-6 (pbk.)
ISBN-10: 0-521-68233-9 (pbk.)
1. Voting – Economic aspects.   2. Elections – Economic aspects.
I. Eijk, C. van der.   II. Franklin, Mark N.   III. Title.
JF1001.B745   2007
324.9–dc22   2006030222

ISBN   978-0-521-86374-2 hardback
ISBN   978-0-521-68233-6 paperback

The Economy and the Vote
Economic Conditions and Elections in Fifteen Countries

Economic conditions are said to affect election outcomes, but past research has produced unstable and even contradictory findings in this respect. This book argues

He founded the Public Opinion and Participation Section of the European Union Studies Association, has been a director of the European Election Studies project since 1987, and has served on the editorial boards of six journals.

Contents

Preface

Science is the product not only of reason, but also of sentiments and passions. This particular book is the offspring of two opposite sentiments: disenchantment and enthusiasm. Disenchanted though we were with much of the literature in the field of economic voting, our enthusiasm derived from newly emerging possibilities for systematic comparative studies of electoral processes.

Many of the publications in the field of economic voting are highly sophisticated in their modeling and analyses of empirical data, yet – in our view – often highly implausible when approached from first principles in the light of straightforward observations of the political world, and in the light of what we believed we had learned from our own earlier comparative analyses of voters and elections. As a case in point, analysts commonly group parties in two categories, those in government and those in opposition. This crude dichotomy obviously does not reflect the kind of choice that voters are faced with in multiparty systems. Moreover, when analyzing the effects of "the" economy on voters, categorizing the world in this way has the effect of discarding and disregarding all sorts of other characteristics of parties that are likely to contribute to party choice. Moreover, election results show that, more often than not, the electoral fortunes of coalition partners diverge considerably, thus calling into doubt the simple logic that government parties are rewarded or punished for the way the economy performed under their stewardship. In Chapters 1 and 2, we set out the common approaches to the study of economic voting and why we find them in many ways unconvincing.

The other sentiment that can claim parentage to this book is our enthusiasm for and fascination with the possibilities for systematic comparative electoral studies that have been generated by the European Election Studies project (see also Chapter 3 and Appendix A). The electorates of the member states of the European Union (EU) have now been surveyed a number of times in the immediate aftermath of European elections. These surveys are of importance not only for studying European integration and the peculiarities of second-order national elections, but also for comparative electoral research in general. Their high degree of comparability – far surpassing that of national election studies that differ widely in contents and operationalization, even in a single country over time – allows us to make optimal use of the natural "laboratory" that the EU and its member states provide for research. Each country offers a different context, characterized by its own parties, its own electoral system, its own government composition, and, in spite of increasing convergence, its unique economic conditions. In important respects, this comparability of information encompasses not only different countries, but also different election years, thus providing unique opportunities for simultaneous comparison over time and space.

The course of our disenchantment and enthusiasm found its confluence in the possibilities offered by the European Election Studies project for assessing whether our misgivings about existing approaches to economic voting were justified and for testing a different approach. Both required a wider variety of contexts and a more extensive measurement of voters' party preferences and choices than are common in many studies. And both were provided by the European Election Studies project. Indeed, at the end of the day, we feel that we can now do more than just formulate misgivings about conventional approaches. We can specify where, when, and why they will provide inconsistent, unstable, or outright misleading results. At the same time, we can demonstrate with our own approach that the economy indeed affects the behavior of voters, but in more subtle and variegated ways than have been proposed thus far, and with more sensitivity to political and contextual circumstances than citizens are usually given credit for.

This book could not have been written without the extraordinarily rich data that have been generated by the European Election Studies workgroup. We are grateful to our colleagues in that endeavor for their friendship and academic stimulus, but also for indulging our claims on scarce questionnaire space for the extensive measurement of voters' preferences and choice. Some of the analyses in this book were presented at the annual conference of the American Political Science Association in Washington, DC, in 2000 and at three workshops of the European Consortium of Political Research (ECPR): Canterbury (2001), Turin (2002), and Edinburgh (2003). We are grateful to virtually all the panelists and workshop members for comments and suggestions that have been immensely helpful in sharpening our thinking. At other occasions too, many colleagues have provided us with valuable feedback; we would like to express our gratitude to Paolo Bellucci, André Blais, Ray Duch, Orit Kedar, Martin Kroh, Bob Luskin, Tony Mughan, Philip van Praag, Hermann Schmitt, Randy Stevenson, Jacques Thomassen, Bernard Wessels, and Paul Whiteley. Special mention has to be made of our gratitude to Michael Marsh and Eric Browne, whose incisive comments were of strategic importance, and to Guy Whitten, who provided the data on clarity of responsibility. While finalizing this book, Wouter van der Brug spent one year as a Fellow at the Netherlands Institute for Advanced Study in the Humanities and Social Sciences (NIAS). He benefited enormously from its facilities and from the support of its staff. We must also thank two anonymous referees who provided invaluable comments on an earlier draft of the book, as well as Wenonah Barton for her assistance in preparing the manuscript in its final form.

We want, finally, to acknowledge the importance to this book of a scholar who is probably unaware of his contribution but who nevertheless crucially influenced our own thinking in this and earlier work. Anthony Downs demonstrated as long ago as 1957 that modeling voter choice and election results requires the distinction between voters' propensity to support parties ("utility," in his terminology), on the one hand, and their choices on the other. Although citations of his work have become ubiquitous, this distinction has been largely ignored, forgotten, or plainly not understood by students of voters and elections. His distinction lies at the heart of the approach that we advocate in this book, and we gladly acknowledge our indebtedness.

July 2006
Wouter van der Brug (Amsterdam, the Netherlands)
Cees van der Eijk (Nottingham, UK)
Mark Franklin (Florence, Italy)

Introduction

Conventional wisdom asserts that economic conditions are closely linked to election outcomes. Bill Clinton turned this conventional wisdom into a cliché when, as a candidate in the 1992 American presidential election, he had his campaign staff put up a banner that hung across their campaign headquarters emblazoned with the words "It's the economy, stupid!" This conventional wisdom is supported by much academic research. At least since the 1930s, voters in a variety of democratic countries have tended to hold governments accountable for bad economic times, reducing their support for parties holding government office in conditions of high unemployment or inflation or of low economic growth (Tufte 1978; Chrystal and Alt 1981; Hibbs 1977; Fair 1988; Lewis-Beck 1988; Markus 1988, 1992; Erikson 1989; Mackuen, Erikson, and Stimson 1992; Nadeau and Lewis-Beck 2001; Dorussen and Taylor 2002). These general findings hold whether the effects of economic conditions are modeled in terms of votes for government parties (generally referred to as "vote functions") or in terms of government standing (generally referred to as "popularity functions").

But it is clear that the economy does not always determine either government popularity or vote shares. In the American presidential election of 2000, Al Gore failed to win decisively as the incumbent party standard bearer despite a booming economy. In the Netherlands in 2002, all three members of the governing coalition lost votes in similarly excellent economic conditions. In Britain and Ireland in 1997, ruling parties also failed to win reelection despite booming economies. And in Britain in 1992, a ruling party succeeded in winning reelection despite an economy that was languishing. Turning to government popularity, it is clear that this often reflects voter concerns that go far beyond the economy. Support for George Herbert Walker Bush reached over 90 percent in the months immediately following the first Gulf War, despite a languishing economy.

These are exceptional cases, of course. The academic literature cited earlier has established that the conventional wisdom holds more often than not. However, even when governments as a whole gain or lose in accord with expectations, the individual political parties that are members of governing coalitions seldom find either their popularity or their vote shares moving in step. With coalition governments, it is often the case that some members of the coalition lose votes in an election, while others gain. The same goes for the major opposition parties in a multiparty system. Some of these may appear to benefit from a slow economy, but others do not.

Moreover, while government fortunes may appear more often than not to respond to economic conditions in general, there are numerous instances of countries with endemically high unemployment (for example, Spain, Greece, and Portugal) or persistently stagnant economies (for example, Japan) where these conditions did not lead citizens to vote ruling parties out of office. Indeed, from 1989 to 1999, in countries that are members of the European Union, the level of unemployment was repeatedly found in survey research to be viewed by voters as by far the most important problem facing their countries. Yet in all that time, few, if any, election outcomes were reported as having been determined by a government's failure or success in tackling high levels of unemployment.

Why are some election outcomes apparently the result of economic conditions, while others are not? Why are some governing parties apparently hurt more than others by bad economic conditions, and why do some opposition parties appear to gain while others do not? Why do some sorts of economic conditions appear to determine election outcomes, while others (at least at certain times) do not? In this book we address these questions.

Parties compete for votes and in so doing provide the means for voters to hold governments accountable. Many voters see the management of the economy as one of the prime responsibilities of government. So an understanding of how voters react to parties in the light of economic conditions illuminates a central feature of democratic governance. Moreover, these questions have an importance to political science that goes beyond their obvious everyday relevance. Even though past research has established a general relationship between economic conditions and election outcomes, the evidence has been by no means conclusive and has given rise to a series of protracted debates in the literature, none of which shows much sign of convergence. This is the case for almost any topic that students of economic voting are concerned with. For example, we do not really know whether voters hold governments responsible for the general economic situation in their country or whether they are more immediately concerned about their own financial situation (whether economic voting is sociotropic or egocentric). Nor do we know with confidence whether voters respond retrospectively (holding governments responsible for past successes and failures) or prospectively (choosing parties for their economic expertise and policies) to economic conditions. Moreover, the modeled forms of vote and popularity functions differ considerably – within as well as between countries – as do the estimated effects of changes in these conditions.

The instabilities in the results of different studies made the editors of a recent symposium exclaim: "We all prefer to think that the instability is *apparent* only. That is, it is due to something we are missing or doing wrongly – if we could just find the 'trick', everything would be well" (Lewis-Beck and Paldam 2000: 114).

We do not presume to claim that we have found the "trick" that makes everything well, but we do believe that we have taken a major step in the right direction. In this book we argue that, indeed, past researchers have been doing something wrong. We assert that most existing studies in the field of economic voting *mis-specify* the dependent variable in their analyses and that many of the instabilities in the findings are a consequence of this mis-specification. Studies at both the aggregate and the individual levels have generally relied on a very crude distinction between the standing of (or votes for) governing parties and the standing of (or votes for) opposition parties. Obviously, this crude distinction does not adequately describe the choice process in multiparty systems. Anderson (1995) and Stevenson (2002) do distinguish between parties that are members of a coalition government, but neither of these authors distinguishes between opposition parties, thus still failing to fully specify the choice process. In Chapter 1, we will review the literature and explain how and why the customary specification of the dependent variable can be expected to yield invalid estimates of the effects of economic conditions.

Past studies of economic voting have looked in detail at variations across political systems and at variations across voters – see the outline of the edited volume by Dorussen and Taylor (2002), who organize their book around this distinction. Our study, by contrast, while conducting its analyses at the level of individual voters, explicitly focuses on *competition between parties*. We analyze the effects of economic conditions on electoral support for each of a country's parties, treating government/opposition status as a variable that helps us to understand the different impact that the same economic conditions have on different parties. Government versus opposition status is, however, not the only characteristic of parties that we distinguish; we also look at their size, ideological complexion, and whether they control government ministries with responsibility for economic affairs. We will show – by estimating aggregate election outcomes on the basis of our individual level models – that particular opposition parties as well as particular government parties are affected very differently by improving or deteriorating economic conditions. We will even show instances of some governing parties gaining votes (at the expense of other governing parties) as a result of a worsening economy.

Because different countries have governments that are composed of very different types of parties (and parties that find themselves in very different competitive situations vis-à-vis each other), similar economic developments can have very different implications for individual voting decisions (and hence for election outcomes) in one country than in another. Such developments can even have different implications within one country at one election than at another. We will show that the character and competitive situation of individual parties make a big difference to the consequences of economic developments. It is no wonder, therefore, that highly unstable findings are reported in studies that take no account of distinctions between parties.

Another source of instability in the findings of past studies is that many of them were conducted in venues that contained a great deal of nonrandom "noise." Studies of vote choice at the time of an election need to take account of all the factors that influence election outcomes, so that effects of the economy can be isolated after having controlled for everything else. The problem here is that we simply do not know what all the factors are that influence election outcomes. Although we have a fairly good understanding of what makes people vote the way they do, when estimates derived from this knowledge are aggregated to the level of the election outcome we do not, in general, reproduce the results, in terms of vote shares for different parties, that occurred empirically (Anker 1992; Dalton and Wattenberg 1993; Erikson 2002). We understand voting behavior in general, but the track record of political scientists in predicting the outcomes of specific elections is almost as bad as their track record in establishing consistent effects of economic conditions. Specific election outcomes appear to be determined not only by general forces but by all sorts of factors, such as campaign slogans, political scandals, and candidate traits that may be specific to particular elections. So, our knowledge is by no means sufficiently detailed to serve as a basis for controlling all the factors that could contaminate our findings – especially if the effects we are looking for are rather small.

We believe that we have found a venue for studying economic effects on election outcomes that is not subject to nearly so much nonrandom noise as the conventional venue of voting choice at national elections. Specifically, we study voter behavior not at the time of national elections, but rather at the time of elections to the European Parliament. For reasons to be discussed more fully in Chapter 2, our findings nevertheless allow us to draw conclusions about voters' actual choices in national elections. It has been established in past research (van der Eijk and Franklin 1996) that the low saliency of European Parliament elections provides scant stimulus that would divert voters from their baseline national party preferences. Elections to the European Parliament are thus not genuinely Europe-wide elections but rather what have been termed "second order national elections" (Reif and Schmitt 1980; Reif 1984). For that reason, what we see at these elections are the same effects that are relevant in national elections but uncontaminated by the idiosyncrasies of national election campaigns. Because we study voters resident in fifteen different countries at three points in time – 33,000 of them in all – our study has the power to evaluate effects that are expected to be quite small. We will enlarge on our research design in later Chapters.

Our design also enables us to address another problem arising from past research, which is that the main finding from aggregate-level studies (that good economic conditions benefit incumbent government parties) has never been unambiguously replicated at the individual level. Individual-level studies (Fiorina 1978; Kinder and Kiewiet 1979, 1981; Lewis-Beck 1988; Nadeau and Lewis-Beck 2001) generally assess the effect of respondents' assessments of economic conditions on their support for a government or an opposition party. But these assessments of economic conditions themselves turn out to be strongly affected by preferences for the governing party or parties (Wlezien, Franklin, and Twiggs 1997; Bartels 2002; Duch and Palmer 2002). Only for the United States, looking at a sequence of up to ten presidential elections, has evidence been found for an effect of real economic conditions on individual voting decisions (Markus 1988, 1992; Nadau and Lewis-Beck 2001).[1] A major objective of this book is to determine the effect of objective economic conditions on individual-level vote choice across a much larger number of electoral contexts (we study forty-two contexts in all).

Plan of the Book

In Chapter 1, we will review the literature on economic voting and develop our argument regarding why and how past studies mis-specify the choice process, pointing out how this mis-specification will in many cases have biased the results of such studies. We show how a focus on political parties as the primary objects of electoral contestation enables us to examine the process by which individuals make their electoral choices – a process that must be properly specified if the role of economic conditions is to be discovered – and how a failure to do so inevitably results in unstable and sometimes incoherent findings. In order to be able to focus on political parties, in this book we adopt a

---

[1] These studies are limited in scope by the small number of different data points relating to economic conditions, resulting in the use of only one economic indicator – personal income. The analyses also employ a very underspecified model of individual vote choice for reasons that are not clear. We will give more space to this model in Chapter 1.

two-stage model of vote choice based on the work of Anthony Downs (1957) that will be introduced in detail in Chapter 2. In that chapter, we also explain how this model meets the conditions set out earlier so as to remove or at least ameliorate the various problems enumerated in Chapter 1. We believe that this model has a good chance of arriving at stable and consistent estimates for the effects of economic conditions. In Chapter 3, we will describe in greater detail the theoretical expectations that govern our choice of variables for the model, the hypotheses that we derive from this theoretical reasoning, and the data we employ to test those hypotheses. Most of the hypotheses pertain to individual-level behavior and relate either to expected effects of economic conditions (and alternative ways of specifying those effects) or to the influence of control variables that our model needs to take into account. These hypotheses are tested in Chapters 4 and 5, which deal with individual-level behavior. There is one hypothesis, however, that concerns the outcomes of elections and the way in which those outcomes are affected by economic conditions. That hypothesis is tested in Chapter 6, while Chapter 7 concludes. In an Epilogue, finally, we sketch out how further research into economic voting might be designed so as to avoid the endemic errors that have characterized the field up to now.

I

Studying Economic Voting

In this chapter, we develop our argument that previous investigations into economic voting have been hobbled by model specification problems. We believe that the main problem in previous work has been a failure to focus on political parties as actors that compete for votes. This failure means that previous research has been unable to take account of the extent of party competition (which can vary from election to election). We argue that this failure to take account of party competition leads to models that are intrinsically mis-specified and that this is one of the root causes for the unstable and sometimes incoherent findings in the literature.

In what follows, we diagnose the deficiencies we see as endemic in existing studies of economic voting (many of these deficiencies apply to other studies of electoral behavior as well) and set out our ideas about what a viable approach should look like in general terms. This will set the scene for Chapter 2, in which we present our own approach to the study of economic voting and describe the ways in which it mitigates or eliminates the deficiencies of past studies.

Conceiving the Dependent Variable

Studies of economic voting have been conducted at the aggregate level, treating the country or election as the unit of analysis, and at the individual level, treating the survey respondent as the unit of analysis. In aggregate-level studies, the dependent variable has been the proportion or percentage voting for the government party (or parties in the case of coalition governments), while in individual-level studies the dependent variable has been a dummy variable indicating whether the respondent voted for a government party or not. Aggregate-level studies try to account for variations in government support on the basis of economic conditions (generally inflation, unemployment, and economic growth), sometimes with controls for systemic characteristics. Individual-level studies try to account for variations in government support by means of a "standard model" consisting of a variety of independent variables found empirically to be important in explaining support for particular parties, together with measures of economic perceptions – the assessments given by individuals regarding the state of the economy at the time of the survey (and perhaps over the recent past and/or near future).

The most important problem that is common to both approaches is that they fail to take account of competition between parties, as already mentioned. This root problem manifests itself in two different ways: a focus on support for the government and a focus on electoral choice.

In existing approaches to economic voting, the dependent variable is defined as a choice between government and opposition parties. The focus on this dichotomy seems to make sense because researchers assume that, if economic conditions have any influence on the voting act, this influence must involve an assessment of who is to be credited or blamed for the state of the economy (Anderson 1995). Here the supposed role of governments in economic management is generally taken for granted and, because of this, it seems natural to construe the dependent variable in terms of the distinction between government and opposition. But this supposes that all members of a governing coalition will benefit equally from good economic times and will suffer equally if economic times are bad. Empirically, however, it turns out that parties sharing government power often fare very differently at the same election. Some government parties lose votes while others gain, and similarly with opposition parties. Moreover, at the time of an election voters are not presented with the opportunity to cast their ballot for or against the government but rather to vote for a party or candidate. In a two-party system, such as exists in the United States, elections may be conceived as providing voters with the opportunity to support or reject the government by casting their ballot either for the party of the president or for the other major party, but even in that system the choice that voters face is rarely presented in such terms. In other countries, where multiple parties vie for voters' favor, the government – opposition dichotomy does not adequately represent the choices on offer.[1] Where several parties share power in a coalition government, it is abundantly clear that casting a ballot involves more than choosing between government and opposition. In such cases, each voter can choose to support only one of several government parties. Even when the government consists of a single party, there will generally be more than one opposition party; yet, each voter can choose to support only one of these parties.

If we only focus on whether the government gains or loses support, as most previous researchers have done, then we fail to examine the actual decision-making process that voters experience. Any model that focuses on the choice between government and opposition is bound to mis-specify the choice process. Yet that is what most existing approaches to the study of economic voting do. Exceptions (for example, Duch and Stevenson 2003) that attempt to focus on party choice by employing multinomial or conditional logit methods suffer from other problems that we will detail in Chapter 2.

The second way in which existing approaches fail to adequately represent political parties is caused by their exclusive focus on the actual choices that voters make (or the aggregated counterparts of these choices in terms of the share of the vote given to each party). This focus also seems natural, since voters generally have to choose a single recipient of their vote. But choice informs us only (and in a very crude way) about a voter's orientation toward a single political party. It does not reveal anything about that voter's orientation toward other parties, except for the fact that they were not chosen. Bingham Powell (2000) has eloquently argued that, by focusing only on the choices made by voters, analysts have assumed that these reveal all we need to know about voter preferences; but this is not so (2000: 160).

---

[1] In most countries, voters are asked to make a choice not only in terms of parties but also in terms of candidates. Candidates, however, almost invariably stand as representatives of a party. Moreover, in most established democracies, party characteristics are regarded as more stable over time than the idiosyncratic characteristics of their candidates. It is therefore common in much electoral research to focus on parties and consider the impact of candidate traits as part of the residual variation. We follow this tradition.

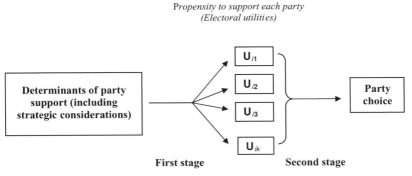

FIGURE 1.1. A two-stage model of electoral choice.

The focus on choice ignores the careful reasoning of Anthony Downs (1957), who argued that the voting act contains two aspects, only one of which manifests itself in observable behavior. Choices are observable, but just as important in his conceptualization of the voting act is the process by which preferences for parties are formed, which is not directly observable in the same way and can be thought of in terms of the propensities that people have to support different parties. Downs argues that voters cast their ballot for the party they prefer the most, but this implies the possibility that there is more than one party that they prefer to some degree. A voter's structure of preferences encompasses parties that are not chosen as well as the party that is chosen, as illustrated in Figure 1.1, which breaks the voting decision into two stages. In the first stage, individuals (identified by the subscript i) assess the strength of their support for each of the parties (1 through k) competing in the election. In the second stage, individuals choose the party that will actually receive their vote. The process is generally presented in terms of party utilities, as we have done in Figure 1.1, where the concept of utility assumes that the contributions of all relevant factors to the overall attractiveness of an alternative can be reduced to a single measure (the utility of voting for the party) so that the attractiveness of a vote for one party can be straightforwardly compared with the attractiveness of a vote for a different party (Ben-Akiva and Lerman 1985: 37). In this way, individuals can readily determine which party, if voted for, would yield them the highest utility. A less convoluted way of saying the same thing is that people vote for the party they support the most.[2] In this book we will refer to "propensity to support a party" (or simply "party support") when we refer to the Downsean concept of party utility, because the word "utility" has in recent years acquired an overlay of additional meanings from its use in the rational choice approach to theory construction that are too restrictive for our purposes (see Chapter 2).

Even in a two-party system, in Downs's view, it makes a lot of difference whether we look at preferences or votes. This is because a voter whose preferences for two parties are tied, or almost so, is in a quite different electoral situation from one who very much prefers one party to the other. In particular, a voter whose preferences are closely tied is more likely to change her vote as a result of a change in preferences than is a voter whose preferences for the two parties are very different. This is because the structure of a voter's preferences encapsulates the situation of that voter in regard to the competition between parties, as illustrated in Figure 1.2. This shows how strengths of party support translate into party choices for five imaginary voters involved in two consecutive electoral contests between just two parties: Party A, which happens to be the government party, and opposition Party B. The situation at the first election is illustrated in the left-hand panel of Figure 1.2. The right-hand panel relates to a later election after an economic recession has occurred.

Let us for the sake of simplicity assume that we can measure the strength of support for each of these parties on a 10-point scale and that members of the electorate vote for the party they support the most. The economic recession has the effect of lowering by 2 units the support that all voters show for Party A. Figure 1.2 shows the consequences of these (first-stage) shifts in support for the voters' (second-stage) actual choices.

In the hypothetical example, Party A's handling of the economy is evaluated negatively by *all voters*. Moreover, this evaluation has *the same effect* on all voters' propensities to support Party A. In every row of the table, we see the same decline of 2 points in support for party A

---

[2] Downs's concept of "party utility" (the benefits – subjective or objective – that a voter gets from voting for a particular party) is often referred to interchangeably with the notion of party preferences (how much parties are preferred in relation to each other). The concept of party utility has the advantage of connoting a value that can be measured rather than a set of options that can only be ordered.

	Propensities and choices before the economic recession			Propensities and choices after the economic recession		
	Strength of support for party A	Strength of support for party B	Vote choice	Strength of support for party A	Strength of support for party B	Vote choice
Voter 1	9	4	Party A	7	4	Party A
Voter 2	8	5	Party A	6	5	Party A
Voter 3	7	6	Party A	5	6	Party B
Voter 4	6	7	Party B	4	7	Party B
Voter 5	5	8	Party B	3	8	Party B

FIGURE 1.2. Hypothetical effects of an economic recession on propensities to support two political parties and choices made between those parties.

between the left-hand and right-hand panels. Yet, the consequences for party choice of this decline in support for Party A are *not the same* for each voter. The original difference in strength of support for Party A over Party B is so large for Voters 1 and 2 that Party A's poor handling of the economy does not provide enough reason for them to change their vote. Voters 4 and 5 started out with stronger support for Party B than Party A and, even though their conviction that Party B is the better choice has strengthened, this also does not change their vote. Only for one of the five individuals does the actual vote choice change as a consequence of Party A's handling of the economy. This difference in consequences for vote choice is due to differences in the competitive situation in which different voters find themselves. Four out of the five votes are simply not in contention because of the initial structure of the party preferences involved. For only one of the five, Voter 3, is it the case that levels of support for each party are sufficiently closely tied as to make it possible for even a quite a large change of party support in the appropriate direction to affect her actual party choice. And this is what happens, as can be seen by scanning the shaded row in Figure 1.2 – the only row to show a change in vote choice between the left-hand and right-hand panels.

A focus on choice would be an adequate representation of voters' relations to parties only if voters were to totally reject all parties that they do not vote for. But we know from voter studies that this is not the case (e.g., van der Eijk and Oppenhuis 1991). Many voters are cross-pressured, so that they hesitate and waver between more than one party, as was the case for Voter 3 in Figure 1.2. This reflects the fact that elections involve competition between parties that vie with each other for the votes of at least some cross-pressured individuals. But an exclusive focus on choice is unable to take into account whether or not that choice was the result of a difficult process of choosing between almost equally attractive alternatives (as it was for Voter 3) or the much easier process of simply reaffirming a past preference (as it was for the other voters in Figure 1.2). Thus, it lumps together, on the one hand, parties that were not chosen but were nevertheless viewed quite positively by voters and, on the other hand, parties that were not chosen because they were viewed negatively. A focus on choice is equally unable to determine whether the party that was actually voted for was one that a voter was really positive about or whether it was voted for because of the absence of any attractive alternative. By focusing on choice, these distinctions are ignored, resulting in substantial heterogeneity within the categories of the choice variable – a heterogeneity that is increased further if the variable is subsequently dichotomized into government versus opposition categories. This heterogeneity cannot but contribute to the instabilities and inconsistencies that are so problematic in the existing literature.

The problem is not overcome by studying government or party support at the aggregate level. Measures of government or party support are derived from aggregating individual choices. The impact of economic conditions on the aggregate measure will be affected by the proportion of voters who are tied (or nearly tied) in their preferences for different parties – something that cannot be observed at the aggregate level. This is obvious if we consider two countries, each with two political parties. If, in one of these countries, the preference structure of the voters is such that none of them would ever consider voting for any other party than the one they had always voted for, then changes in economic conditions will have no electoral consequences there. If the other country is one in which many voters are strongly cross-pressured so that they are closely tied in their preferences for the two parties, then changes in economic conditions can cause a considerable change in choices and election outcomes. The fact that the structure of voter preferences cannot be seen in aggregate-level data suggests a fundamental problem in trying to understand voting behavior purely on the basis of election outcomes.

Model Specification and the Instability of Past Findings

What can we learn from this? The most obvious, and not very new, insight is that models of party choice should control for all the important determinants of party preferences. A properly specified model needs to include variables that account for why Voters 1 and 2 in Figure 1.2 support Party A so much more strongly than Party B and why this is the other way round for Voters 4 and 5. A more important lesson to be learned, however, is that if we analyze vote choice as a dependent variable in our models, we may not be able to find effects that are really there. When there are many voters whose choices remain unchanged (like Voters 1, 2, 4, and 5 in Figure 1.2) and very few voters with a structure of preferences similar to that of Voter 3, we may wrongly conclude that the economy has little effect. But the economy might actually be having quite a strong effect, though with consequences for party choice that applied to only a small number of voters.

Even more importantly, looking at effects on vote choice may lead us to ask what it is about people like Voter 3 that explains why those individuals are affected by economic conditions (or any other independent variables) and others are not. Trying to answer this question can only lead us astray. Voter 3 is no more affected by the state of the economy than other voters are. She merely finds herself in a different situation in terms of the competition between parties. Along much the same lines, looking at effects on vote choice may lead us to ask what it is about some parties that makes them lose (or gain) more votes than others. (Illustrating this would require a slightly more elaborate example than Figure 1.2. in which only two parties are depicted.) Quite often, such differences are not attributable to the characteristics of individual parties, but rather to the patterns of electoral competition between them.

This brings us to our most crucial point. As mentioned in the Introduction to this book, two edited volumes have recently appeared that provide an overview of the state of the art in studies of economic voting. The first was a special issue of *Electoral Studies*, edited by Lewis-Beck and Paldam (2000), and the other was a book edited by Dorussen and Taylor (2002). In both volumes the editors mention as one of the biggest puzzles in the economic voting literature the instability of results across countries and over time (Lewis-Beck and Paldam 2000: 114; Dorussen and Taylor 2002: 1). We would argue that the instability of findings – across different elections in the same country, but particularly across different countries – is due largely to the fact that these findings arise from models that focus only on choice and are thus not able to take party competition into account. In some countries, there are many individuals of the Voter 3 type, who find themselves cross-pressured between competing parties so that changes in economic conditions may result in a change in their choice of parties, whereas in other countries there are few such voters. Even within one country, some elections are more competitive than others. In a highly competitive election, where many voters are undecided between the competing parties, even a quite small effect of an incumbent party's handling of the economy could have large consequences for the vote. In a less competitive election, the same effect of economic conditions would have much less impact on the outcome. If differences in the extent of party competition are not controlled for, the findings could be quite contradictory – as contradictory, indeed, as the extant findings in the economic voting literature.

Of course, it is not just in studies of economic voting that scholars have mis-specified the decision process that underlies voters' choices between parties. But the economic voting literature constitutes the branch of voting studies most deeply engaged in cross-national research, where the consequences of failing to distinguish between the two aspects of the voting process (propensities and choice) have been most apparent.

Asymmetric Effects and the Concept of Electoral Potential

Voters base their support for parties on many factors other than the economy, as we will discuss more fully later in this chapter. Whether the economy trumps these other concerns depends on the salience of the economy in comparison with other considerations. Thus, it has been suggested that the economy may be less salient in good economic times creating an asymmetry between a strengthening and a weakening economy: the latter is thought likely to have greater effects on vote choice than the former (Bloom and Price 1975; Stevenson 2002). This idea ties into a social psychological literature (e.g., Kahneman and Tversky

1979) that posits a grievance asymmetry in individual assessments of circumstances of all kinds (see also Price and Sanders 1994; Nannestad and Paldam 1997, 2002).

Such psychological asymmetries may exist in regard to assessments of the economy. However, much more important to our minds are quasi-mechanical asymmetries that are the consequence of the competitive situation in which parties find themselves. Such asymmetries arise because parties fluctuate in the extent to which they are able to attract all of the voters who might have been induced to vote for them. The electoral support for any individual party is at its maximum when all the other parties with which it competes for votes receive minimal support. These maxima and minima fluctuate over time, but at any one point in time they place a floor under the losses a party can suffer as well as a ceiling over the gains it can make. We call the maximum electoral support that a party can receive the "electoral potential" of that party (van der Eijk and Niemöller 1984; van der Eijk and Franklin 1996). A party's electoral potential is almost always higher than its actual vote. Put another way, parties seldom mobilize their full potential because competitor parties are successful in drawing some of those votes away.

Where a party stands in relation to its electoral potential depends on many factors other than the state of the economy, and it is important to realize that a governing party that has already mobilized close to its full potential cannot readily improve its position no matter how well the economy performs. By contrast, an opposition party that is close to the nadir of its potential, having gained the votes only of its bedrock supporters, has a large pool of potential supporters from which it can gain votes in bad economic times. Since government parties generally are parties that did well in their most recent elections, and opposition parties are generally parties that did badly at that time, it follows that the potential benefit to opposition parties from a bad economy might well be greater than the potential benefit to government parties from an economy that does well; and the potential cost to government parties from a bad economy might well be greater than the potential cost to opposition parties of a good economy. Such asymmetries would have nothing to do with psychology and would apply to political developments of all kinds, not just economic ones.

The extent of these asymmetries is, of course, an empirical matter. An unpopular party may well be included in a governing coalition despite its lack of popularity, and such a party may not be hurt by bad economic times because its support is already so low in relation to its potential. Conversely, a party may have been quite successful in drawing the support of most of its potential voters without becoming a government party, and such an opposition party may stand to gain little from bad economic times. In terms of the illustration we presented earlier, such asymmetries would show themselves in the proportion of a party's supporters whose support propensities resemble those of Voter 3, the swing voter in Figure 1.2, as opposed to the proportion whose support propensities resemble those of Voters 1 and 2 in regard to Party A. Failure to take account of such asymmetries can only have exacerbated the instability of findings in the extant literature.

Taking Account of Party Characteristics

The failure of existing approaches to adequately take account of political parties as the objects from which voters must choose in elections, and as actors that compete with each other for votes, causes additional problems. One is the difficulty of including in the analysis certain independent variables that we believe should influence the way in which voters take economic conditions into account. In particular, we expect some of the characteristics of parties to be relevant to voters, such as their importance as players in the game of politics (generally seen as being determined by the number of seats they command in the legislature). And it might matter to voters how long a party had been in government. Such characteristics cannot be taken into account when the dependent variable is whether one voted for a government party or not. And even when parties are viewed individually as recipients of citizens' votes, still their sizes and other characteristics cannot readily be taken into account so long as party choice is the dependent variable, because then the identity of the party is often coterminous with its characteristics. The same is true of a number of other characteristics of parties, such as their ideological complexion or their stature within a governing coalition (the number of ministries they control). It is noticeable that few models of vote choice, whether at the individual or aggregate levels, contain any variables at all pertaining to the parties that are chosen (or not). In studying economic voting this is particularly troublesome, since voters who are trying to attribute credit or blame for economic conditions would be expected to take account of a party's role within a governing coalition (whether it controls the prime ministership, for example); and if voters take account of a party's role, then researchers need to be able to do so too.

Just as important as characteristics that derive from a party's governing status (which can vary radically over very short periods) are longer-term characteristics such as their ideological complexion. It has several times been suggested that left-wing governments will be particularly held responsible for rises in unemployment, while right-wing governments will particularly be held responsible for rises in inflation (Hibbs 1977, 1982; Powell and Whitten 1993; Whitten and Palmer 1999). But governments do not always consist of ideologically coherent parties. Not only in famous instances such as the German 1967 "grand coalition" of socialist and conservative parties (SPD and CDU/CSU, which took office again in 2005), but in quite a large number of other instances, governments span the division between left and right.[3] This could well explain why the fortunes of coalition members at ensuing elections are not necessarily consistent. In a period of strong economic growth coupled with high inflation, for example, right-wing members of a government might suffer electorally, while left-wing members gain (for reasons that will be explored in Chapter 4). Clearly, the conventional approach to economic voting is not able to address such developments because it cannot treat the members of the government individually.

Taking Account of Voter Characteristics

The failure to distinguish between preferences and choice also prevents analysts from taking account of certain features that apply to voters. In particular, voters have been found to differ in the extent to which they are open to the possibility of switching their votes and supporting a different party than they supported last time (Butler and Stokes 1974; Franklin, Mackie, Valen, et al. 1992). This difference between voters in what might be called their "propensity to switch" is associated with the life cycle, with older people being more likely to be set in their ways and hence in their propensity to support only a single party

---

[3] How often this is seen to happen depends on how far to the left or right a party has to be in order to be classified as left or right. If we divide parties according to which side they fall on the simple midpoint of a left–right scale then, in our data, eighteen out of forty-two governments were split in these terms.

(Franklin, Mackie, and Valen 1992). At the individual level, when the dependent variable is party choice, the extent to which individuals are open to the competition between parties cannot be straightforwardly taken into account.[4] At the aggregate level, the focus on vote shares given to different parties prevents analysts from allowing for the extent to which particular parties are subject to electoral competition. A party all of whose supporters come from a particular social group whose members would never consider voting differently can neither gain nor lose as a result of its performance in office, whereas a party that makes appeals to different groups whose members have realistic electoral alternatives is in a very different electoral situation. As already explained, such differences between parties cannot be ascertained on the basis of aggregate-level vote shares any more than in individual-level designs that focus on party choice.

Research performed at the aggregate level is particularly at risk of employing models that are underspecified in failing to take account of the many considerations found empirically to affect party choice at the individual level. If variables such as social structure, ideology, or issue preferences affect individual-level vote choice, then they can in the right circumstances affect election outcomes. But if election outcomes are affected by such variables, then their omission from aggregate-level analyses of economic voting will result in underspecified models that fail to find consistent effects of economic conditions – precisely what has been observed in practice (Lewis-Beck and Paldam 2000). Had those missing variables somehow been included, the resulting models might well have produced different (and possibly more consistent) estimates of the effects of economic conditions.

Another concern that aggregate-level studies cannot address is whether voters are assessing the economic situation prospectively or retrospectively. Those studies make the (generally implicit) assumption that voters take account of the economy only in a retrospective fashion: punishing the party (or parties) in power when times are bad

---

[4] One could think of partitioning data so as to look at voters with a high propensity to switch separately from voters with a low propensity to switch, but this smacks of controlling on the dependent variable, which would yield all sorts of model specification problems, as would a set of interactions between propensity to switch and various independent variables. More importantly, we observe that these kinds of considerations are absent in the existing literature on economic voting.

and rewarding them when times are good. This may indeed be the way in which economic conditions impact the vote. But even within the existing literature there are hints that voters' economic concerns may not just be retrospective.

As already mentioned, it has been argued that voters will expect a party of the right to be more concerned about inflation and a party of the left to be more concerned about unemployment (Hibbs 1977, 1982; Powell and Whitten 1993; Whitten and Palmer 1999). If this is true, it has prospective as well as retrospective implications. A right-leaning party may indeed not be held as responsible for unemployment as a left-leaning party would have been, but in times of unemployment voters may be more likely to elect a left-leaning party because they view such a party as being more likely to do something about unemployment. This consideration could mitigate or even reverse the negative effects that such a party might otherwise have suffered as a consequence of any responsibility it might have had for allowing the unemployment rate to rise. And opposition parties might gain particularly from unemployment if they are left-leaning parties (or from inflation if they are right-leaning parties) if voters are taking a prospective view. Conventional research strategies that simply distinguish between government and other parties cannot take account of choices made among opposition parties and thus cannot take account of these possibly prospective orientations.

Measuring the Economy

Research performed at the individual level has particular difficulty measuring the independent variables relating to the economy. Such research has generally employed survey data for individual countries, and single-country studies generally rely on measures of economic perceptions rather than of economic conditions, substituting subjective evaluations of how well the economy is performing for objective measures. This seems to make sense because individual voters can only hold government parties accountable for the state of the economy to the extent that they have some awareness of economic conditions, in which case that awareness will manifest itself in terms of perceptions. But the logic underlying this substitution of perceptions for actual conditions is rather odd and has seldom been closely examined. Since the state of a national economy is the same for all respondents in a national survey, all these assessments would be the same – apart from random error – if everyone responded to the same reality and if everyone had the same perception of this economic reality. So, what is reflected by different responses? One possibility is that people respond differently to the question because they have different aspects of the economy in mind. Some may think of unemployment when reporting their perception of the state of the economy, others may think of inflation, and so on. If this were the case, the responses would not be comparable, thus rendering their content validity highly dubious. After all, in this case, differences in responses would not reflect different economic circumstances – which the measures should reflect if we want to estimate the effect of economic conditions on the vote – but rather different interpretations of the survey question.[5]

Alternatively, differences between responses about the state of the economy may derive from respondents incorrectly assessing economic conditions. In that case, a study of economic perceptions runs the risk of contamination from whatever it is that causes voters to misperceive the actual state of the national economy. One likely source of contamination would be the cues arising from party identification, where voters perceive the economy as doing well if their preferred party had a hand in governing the economy and badly if the government is composed of parties they abhor. Research has shown that this indeed happens (Wlezien, Franklin, and Twiggs 1997; Bartels 2002; Duch and Palmer 2002; van der Eijk, Franklin, Demant, and van der Brug 2004; Zaller 2005), rendering problematic any attempt to use subjective economic assessments as independent variables in a model of party support.[6] Subjective measures of the economy are also problematic from a theoretical and normative perspective. Theories of economic voting are inextricably linked to the notion of democratic accountability, which

---

[5] One might suppose that had the perceptions been measured in different economic circumstances, they would have reflected variations in those circumstances. Elsewhere we demonstrated that this is not the case (van der Eijk, Franklin, Demant, and van der Brug 2004, 2007).

[6] In technical terms, this is referred to as an "endogeneity problem": the independent variables are not measured independently of the dependent variable, and may even be regarded as the consequence of party preference rather than its cause. Using such variables as though they were truly independent measures constitutes a specification error that will generally serve to exaggerate the apparent political consequences of economic conditions.

implies that parties and politicians are held to account for the actual consequences of their actions. Economic voting – voters rewarding positive consequences and punishing negative ones – therefore fosters democratic accountability. But this requires *actual* economic conditions to be the benchmark for electoral punishment and reward. If punishment and reward are meted out on the basis of subjective, idiosyncratic, or incorrect views of economic conditions, this might help to explain voting decisions, but the resulting votes could not properly be regarded as "economic voting" in the same sense as those words are used in the aggregate-level economic voting literature.

Substituting measures of the "real economy" for economic perceptions at the individual level brings different problems. Doing so is only possible when there is variation in economic conditions. This can be obtained by conducting a series of surveys within a single country or by combining surveys from different countries, each survey being conducted under different economic conditions. The first of these alternatives is hampered by the generally small number of elections for which we have appropriate survey data (nowhere as many as fifteen at the time of writing). The problem with such a dataset (employed, for example, by Markus 1988, 1992; Nadeau and Lewis-Beck 2001; Zaller 2005) is that, although the analysis is conducted at the individual level, the small number of different survey contexts makes it problematic to employ more than a very few independent variables defining those contexts. Moreover, when aiming at an analysis that has wider relevance than a single national context, there are a number of contextual factors that should be controlled for in a properly specified model. Ten, twelve, or even fifteen contexts (all that are available in most series of national election studies) are simply not enough to permit evaluation of these factors. Consequently, the models actually employed to investigate the effects of economic conditions using such datasets have been very underspecified. Some of the few analyses employing a series of surveys for a single country (Markus 1988; Nadeau and Lewis-Beck 2001) were additionally mis-specified because they used very few of the individual-level independent variables that are known to affect preferences (and thus, indirectly, choice), perhaps because of problems of comparability across surveys (see footnote 7).

The second way in which measures of the real economy could be employed in individual-level studies would be by combining surveys from different countries. That approach is only possible, however, when the countries' party systems are somehow made comparable. In past research, this has been accomplished by simplifying the choice options in a government–opposition dichotomy, so that differences between party systems do not have to be accommodated. But that brings us back to the problems discussed earlier.

Taking Account of System Characteristics

We have been critical in this chapter of conventional approaches to the study of economic voting. Conventional approaches are not without benefits, however. One advantage of taking a government–opposition dichotomy as the dependent variable lies in permitting comparability across political systems, as just mentioned; and the pooling of multiple surveys across multiple political systems is one way of providing adequate variance in real economic conditions. Moreover, the use of multiple political systems does more than permit us to take account of real economic conditions. It permits the inclusion of multiple contextual indicators, which we have said would be desirable (though the use of multiple contextual indicators has not been common in such studies). At the aggregate level, it has been found that the ease with which governments are held to account (what has been called "system clarity" by Powell and Whitten 1993; Whitten and Palmer 1999) plays an important moderating role in economic voting. We can imagine other systemic characteristics that might play a similar role, as will be explained in Chapter 3. But the comparability across political systems that is a feature of past studies comes at a high price, as we have seen. Any change in the research design that moves away from the focus on government–opposition status, while still maintaining a cross-national perspective, will have to find an alternative means of achieving comparability since the fact that different countries have different party systems makes it problematic to pool the data from different countries into a single dataset. And without pooling the data, we have no way to provide a measure of economic conditions that varies across cases.

Homogeneous versus Heterogeneous Effects of the Economy

It is generally assumed (though this assumption is usually unstated) that effects of the economy on individual voters are largely homogeneous.

That is, all classes and conditions of voters are expected to bow to the same "economic wind" and respond in the same way to changes in economic conditions. Indeed, the presumed homogeneity of effects of economic conditions is one of the reasons for widespread interest in this topic, since it permits aggregate-level analyses that need not take account of differences between voters at the individual level. Yet there are scholars who have proposed that effects of the economy would not be homogeneous at all, but rather that they would be quite heterogeneous in nature, with different types of individuals reacting differently to economic conditions. These suggestions build on findings of some of the earliest voting studies to the effect that more sophisticated voters tend to be relatively immune to campaign and other effects on their vote, so that vote switching is rather concentrated in the less sophisticated segments of the population (Berelson, Lazarsfeld, and McPhee 1954; Campbell, Converse, Miller, and Stokes 1960; Converse 1964, 1970). Zaller (2005: 193) built on these findings when he showed that "low information voters are at least as responsive to election-specific content as high information voters and most likely more so." His explanation is that high-information voters are more ideological; hence, "small-election specific changes do not impel them to change sides" (194). This explanation is quite convincing, but it underlines the problematic nature of an approach such as Zaller's, which focuses on choice rather than on preferences. His analyses demonstrate that low-information voters are more likely to change sides, but not whether they are more responsive to economic conditions.

Along a rather different track, Dorussen and Taylor (2002) have suggested that certain groups of voters may be more responsive to changes in economic conditions because they themselves are liable to be more affected by those changes. If "pocketbook" voting of this kind exists, that also would create distinctions among voters in terms of which ones would be expected to react most strongly to changes in economic conditions.

These ideas, if true, could join with the other deficiencies enumerated earlier to undermine even further the ability of scholars to find consistent effects of economic conditions in countries whose populations differ in terms of the demographic character of their voter profiles if this implies that some countries would have more voters in categories that respond to changes in economic conditions. Evidently, it is important to assess whether voter responses to economic conditions do indeed differ between different types of voters and, if so, to find some way to take account of these differences.

Features of an Improved Approach

The litany of defects we have outlined in this chapter, characterizing the methods employed in past investigations of economic voting, makes it easy to understand the inconsistencies and instabilities in past findings. We conclude with a brief overview of the implications we draw from this list of defects for the way in which future research on economic voting should be designed if it is to have a better chance of arriving at consistent and stable findings. It should be clear from our discussion that an ideal approach to the study of economic voting would marry desirable properties from the aggregate-level and individual-level designs used in past work and add new features that have not previously been employed.

First and foremost, such a research design must adequately represent the relations between voters and political parties that define the electoral process. As discussed at length, this implies that the dependent variable should not group parties together in any way (such as dichotomizing them into government versus opposition parties, as has been common in past research), nor should it focus just on the choices that voters make between parties; it must also take into account the structure of preferences that voters have for the parties that compete for their votes. A second feature of an adequate research design is that it avoids using subjective indicators of economic conditions, since these are strongly contaminated and subject to severe endogeneity problems. A third desirable feature is that research should nevertheless be based on individual-level data. The main reason for this is to avoid falling prey to a multitude of aggregation artifacts that otherwise would complicate (and potentially undermine) the validity of whatever causal inferences we would like to make. One of these aggregation problems has been highlighted in this chapter: the inability to deduce from data about parties' vote shares the patterns of electoral competition that determine the extent to which changes in economic conditions are able to have palpable effects on party choice.

The combination of the second and third of these desired properties of an adequate research design implies the need for data about multiple electoral contexts. Individual-level data derive from surveys, and the real economy is the same for everyone included in a given survey. Because for many countries the longest adequate and comparable series consists of no more than about ten to twelve surveys, the need for multiple contexts can most easily be satisfied by using comparable survey data from different countries. This would have the additional advantage (if the number of contexts is sufficiently large) of permitting the assessment of possibly moderating effects of system characteristics on how economic conditions affect voter preferences and choice.

Finally, an adequate design for the analysis of economic voting requires rich data, permitting the analyst to take account of all sorts of factors that – on the basis of first principles or from suggestions in the literature – could not be ignored without risking omitted variable bias in the measurement of effects of interest. In terms of individual-level data, this means that the surveys on which studies of economic voting are to be based should allow us to take account of as many factors as possible that are known to affect voters' party preferences. At the very least, appropriate models would include as independent variables the normal demographics of age, education, religion, and social class, as well as left–right location and enough issue variables to enable researchers to place respondents in terms of their issue concerns. Moreover, this individual-level information must be highly comparable between the surveys from different contexts. In practice, this will be one of the more daunting requirements, as the actual comparability of many ostensibly comparable datasets is usually much less than is often assumed.[7]

In addition to rich individual-level data, an adequate design for the study of economic voting requires plentiful information about parties and about contexts. Such information can very well come from sources other than surveys. As far as parties are concerned, information is needed regarding all those attributes that have been suggested in the literature as relevant for economic voting or, more generally, as relevant for generating party support among voters. Many of these variables are based on the notion that not all parties are equally held accountable for

[7] The comparative studies reported by Franklin, Mackie, and Valen, et al. (1992) and Thomassen (2005) testify in vivid detail to these problems, which we suspect were also responsible for the underspecified models used in individual-level studies of economic voting across time, as suggested earlier.

the state of the economy, but that the extent to which each party is held individually accountable is dependent on factors such as whether it is part of the government, what portfolios it holds, and how long it has been in office. Moreover, we expect parties' sizes to be relevant for the degree to which voters attribute to them credit and blame for economic conditions, perhaps encapsulating other party characteristics such as the ministries they control.[8] We have already referred to the suggestion that left-wing governments will be particularly held responsible for rises in unemployment, while right-wing governments will particularly be held responsible for rises in inflation.[9] In view of our argument that individual parties rather than governments should be the focus in analyses of economic voting, this necessitates taking into account the ideological complexion of individual parties.

Given the need for individual-level data from a variety of contexts – so as to have sufficient variation in measures of the real economy – properly specified analyses also require sufficient relevant information about these contexts. Primary among these contextual variables are, of course, the economic conditions whose effects on voting and election are the objects of concern. But contexts vary also in other respects that may be expected to have a direct impact on economic voting or that may have to be controlled for in order to avoid aliasing effects. In particular, it has been hypothesized that the clarity of responsibility for (economic) policy in a system – widespread knowledge of who to hold accountable – is a necessary precondition for economic voting (Powell and Whitten 1993; Whitten and Palmer 1999). Other distinctions between political systems may also have to be assessed, such as, for example, Lijphart's (1999) classification of consensus versus majoritarian democratic systems or Powell's (2000) classification of systems that adhere more to proportional as opposed to majoritarian visions of democracy. Esping-Andersen's (1990) distinction between liberal, social democratic, and conservative welfare states may be relevant because in some of these countries citizens have less to fear from a deteriorating economy than in other countries, which may be reflected in how voters react to economic conditions. Finally, all these different kinds of data – at the level of individual respondents, political parties,

---

[8] See, e.g., Anderson (1995).
[9] Cf. Hibbs (1977, 1982), Powell and Whitten (1993), Whitten and Palmer (1999).

and contexts – have to be integrated into a structure that allows them to be analyzed in conjunction.

In summary, then, from the aggregate-level approach, we would wish to see adopted the measures of economic conditions used in those studies: measures of economic growth, unemployment, and inflation published by the Organization for Economic Cooperation and Development (OECD). We would also wish to see the inclusion of other variables that distinguish between different types of political systems in which effects of the economy might be rather different. Using measures of the real economy and of systemic characteristics implies the need to employ a relatively large number of units at the systemic level. From the individual-level approach, we would wish to see adopted a "standard model" of voting behavior that includes all of the many variables found in past work to influence the voting act. This implies the need for survey data and, indeed (given the need for a large number of units at the systemic level), a rather large number of different surveys that nevertheless contain as far as possible the same individual-level measures of concepts employed in the standard model.

Going beyond any approach used to date, we would wish to see an approach that took account of the characteristics of those political parties that vie for the votes of the individuals included in the surveys. This implies the need for a dependent variable other than the conventional measure of party choice so that, for each party, there is a measure of the extent to which that party was supported by each voter. This implies a unit of analysis below that of the survey respondent: a unit of analysis at the intersection of parties and voters. Only at such a level of analysis can the characteristics both of parties and of individuals (in addition to the characteristics of political systems) be taken into account. At that level of analysis, investigators could code not only the characteristics of individuals, and in particular those that are generally understood to condition their choices between parties, but also the characteristics of the parties themselves, and in particular those that make parties likely to be held accountable for the performance of the economy. At such a level of analysis, it should be possible to properly specify the conditions that govern the responses of voters to changing economic conditions.

In Chapter 2, we will describe the model we employ in this book and explain how it meets the conditions set out here so as to remove

or at least ameliorate the various problems enumerated in this chapter. We believe that this model has a good chance of arriving at stable
and consistent estimates for the effects of economic conditions. Then
in Chapter 3, we will describe in greater detail the theoretical expectations that govern our choice of variables for the model, the hypotheses that we derive from this theoretical reasoning, and the data we
employ to test those hypotheses. Most of the hypotheses pertain to
individual-level behavior and relate either to expected effects of economic conditions (and alternative ways of specifying those effects) or
to the influence of control variables that our model needs to take into
account. These hypotheses are tested in Chapters 4 and 5, which deal
with individual-level behavior. There is one hypothesis, however, that
concerns the outcomes of elections and the way in which those outcomes are affected by economic conditions. That hypothesis is tested
in Chapter 6, which investigates election outcomes. Only after that, in
Chapter 7, will we be able to evaluate our approach in terms of whether
it has indeed solved the methodological and other problems that led
past researchers to produce such unstable findings. In the Epilogue,
finally, we sketch out how further research on economic voting might
be designed so as to avoid the endemic errors that have characterized
the field up to now.

2

Party Choice as a Two-Stage Process

In the Introduction to this volume, we reported that instabilities in the results of past studies have led researchers to call for a methodological fix – a "trick" that would give stability to their findings. We believe that one way to find this trick is to employ an approach that solves the various problems outlined in Chapter 1. Whether such an approach would be the required trick – the ideal approach that would yield stable findings – remains to be seen. By addressing the problems we have enumerated, however, we will take a major step in the right direction. On the basis of our discussion of these problems, and summarizing the conclusions we reached in Chapter 1, we can reiterate some of the properties that an ideal approach would have.

The first property of an ideal approach is that it should allow us to combine information from different countries in a single dataset that contains data at the level of individual respondents. Such a dataset would permit us to use objective national economic indicators to measure economic conditions. In order to obtain sufficient variance in economic conditions for reliable effects to be measured, the number of different elections needs to be quite large. How many elections we need to study in order to acquire adequate variation in economic conditions is not something that can be definitively stated. It would also be desirable if these elections were spread out over a number of countries to provide us with meaningful variance in country characteristics. Again, it is not possible to say a priori how many countries it would take for the variance in their characteristics to be meaningful. In this study, we pool the data from forty-two different elections conducted in fifteen different countries – generally three elections per country. We believe that this dataset (described in more detail in the next chapter) provides adequate variation, but this will be a matter for empirical investigation.

A second property of an ideal method is that it should allow us to go beyond the distinction, commonly made in past studies at whatever level of analysis, between government and opposition. An ideal approach would permit individual political parties to be represented in the data so that we can take account of a series of party characteristics that might influence party standing with the voters. In Chapter 1 we mentioned some of the party characteristics that we consider to be relevant. By distinguishing individual parties and their attributes, we can assess whether and how party characteristics moderate the effects of economic conditions on electoral decisions, as has been suggested by Anderson (1995), Powell and Whitten (1993), Whitten and Palmer (1999), and some others.

A third property of an ideal method is that it should allow us to distinguish between electoral preferences for parties on the one hand and discrete vote choice on the other. We argued in the previous chapter – and illustrated our argument by means of Figure 1.2 – that the extent to which vote choice responds to economic conditions is only partially a function of voters' reactions to economic conditions. Actual votes can only be affected by the economy if there is sufficient electoral competition, which manifests itself in voters having propensities to support more than just a single party. Since this is not something about voters or parties but rather about the state of party competition, we need to be able to study preference formation separately from party choice. Equally, in order to understand election outcomes, we need to be able to study party choice separately from preference formation. So we need a method that allows us to analyze the level of support that voters have for different parties but that also allows us to link that support unambiguously to actual electoral choice. Such a method – which would effectively implement the distinction between the two aspects of voting behavior that we referred to in Chapter 1 in terms of Downs's (1957) two-stage model – would allow us to assess not only how changing electoral circumstances impinge on electoral preferences, but also how changes in electoral preferences affect election outcomes.

In this chapter, we describe a procedure for implementing such a two-stage model and explain how we operationalize it in practice. But before we turn to that, we need to address two fairly recently developed approaches to studying party choice in multiparty situations (multinomial logit and conditional logit) that have been employed in past studies to address at least some of the same problems that concern us here. In the next section, we will first discuss these well-known mainstream approaches and explain why neither is appropriate in our case.

Why Do We Not Use Logit Models?

Increasingly, multinomial logit and conditional logit methods are seen as the de facto standard for analyzing party choice in multiparty systems. These methods are usually described as regression models for nominal-level dependent variables, offering all the versatility and multivariate power that are commonly associated with regression techniques. Because each of these techniques permits us to distinguish separate political parties, they seem indeed particularly suitable for studying multiparty situations, thus addressing the second of the desirable properties listed earlier. However, multinomial logit appears quite deficient in terms of the first of those desirable properties because it cannot pool information from different countries with different party systems. Such models only permit an analysis of each electoral context separately, and within each of those contexts the real economy will be a constant whose effects cannot be analyzed.[1] One way around this last problem is to employ subjective indicators of the state of the economy, generated by asking respondents for their perceptions of how the economy is performing. This has been done, for example, by Duch and Stevenson (2003). As mentioned in Chapter 1, however, we consider this to be an inadequate solution. The variations in economic perceptions cannot and therefore do not in any way reflect variations in the

---

[1] If the set of parties is identical across elections, it is possible to pool survey data from different elections in the same country, yielding variation in real economic conditions. Given that there are no series of suitable election studies covering as many as even fifteen cases (see Chapter 1), this variation in economic conditions would be quite restricted, however. Moreover, such a dataset would also provide too few degrees of freedom to permit inclusion of the necessary contextual controls, as discussed in Chapter 1.

real (national) economic context (or specific aspects thereof), which is after all the same for all respondents to a specific survey. Moreover, such perceptions are fraught with endogeneity problems (see Chapter 1, footnote 5). Because multinomial logit methods would require us to substitute subjective perceptions for real economic indicators, we would be unable to address the problems discussed at length in Chapter 1. Moreover, multinomial logit methods also share some of the problems that plague the conditional logit technique, which we will turn to next. So, multinomial logit does not meet the requirements set out at the end of Chapter 1 for an adequate approach to the study of economic voting.

Conditional logit is the second method sometimes used for analyzing party choice in multiparty systems. In principle, this method does permit the analysis of voters taken from multiple contexts, making it possible to employ measures of the real economy (which would take on different values in different contexts). In spite of the fact that this method has so far hardly been used in comparative electoral analyses,[2] its potential for doing so is obvious. This comparative potential, and the near-canonized status of this method as the way par excellence for analyzing choice in multiparty systems, merit a somewhat more extensive discussion of conditional logit than its scant usage in extant comparative studies would seem to justify.

The use of conditional logit models has a number of drawbacks that are often overlooked. One of these is that the method requires independent variables to be defined as relationships between respondents and parties. Where this is not possible, the analyst either has to omit such variables or resort to a mixed model that combines conditional logit and multinomial logit components.[3] The latter option loses the potential for jointly analyzing data from different party systems, and the former leads to mis-specification of models owing to omitted variables. An additional problem (which applies equally to multinomial

---

[2] The major exception is Kroh (2003), who analyzes data from thirty elections in twenty-seven countries in a single model. Although his study did not focus on the effects of economic contexts, his analyses demonstrated the potential of doing so.

[3] Our own method, which is described later in this chapter, requires this also. But the solution we developed that accomplishes this for all kinds of independent variables cannot be applied straightforwardly in a logit-based context.

logit) is that the method requires the elimination from the analysis of parties that have been chosen by only a handful of respondents in order to prevent the estimated parameters from becoming too unstable. Because of the small proportion of voters involved, this restriction is generally considered to be unproblematic. Yet, the decision to leave out some choice options (i.e., parties) is less innocuous than it seems at first sight. It changes the nature of the phenomenon under investigation, and one ends up investigating choice from among the larger parties rather than party choice as such. In practice, this also means that only those respondents who voted for one of the larger parties are included in the analyses – a form of selection on the dependent variable. This generally reduces the variance of independent variables, which leads to smaller estimated effects than otherwise would be found. The magnitude of such biases is occasionally very large.[4] Moreover, the character and extent of such selection biases will generally be different between contexts, as the parties that will have to be excluded from the analysis will be unique for each of the contexts and the numbers of respondents involved will vary as well. This undermines the effectiveness of pooling individual-level information across different countries.

A quite different set of problems besetting conditional logit models (and multinomial logit models too) is that they are not really regression models for nominal-level dependent variables. Choice is not the dependent variable in these models, but rather the utility of the choice options, while choice is assumed to be determined by utility maximization. As will be clear from our discussion in Chapter 1, this fits with the Downsean two-stage approach that we advocate for studying voters' choices. However pleasing this may be, the dependent variable (utility) is not observed at all, but rather deduced post hoc from the data. This procedure yields unbiased estimates of utilities – and subsequently of the effects of independent variables – only if *all* relevant characteristics of voters and of parties are known and included

---

4 Van der Eijk, van der Brug, Kroh, and Franklin (2006) find that elimination of smaller parties in ways that are often practiced yields biases in estimated coefficients of as much as ten standard errors, which is statistically highly significant. The ordering of independent variables (from most to least important) changes as well.

in the model (for a more detailed discussion, see van der Eijk, van der Brug, Kroh, and Franklin 2006). This is obviously a tall order: a fully specified model is in practice unattainable.[5] Moreover, these models yield unbiased estimates of the effects of the independent variables only if their central assumptions are not violated. Some of these – most notably the assumption of independence of irrelevant alternatives – are exceedingly implausible.[6] The greater the electoral competition – that is, the more that support for one party overlays with that of one or several other parties – the more likely it is that this assumption will be violated.[7]

A final undesirable property of discrete-choice models such as conditional logit (and multinomial logit) is that their parameter estimates are not comparable between models and datasets as a consequence of the procedure they employ to estimate the (unobserved) utilities that function as the dependent variable (for a detailed discussion of this point see Train 2003: 28–9). Thus, when models differ in the absolute magnitude of an estimated parameter, one may not conclude that the larger (absolute) value represents a stronger effect. This would make it hard to reach conclusions based on comparisons between the effects found in different models.[8]

---

[5] This is not the ordinary omitted variable problem that affects all analysis of causal effects, including our own. In discrete choice models, omitted variables bias the dependent variable itself, as utility (the dependent variable) is not empirically observed but derived from the data under the assumption of having a fully specified model. In our own procedure, we do not rely on inferred measures of utility, but on empirical observations instead. As a consequence, our procedure is less vulnerable to a cumulation of omitted variable problems than discrete choice models are.

[6] A useful and accessible discussion of the role of this assumption in various kinds of discrete choice models can be found in Alvarez and Nagler (1998).

[7] The problematic nature of the independence of irrelevant alternatives (IIA) assumption is often illustrated with the so-called red bus–blue bus example. If IIA holds, the ratio of commuters choosing to travel by train versus by (red) bus should be unaffected by the appearance on the market of a competing (blue) bus service. This assumption will be less likely to hold the more similar the two bus services are (in this stylized example they differ only in the color of the bus). Had the new transport possibility been of a different nature (e.g., a boat), the IIA assumption might more easily be fulfilled. In the political realm, we know that parties compete for votes by making similar appeals on many issues. But the stronger such similarities are, the more the relationship between parties will resemble the relationship between busses in the red bus–blue bus analogy, in which case the IIA assumption patently does not hold.

[8] Lack of awareness of this feature of discrete-choice models has led to a number of incorrect substantive conclusions in the empirical literature.

Our Alternative: Measuring Electoral Utilities

As we just explained, logit models estimate (unobserved) utilities on the basis of respondents' choices and their scores on independent variables that are included in the model. In view of our doubts about the merits of these approaches, we propose a method that, instead of estimating utilities, aims to measure them directly by means of questions included in mass surveys. In order to emphasize the distinction between direct observations on the one hand and estimates of unobserved variables on the other, and for reasons elaborated in Chapter 1, we refer to these empirically observed measures as "party support propensities" or the "level of party support." On the basis of these measures, it is possible to derive voters' preferences for different parties, so (where this does not cause confusion) we will also occasionally refer to them as "party preferences."

Party support levels can be observed by standard survey methods. This involves asking respondents to report the strength of their support for each party in turn. The problem here, however, is how to formulate such questions. Words such as "support," "utility," "preference," and "choice" are quite common in everyday language, but their colloquial meanings are largely overlapping and quite distinct from their meaning in theories of electoral behavior. Citizens think and talk about voting and party preferences more often in terms of party choice than anything else. Consequently, survey questions intended to measure party support may be better cast in terms of choice in order to be comprehensible to respondents. To have such questions nevertheless pertain to the propensity that voters have to support each party – that is, to the Downsean notion of the utility that voting for a party would yield – respondents must be freed from familiar restrictions that apply to the real act of voting (especially the normal restriction that one can vote for only a single party) but that do not apply to utilities. In the early 1980s, experiments were conducted that employed projections into an undefined future that would, it was hoped, accomplish this (van der Eijk and Niemöller 1984). These researchers settled on a formulation that has been used in an increasing number of studies in recent years: all Dutch Parliamentary Election studies since 1982 (seven studies in total at the time of writing), the European Election Studies of 1989, 1994, 1999, and 2004, and a growing number of (national) election studies including those in Britain, Ireland, Spain, and Germany. In this formulation, respondents are asked to indicate on a 10-point scale how likely it is that they will "ever" vote for each of the parties in their country. In the surveys that we analyze, this question was formulated as follows:

We have a number of parties in [name of country] each of which would like to get your vote. How probable is it that you will ever vote for the following parties? Please specify your views on a 10-point-scale where 1 means "not at all probable" and 10 means "very probable." You may use any number between 1 and 10 to specify your views.

This question was then asked for each of a series of parties, usually all plausible contenders for parliamentary representation.

As voters are not expected to have prognostic powers, the responses are thought to express their current support for the parties to which the question refers. Indeed, as we shall see, much research has established that these questions (despite their use of the word "ever") do precisely tap respondents' orientations to the current electoral context only. Minor variations in question wording seem not to affect this question's validity as long as two conditions are fulfilled. First, the "ever" has to be left unspecified, and not related to a specific upcoming or recent election or to a given time period. Second, the responses for each of the parties should in no way constrain each other: a high score for one party should not require that lower scores be given to other parties, and the scores should not be required to have a constant sum or anything like that. In spite of the fact that the question wording seems at first sight to elicit choice probabilities, so long as the period about which the voter is questioned remains undefined, this appears to ensure that the scores that respondents give each party are not in fact probabilities but rather relate to strengths of support for parties that can vary independently of each other.[9]

---

[9] We want to emphasize the difference between our measurement of party support and the data provided by a different question that at first sight seems very similar. Sometimes respondents are asked to indicate choice probabilities with respect to *intended* voting behavior in an upcoming election (Maas, Steenbergen, and Saris 1990; Burden 1997). In these questions the set of responses must satisfy some constraint, e.g., when requested in the form of percentages, that they sum to 100. Such questions do not yield measures of party support (or utilities in Downsean terminology) but probabilities. These are quite different measures, because support pertains to single parties, whereas the constraint that probabilities sum to 100 percent gives them a relational

In order to be useful as measures of electoral support, responses to these questions should fulfill two criteria. First, the empirical relationship should hold that actual party choice at the time of the survey coincides with the party to which respondents award the highest score. This implies that actual choice should ideally depend only on the responses to these questions; no other empirical factors should impinge on actual choice after controlling for electoral support measured in this way. The responses we obtain fulfill this requirement with flying colors. In the European Elections Study of 1994, for example, the percentage of respondents that actually (said they would) vote for the party that they most strongly support ranges from 93 percent to 99 percent across the different member states of the European Union (EU) (van der Eijk, Franklin, and van der Brug 1999). Similar findings were obtained in the 1989 study (van der Eijk and Franklin 1996, Ch. 20) and the 1999 study (van der Brug, van der Eijk and Franklin forthcoming).[10]

A second criterion is that respondents should not routinely give a "certainly never" response in the case of parties they do not vote for, because the combined answers would then yield no more information than answers to the ubiquitous party choice question. We do indeed find that in all member states of the EU there are substantial numbers of voters whose preferences for their second most preferred party lag only minimally behind their preferences for their most preferred one (the party they actually vote for). For some this is also the case for their third most preferred party. Consequently, for these voters, small fluctuations in party support may change the rank order of the propensities they have to support each party and hence the choice they finally

(or ipsative) character. Support (or utility in the Downsean meaning of the term) should be reflected in nonipsativity of observations (i.e., the number of observations equals the degrees of freedom). Probabilities are obviously ipsative, owing to the fact that they sum to a fixed total (so degrees of freedom are less than the number of parties). In many standard forms of analysis this generates a violation of basic statistical assumptions.

[10] That still leaves a discrepancy of up to 7 percent between the theoretical expectation and its empirical manifestation. Extensive analysis has not shown that the size of this discrepancy is systematically related to any of the independent variables of interest to us in this or other research. It thus reflects (a small degree of) random error in the measurement of vote propensities. Therefore, we consider this measure to be a valid operationalization of our concept of support and thus also of the Downsean concept of utility (van der Brug, van der Eijk, and Franklin forthcoming).

make.[11] The number of parties that are close together in utility and at the top of any particular voter's preference order is usually quite small. Most parties further down a voter's preference order lag so far behind in terms of support that the difference is unlikely to be made up by minor fluctuations. Above all, the second criterion required for a useful measure of utility is fulfilled: in addition to indicating party choice (the party with the highest score), they also provide information on the extent to which respondents are subject to competing pressures from more than one party. The proportion of respondents who would derive high utility from several choice options (the pivotal Voter 3 in Figure 1.2) varies between countries and between election years (see, for example, van der Eijk and Oppenhuis 1991; Kroh, van der Brug, and van der Eijk forthcoming). So does the proportion of voters whose structure of preferences places them effectively beyond the reach of electoral competition. In addition to these two most obvious criteria for interpreting the responses as electoral utilities, a large number of additional validating analyses have been reported elsewhere, most importantly by Tillie (1995) and by Oppenhuis (1995).

Despite the fact that we think our measures of electoral support for political parties are unbiased indicators of what in Downsean terms would be called "electoral utility," we do not generally in this book refer to them as such. We want to avoid using the term utility because there is considerable confusion in the political science discipline as to what the concept of utility actually refers to. Moreover, the term is often used somewhat differently again by economists, who also actively contribute to the literature on economic voting. Finally, the term utility is frequently associated with the so-called rational choice approach to social science theorizing, an approach that is rather different from the one we employ in this book. As stated earlier, we will therefore refer to our measures as party support propensities or party support.

A Design to Analyze Variation in Party Support

Voters' propensity to support political parties is measured in each electoral context for a large number of parties, and each of these parties yields a separate variable. Yet, these variables should all be analyzed

---

[11] These asymmetries will be illustrated in great detail in Chapter 6.

simultaneously as if they were a single (dependent) variable. The logic of the party support concept suggests a common foundation for the factors that yield support rather than party-specific foundations, and only if support for different parties is treated as a single variable can we discover whether this is true.[12] We want to know what it is that leads people to differ in their support for parties, and we would like the answer to this question to explain equally why some parties are strongly supported and others are not. If we are clever in formulating the independent variables in such a way as not to be party specific, it would be theoretically possible for us to completely eliminate the need for party-specific explanations of party support. Obviously, it is an empirical question to what extent support for different parties can be explained by common factors, and to what extent party-specific factors still play a role, but this empirical question can only be answered by a single analysis for all these variables combined.

Treating all the different party support variables for each individual as a single dependent variable can be achieved by a variant on the technique suggested for regression in time and space (Stimson 1985). In practical terms, this involves no more than performing a regression on a "stacked" data matrix (the same operation as performed in conditional logit analysis). This matrix is derived from a "normal" survey data matrix, in which the unit of analysis is transformed from the respondent to the respondent * party combination, as illustrated in Figure 2.1, where transformations are indicated by arrows. In this way, each respondent appears as many times as there are parties for which support propensities were measured, and the level of analysis is effectively changed from the individual level to the individual * party level – a level of analysis called for in our enumeration in Chapter 1 of the requirements for an adequate approach to the study of economic

---

[12] Conditional logit models likewise assume a common foundation in terms of the (unobserved) utilities rather than party-specific foundations. However, in those models, the validity of that assumption is hard to test since it lies at the root of the procedure employed to estimate the unobserved utilities. In our approach, we can establish empirically whether a single set of common factors adequately explains support for each of the parties or whether the foundations of party support are party specific. The way we test this assumption is by assessing the significance of interactions with dummy variables identifying each party. In the analyses reported in this book, such interactions were not found to be statistically significant. Equivalent tests cannot be conducted when conditional logit models are employed.

Original Data Matrix

resp-id	Age	left/right (L/R) position respondent	perceived L/R-position pty 1	perceived L/R position pty 2	perceived L/R position pty 3	L/R dist. to party 1	L/R dist. to party 2	L/R dist. to party 3	vote choice	support for party 1	support for party 2	support for party 3
1	59	4	4	6	7	0	2	3	1	9	5	4
2	40	6	3	7	8	3	1	2	2	5	9	7
3	22	9	3	6	8	6	3	1	3	2	4	7

Stacked Data Matrix

resp-id	id-of-party	Age	left/right (L/R) distance	vote-choice	party support
1	1	59	0	1	9
1	2	59	2	1	5
1	3	59	3	1	4
2	1	40	3	2	5
2	2	40	1	2	9
2	3	40	2	2	7
3	1	22	6	3	2
3	2	22	3	3	4
3	3	22	1	3	7

FIGURE 2.1. Structure of the stacked data matrix.

voting. Separate identifiers are added to this stacked data matrix to identify the respondents and parties in question.

The dependent variable in the analyses is the observed strength of support of the respondent involved in each respondent * party combination for the party involved in the same combination. In this data matrix, the dependent variable thus pertains to each of the parties in turn, as well as to each of the respondents in turn, and can be thought of as *generic* party support. In such a data matrix, many of the independent variables that derive from survey data need to be recast so that they pertain not to a respondent or to a party, but to a *relation* between a respondent and a party.[13] Usually, such independent variables have

---

[13] The structure of this data matrix is basically the same as in conditional logit analyses. The only difference is that the dependent variable is dichotomous in conditional logit (a party was chosen by the respondent in question or it was not), whereas it is a

to be specially constructed. Neither a party's position on the left–right scale nor the position of a voter on that scale will, for example, capture in this design the effect of left–right ideology on party support, but a distance between the left–right positions of each voter and each party does capture this effect, and our surveys do measure the locations of parties in left–right terms as well as the locations of voters, so distances between the voter and party in each voter * party combination can be calculated by subtraction. If we later find that stronger support is given to parties whose distance from the individuals concerned is relatively small, we will have established (or confirmed) the importance of left–right distance in determining which parties are preferred.

In principle, similarity (or dissimilarity) measures could be constructed for any variable for which we could relate party characteristics to voter characteristics. For example, a measure of Catholic affinity could be coded 1 for each voter-party record in which a Catholic voter was paired with a Catholic party and 0 otherwise. In practice, we often do not know on theoretical grounds where a party stands in terms of particular independent variables. In such cases, appropriate independent variables for this stacked design can still be constructed by way of an inductive procedure. This procedure predicts the support score for each respondent on the basis of a simple regression analysis for each of the parties in turn in the (unstacked) data matrix, using as the predictor the independent variable of interest. These predicted scores are, of course, measured on the scale of the dependent variable. They can be interpreted as containing two components: a component that consists of the explanatory power of the independent variable in question and a component that reflects the popularity of the party in question that is generated on other grounds than by the independent variable. By eliminating the second component (which is done by centering the predicted scores), the remainders reflect only variations caused by differences in the independent variable. These predicted and centered values (y-hats) are saved and stacked to yield a generic independent variable.[14] This

---

scale here. Moreover, the nature of the independent variables – expressing a *relation* between voters and parties – is identical in our approach and in conditional logit models.

[14] The original regression equation is $y_i = a + b^*x_i + e_i$. In this equation the predicted value $\hat{y}_i = a + b^*x_i$. By substituting $a + b^*x_i$ with $\hat{y}_i$ in the equation, the new regression equation (using the $\hat{y}_i$ as predictors of party utility) becomes: $y_i = \hat{y}_i + e_i$.

independent variable differs from other generic independent variables constructed in the same way only in terms of the identity of the original independent variable that gave rise to the y-hats concerned.[15]

As an example, we constructed in this manner a proxy measure of each voter's proximity to each of the parties in terms of social class by assessing empirically how well respondents' social class predicted their support for each of the parties. So for each party in turn, in each country in turn, a regression analysis was conducted with social class as the independent variable and support for that party as the dependent variable. The predicted values of each of these regressions (y-hats) were centered (see footnote 14), saved, and inserted into the stacked data matrix as new predictors of party support – but now as a single variable pertaining to every respondent * party combination in the stacked dataset, no matter which particular individual or party was concerned.

Stacked datasets were constructed for each separate country and for each separate election for which we had relevant data. To the extent that the same predictors were available in each survey, the same generic variables could be created in all of them. In each of the stacked datasets, the dependent and the independent variables were transformed in this way into a generic form, making them not only comparable across parties but also comparable across datasets. It was then a trivial matter

---

If one estimates this new regression (using the y-hat as an estimator of y), the estimate of the intercept will be 0, the estimated slope will be 1, and e_i (which forms the basis for the computation of explained variance) is unaltered. When stacking the y-hats on top of each other in the stacked matrix, the newly constructed independent variable is not the predicted value (y-hat), but the deviation of the y-hats from their mean for each party. This still encapsulates the variance in party utility caused by the independent variable, but it prevents differences among parties in the average level of utilities from being incorporated in the newly created independent variable. Such differences among parties in average utilities are caused by other factors besides x_i and should hence not contribute to the variance in the newly created predictor. This procedure is also advocated by Iversen (1991) and by Snijders and Bosker (1999). For a more elaborate discussion, see van der Eijk and Franklin (1996, Ch. 20).

[15] The following independent variables were constructed in this way: social class, income, religion, issues, EU approval, and previous national vote. The measured effects (b's) for these variables have no substantive interpretation, but their importance in our analyses is in controlling for the effects concerned. Effects of interest in this book are mainly those of economic variables that are not constructed in this way and whose effects do have straightforward substantive interpretations.

to pool the stacked datasets for different elections and countries, evidently adding additional variables to identify the country and election to which each record belonged.[16] Once suitably stacked data from separate countries had been pooled, we could employ the identifiers for parties and countries as key variables to permit the matching and merging of additional independent variables relating to each party and to each country context. Obviously, party attributes are constant for all respondent * party combinations that pertain to the same party, and country characteristics are constant for all data from the same country. But these attributes and characteristics do vary within the stacked and pooled dataset. In structuring our data in this way, we follow the decades-old advice of Przeworski and Teune (1970) to replace the names of parties and countries with theoretically relevant variables whose values reflect their characteristics. Analyses on the resulting stacked and pooled data have the advantage not only of being able to take account of additional independent variables that would be constant within any one country but also of taking account of a larger range of variation of independent variables than is usually available within each country. Many variables are likely to find their variance truncated within any one country as compared to the variance found over all countries taken together. Analyzed country by country we would find different effects as a consequence of the different distributional characteristics of the same variable in different countries.[17] By pooling the data, we avoid such spurious country differences while at the same time gaining the benefit of extra leverage in analyses whose variables enjoy the maximum available variation.

We are also able to check that all relevant party and country differences have indeed been taken into account by finally adding party and country dummies as test variables that should not have significant

---

[16] We use the word "pooling" to describe the introduction of records (here respondent * party combinations) from one survey to those of a different survey that has been transformed into the same stacked form.

[17] It would be incorrect to interpret such differences as necessarily indicating differences in the strength of effects. To some extent they are the consequence of selection bias, with each country representing a different truncated distribution. This problem was found in the analyses conducted for a study of voter behavior at European Parliament elections (van der Eijk and Franklin 1996), and the solution adopted here was pioneered in that work (see Tables 20.3 and 20.4 in that book).

effects, either individually or in interaction with substantive independent variables, if all relevant characteristics had been taken into account.

Operationalizing the Two-Stage Model of Party Choice

The approach that we have adopted allows us to analyze party choice by means of the two-stage model referred to in Chapter 1. In the first stage, voters determine their propensity to support each of the parties on offer, taking account of all the different factors that generate such support. We can analyze this process by straightforward multivariate modeling of the dependent variable in the stacked data matrix. In these analyses we may use as independent variables (or as components of interaction terms) the relational variables pertaining to respondent * party combinations as well as attributes of voters, of parties, and of contexts. In the second stage of this model, voters compare these propensities and vote for the party that they support most strongly. Though the stacked and pooled data matrix provides us with leverage through its very comprehensiveness, when preferences are turned into choices, those choices are party – and hence country – specific. So, while our understanding of what makes parties valued can be party – and country – independent, that understanding is readily translated into an explanation of why respondents choose to vote for the specific parties they actually vote for in a particular country at a given moment in time.

By stacking respondent * party combinations and pooling these across countries, our data acquire a structure that makes it possible, using ordinary least squares (OLS) regression, to analyze the effects of variables at different levels of analysis in a single integrated model and to assess interactions between variables at different levels.[18] This provides a simple and straightforward way to address questions of contextuality and heterogeneity.[19]

---

[18] Only by pooled analyses can a systematic assessment of characteristics of the effects of contexts (such as countries or time periods) on individual behavior be attained along the lines originally recommended by Przeworski and Teune (1970).

[19] For examples of the use of stacked and pooled design for assessing homogeneity of parties, see van der Brug, Fennema, and Tillie (2000) and van der Brug and Fennema 2003; for examples of assessing homogeneity of voters, see van der Brug, van der Eijk, and Franklin (2002).

Because of the multilevel structure of the data, it might be wondered why we do not employ multilevel analysis methods (hierarchical linear modeling – HLM) that would appear to be ideally suited for these types of data. The main advantage of these models is that they prevent tests of significance from being conducted with inflated degrees of freedom.

Inflated degrees of freedom can spring from two different sources. The first is usually referred to as the "problem of intraclass correlation": contextual characteristics often generate a degree of homogeneity between the individual cases from the same context, which violates the assumption that they are independent observations. The more homogeneous the individual cases are within each context, the less independent information they provide (cf. Snijders and Bosker 1999; Diez Roux 2002; Steenbergen and Jones 2002). This problem affects the use of individual-level independent variables in pooled datasets. Adequate specification of contextual characteristics will account for this homogeneity and remove the danger of testing significance of individual-level variables with inflated degrees of freedom. HLM is helpful in avoiding the inflated degrees of freedom problem only to the extent that context-generated homogeneity remains after accounting for contextual variables. In our case, theoretical considerations derived from previous analyses on the propensity to vote variable allowed us to specify contextual variables that account adequately for intraclass correlation, so that our tests of the significance of individual-level factors in the pooled data are not inflated (the intraclass correlation accounts for only 0.9 percent of the variance in the dependent variable).

The second problem concerning degrees of freedom relates to testing significance of independents of higher-level units. Our stacked and pooled dataset contains more than 237,000 records, but this does not alter the fact that the data represent only forty-two political-economic contexts. One could argue that a test of the significance of contextual factors should be defined on the number of higher-level units. Were we to do so, we would find that none of the economic conditions investigated has a significant effect. Yet, we consider this an unsatisfactory and unjustified basis to conclude that the economy has no effect on voters' support for parties. Most aggregate-level studies of economic voting find effects of economic conditions of the kind reflected in our hypotheses (to be elaborated in Chapter 3). Calculating standard errors for aggregate variables using an N of 42 would thus, without good reason, greatly increase the risk of Type II errors (possibly leading us to conclude mistakenly that there were no effects of economic voting).

One might think that our data contain yet a different form of multilevel structure that requires special modeling considerations. Should the voter * party records in the stacked data matrix be considered as hierarchically nested within individual respondents as higher-level units, and should that be reflected in degrees of freedom? The answer to this question is no. The dependent variable in the voter * party records is not just a characteristic of an individual that is equally reflected in the other voter * party records that are associated with the same individual. It is as much a reflection of characteristics of parties as it is of individuals. The same holds for the independent variables that are distances or similarities (the latter operationalized by way of the y-hat procedure explained earlier). The multilevel structure is therefore not a hierarchical one of voter * party recoreds nested within voters, but is a complete cross-classification of voter * party records nested equally within voters and within parties. This complexity is not easily handled by HLM, so this perspective, too, provides no compelling reason to employ explicit multilevel modeling, particularly as the complexities of the data structure can be handled in a straightforward fashion in OLS by specifying, where necessary, higher-order interaction effects.[20]

Though we do not engage in HLM, we are aware of the fact that disaggregating our data to the level of the individual * party dramatically increases the degrees of freedom that would be present in a standard regression analysis. Therefore, we report robust standard errors for

[20] Testing whether higher-level units (individual respondents) account for residual variation in lower-level ones (voter * party records) is entirely redundant in this case. We do know that we have not exhausted individual-level explanatory characteristics. Some of these were not present in our data (for example, postmaterialism and other value orientations, orientations toward political leaders, information about voters' social networks, etc.). To the extent that we err here, we do so in commission, as such factors are standardly omitted in the extant literature on economic voting. Other omitted variables would include idiosyncratic response tendencies (cf. Saris 1988) that are not of central concern to us here, particularly because there are no indications that such factors are systematically correlated to the independent variables that we do use (in other words, omitting them is unlikely to generate omitted variable bias in our estimates).

our findings, treating the individual survey respondents as units for the purpose of computing standard errors rather than the responses they give for each party they rate. The logic here is that individuals may give different patterns of answers (with several parties tied for first place in the case of undecided individuals, but with much more differentiated ratings for strong party identifiers). This would create problems of heteroskedasticity if the respondent * party combination were used as the basis for computing standard errors. The procedure we employ gives much larger (more robust) standard errors than we would otherwise get. Using panel-corrected standard errors (Beck and Katz 1995), in which each individual is treated as a panel, would be an alternative approach. However, we find that this gives smaller (less robust) standard errors than our approach.

Though some may disagree with the reasoning outlined here that led us to adopt the methods for calculating statistical significance employed in this book, such skeptics might like to bear in mind that the number of coefficients significant at the 0.05 level in an analysis (in Chapter 5) where theory predicted no significant effects was just what would have been found on the basis of chance: about one in twenty (for several hundred coefficients). Had our methods of calculating significance levels set the bar too high or too low, we would not have obtained these results.

In addition to reporting robust standard errors, we consider as significant only coefficients whose standard errors yield significance at the 0.01 level. Given the large number of cases at the individual level in this study (over 33,000 cases), using the more conventional 0.05 level would yield significance even for substantively tiny effects. More importantly, given that we estimate a great many effects, many of these would prove significant at the 0.05 level simply on the basis of chance. By using a more stringent criterion for significance, we ensure substantive importance for our findings and limit the risk of capitalizing on chance.

Returning to the two-stage model, the second stage in modeling voter behavior provides us with additional analytical possibilities. Estimated explanatory models of party support can be used as a basis for assessing the consequences for party choice of changes in the independent variables. This makes it possible to estimate the consequences of variations in economic conditions in terms of the choices that individual voters make and – by aggregating these – in terms of the election results to which those choices collectively give rise. Explaining how this works in practice will be deferred until Chapter 6, where we also present the relevant analyses.

Advantages of Our Approach

We can be quite specific about the ways in which our approach avoids the problems and pitfalls of traditional approaches to the study of economic voting. Its most important advantage is its superior representation of the choice process, which should give rise to superior estimates of the effects of economic conditions because of the separation of that process into two different stages.

The first stage is analytically complex, but by focusing on voters' support for each of the parties that compete for their votes, we can analyze a dependent variable whose shifts in value are not constrained by the competitive situation between parties. We showed in Figure 1.2 how a change in economic conditions might yield uniform shifts in party support even while giving rise to very nonuniform changes in party choice. Abstracting from the combined process just the stage that relates to party support gives us the possibility of detecting effects that would be hard to detect on the basis of changes in party choice. More importantly, it gives us the possibility of properly specifying the process that generates the differences in levels of party support. The level of measurement of the dependent variable, at the confluence of individual and party, enables us to analyze the impact not only of individual characteristics (as has been customary in individual-level studies) but also of party characteristics. And the pooling of multiple surveys from different political contexts enables us to take account of system characteristics that would be constant in any one survey.

Because the dependent variable is a rating scale that can be interpreted as an interval-level measure, it has the advantage (in comparison with a dependent variable indicating the choice between parties) of permitting us to bring to bear the full power of OLS regression analysis in evaluating the effects of economic conditions on party support while controlling for other influences, yielding coefficients that can be straightforwardly compared in terms of their relative magnitudes. In this way, we can discover not only whether the economy affects party support but also whether this is a strong or weak effect relative to other influences.

The second stage is analytically simple, because it is based on a simple maximizing decision rule: voters choose the party that they support the most.[21] However, separating this choice into a separate stage is substantively very powerful. It enables us to take account of the fact that different parties and different voters are situated very differently in terms of the competition for votes. Most voters will not change their votes as a result of changes in their degree of support for the various parties. Some of these changes in support will pertain to parties that are too far from serious consideration to have any chance of being chosen no matter what changes there may be in their level of support. Other changes will be in the wrong direction given the competitive situation of the parties concerned: increasing the support for a party that is already in first place or reducing the support for a party that is already in second or lower place. It matters very much which precise parties see their support changed and where those parties stand in the competition for votes. Distinguishing the choices between parties in a separate stage enables us to take account of such factors. Above all, analyzing party choice at a point at which the structure of party competition for each voter is already known enables us to take account of the

---

[21] The proposition that "voters choose the party that they support the most" seems to fly in the face of numerous observations of so-called strategic voting: situations where voters do not choose the party they prefer most, for instance, because that party has little chance of being elected (cf. Bowler and Lanoue 1992; Niemi, Whitten, and Franklin 1992; Franklin, Niemi, and Whitten 1994; Heath and Evans 1994; Ordeshook and Zeng 1997; Alvarez and Nagler 2000; Karp, Vowles, Banducci, and Donovan 2002). The difference is, however, a matter of different uses of similar terms. Many arguments about strategic voting use a decontextualized notion of support (they refer to people's "true" preferences, irrespective of political context). Our measures of (propensity to) support, however, are situated in a particular context in which one of the parties may well be unlikely to "win" (in any meaningful interpretation of the term). To voters who value winning, the propensity to support that party will therefore be smaller than it would be in a different context where that party had a high likelihood of winning. In our model, therefore, strategic considerations are thus relevant in the first stage, not in the second. Tillie (1995) operationalized voters' strategic concerns and demonstrated that those were of relevance in the first stage, and not in the second stage of models like ours.

extent to which each party has succeeded in mobilizing its full electoral potential. As explained in Chapter 1, the extent to which parties can gain or lose votes as a consequence of changes in economic conditions depends ultimately on where they stand in relation to their potential support. Not being able to take account of parties' competitive situation was the major defect in traditional approaches to the study of economic or any other kind of voting.

The analytical approach of this two-stage model follows very closely the logic of Downs (1957), who also explicitly discusses the importance of distinguishing analytically between party support (generally referred to as party utility, as already mentioned) and party choice. Our approach does not, however, require the analyst to use just those independent variables that Downsean theory suggests. In our models, we do control for one of the crucial independent variables in the Downsean model, left–right proximity to parties, but we also control for social-structural variables such as class and religion, as well as other variables that have no place in Downs's theory. The design of our analyses is similar to the one employed in the analysis of directional issue voting (MacDonald, Listhaug, and Rabinowitz 1991). Ever since their first major publication on this topic (Rabinowitz and MacDonald 1989), these authors have eschewed a dependent variable measuring the binary distinction between the party voted for on the one hand and all other parties on the other, based on the same well-established observation that we cite: in multiparty systems, voters commonly regard several parties as worthy recipients of their vote rather than just a single one. The difference is that while Rabinowitz and MacDonald use "sympathy ratings" (also known as "thermometer scales"), we employ measures of party support.[22]

Our approach permits us to analyze both stages in the Downsean calculus of voting, analyzing first the support that voters give to different

---

[22] The link between sympathy ratings and vote choice is assumed, but not tested in the various publications by Rabinowitz, MacDonald, and their associates. In this study, we employ the answers to questions for which the link with vote choice has been demonstrated empirically (as explained earlier in this chapter). Another difference between our method and theirs is that we also investigate the second stage in the two-stage model: converting individual preferences for all parties into individual choices for each party and aggregating these into election outcomes. This second stage is not investigated in the various publications by Rabinowitz, MacDonald, and their associates.

political parties, which we address in Chapters 4 and 5, and then the choices that they make (and the electoral outcomes that result), which we address in Chapter 6. Before we move to those analyses, however, we need to elaborate our hypotheses and introduce the individual-level data that we employ in this study, along with the various political and economic contexts from which we derive additional variables. That is the subject of Chapter 3.

3

Hypotheses and Data

The Theoretical and Empirical Setting

In this chapter, we will pull together the theoretical expectations we derive from the relevant literature (much of which has already been referred to in Chapter 1) and set them out in the form of testable hypotheses. These expectations mainly concern the effects of economic conditions on voting. They will be complemented, however, by expectations that are included to produce the control variables we need if our models are to be well specified. Having set out the relevant hypotheses, we will then describe the data with which we test those hypotheses, and the economic and political settings from which the data were obtained.

Hypotheses

Our theorizing can be divided into three categories. First is the fundamental expectation upon which all of the economic voting literature is based: that government standing with the voters will be hurt by bad economic times and (perhaps) helped by good economic times (e.g., Tufte 1978; Chrystal and Alt 1981; Hibbs 1977; Fair 1988; Lewis-Beck 1988; Markus 1988, 1992; Erikson 1989; Mackuen, Erikson, and Stimson 1992; Powell and Whitten 1993; Whitten and Palmer 1999; Nadeau and Lewis-Beck 2001), together with its generally unspoken corollary relating to opposition parties (that they should in some way suffer less or even benefit from bad economic conditions). Then we move on to the elaborations of this hypothesis that become possible in the context of models that distinguish between different government (and opposition) parties. Finally, we introduce and develop certain expectations that have nothing to do with economic voting but that would affect the standing of government parties. Variables deriving from these expectations need to be controlled for if our estimates of the effects of economic conditions are to be unbiased.

So, we start with expectations regarding economic voting. Since we hope for better-specified models by focusing on parties rather than on governments, the expectations we derive from the literature referred to in the previous paragraph have to be reformulated in terms of parties, yielding our first hypothesis:

H_1: The state of the economy has effects on voters' support for government parties – positive in the case of economic growth, negative in the case of unemployment and inflation.

Previous research has implicitly assumed that effects on opposition parties would be either zero or opposite to the effects on government parties. We see no reason to expect either regularity. If the relationship between government and opposition is a hostile and uncompromising one, it seems logical that effects would be oppositely signed. If, however, opposition parties can influence government policy, then they should share to at least some extent in whatever credit or blame voters apportion for that policy. Our second hypothesis is thus:

H_2: Effects of the economy on voters' support for opposition parties will be different than for government parties – either smaller in magnitude or differently signed.

As a supplement to these two primary hypotheses, we consider it likely that the extent to which parties will be held responsible for economic conditions will vary according to some of their attributes and according to specific conditions. That is what we turn to now. To start with, we might expect parties that have been in government for a longer period to be held more responsible for economic conditions than parties that have held government office for a shorter period. Particularly in poor economic conditions, government parties will try to externalize blame by pointing to their predecessors or to external conditions outside their control. We expect that such attempts will become increasingly less effective the longer a party has been in government. We have to keep in mind, however, that parties do not necessarily all become part of a government at the same time. Sometimes coalitions change in composition during the course of a parliamentary term, and newer additions may not be held as fully responsible as are members of longer standing. Additionally, if we look beyond a single parliament, we have to deal with the fact that coalitions change their complexion over time but that some parties are almost always included. Some parties, such as the Italian Christian Democrats until the early 1990s (as well as their Dutch and Belgian counterparts), appeared to be permanent government parties, though with a variety of changing partners. Evidently, when assessing responsibility for long-term economic performance, it is quite possible that voters would distinguish long-term government members from those who have been members of the government for a shorter time. This theorizing gives rise to:

H3: Effects of the economy on support for government parties will reflect the length of time the party has been a member of the government.

Even leaving aside time in office, we do not necessarily expect all government parties to be held equally accountable. Single-party governments (as in Britain during our period) might indeed take all credit and all blame for what happens on their watch, but parties that share government power in a coalition need not share responsibility equally. Past research has generally assumed implicitly that all government parties are treated as if each was the only government party (the prime exceptions are Anderson 1995; Norpoth 1996; Wilkin, Haller, and Norpoth 1997). It seems more logical to us that credit and blame would be assigned to coalition partners according to their influence on government policy with respect to the economy: large parties have more control over policymaking and can reasonably be held more accountable for the results than small parties. Moreover, there is no reason to suppose that the electorate would treat opposition parties any differently. Large opposition parties are more likely to find themselves in a position to influence economic policy, and small opposition parties less likely. Large opposition parties may therefore not be exempt from blame for poor economic conditions, particularly if they were in government in the not too distant past. This might even result in negative economic developments impinging upon support for all mainstream parties that are considered to be part of "the regime." On the basis of this consideration, we should distinguish parties not only by their status as government or opposition parties, but also by their size. In all European countries during the period we study, large parties (measured by the proportion of seats they hold in parliament) are also potential governing parties.[1] If economic recession decreases support for mainstream political parties, large opposition parties may well lose support as a consequence of a slowing economy, just as large government parties do.

In addition to size, control over specific government portfolios might be expected to affect the extent to which government parties are credited or blamed for economic conditions. This relates in particular to the prime minister and the minister of finance. These ministers in particular attract media attention when the economy comes under scrutiny, and consequently their responsibility is more visible to the public than the responsibility of other ministers.[2] Our next two hypotheses are thus:

H4a: Effects of the economy on support for all parties will be distributed among them in proportion to their size;

H4b: Effects of the economy on the support for parties that are members of a governing coalition will be strongest for the parties that control the prime ministership or the ministry of finance.

It is even possible that (many) voters would take party size into account to the exclusion of government status, holding larger parties more responsible than smaller ones, irrespective of whether they are government or opposition parties. Particularly in contexts where it is not clear which parties are responsible for the state of the economy (see later), it may be more important for voters to judge parties by their identity as "important players" than by their status as government parties. It is therefore possible that party size, being a considerably more durable party characteristic in most countries than whether a party is in government, would be used by many voters as a cue or

---

[1] We use party size as a proxy for what Sartori (1976) called "players." Other authors have referred to such parties as "system parties" or as "coalitionable." Such parties are generally fairly large, although at times there were relatively large parties that were not coalitionable, such as the Communist Party in Italy and today's Belgian Vlaams Blok. By looking at size as a continuous measure, we extend Sartori's notion from a dichotomy to a measure of how much of a player a party can be considered to be.

[2] Testing this expectation may be complicated, however, by multicollinearity: in our data the largest party always controls the prime ministership and often also the ministry of finance.

proxy informing them whether the party is a player in the policymaking process. So, H4a may turn out in practice to override H1 and H2, at least in certain countries and at certain times.

How parties behave is at least partially determined by their ideologies. These ideologies affect the positions parties take on concrete issues and the types of themes they prioritize, as well as the reputation parties have for solving concrete problems. There are thus good reasons to expect that parties of different ideological complexions will pursue different economic policies. That this will probably be the case is also suggested by the results of content analyses of party manifestos, which have – not altogether surprisingly – shown that right-wing parties emphasize different topics within the economic domain than left-wing parties do (see, for example, Budge, Robertson, and Hearl 1987; Klingemann, Hofferbert, and Budge 1994).

It is possible, of course, that parties would pursue different policies but with the same objectives. Hibbs (1977) argued, however, that left-wing parties pursue different goals than right-wing parties do because of the different interests of their core supporters. He predicted that right-wing parties would give highest priority to low inflation, whereas left-wing parties would give highest priority to fighting unemployment.

To the extent that voters are aware of the priorities of parties, they might hold them accountable in different ways. If supporters of left-wing parties do not expect those parties to give priority to keeping down inflation, they might not mind very much if inflation increases under a left-wing government. However, if the same thing were to happen under a right-wing government that was expected to keep inflation at bay, supporters of those parties could be more dissatisfied.

But governments do not always consist of ideologically coherent parties. As mentioned in Chapter 1, governments quite often span the division between left and right.[3] Therefore, we may expect that support for parties of different ideological complexion will be differently affected by various economic conditions. This could well explain why the fortunes of coalition members at ensuing elections are not necessarily consistent. In a period of strong economic growth coupled with

---

[3] As previously mentioned, if we divide parties according to which side they fall on from the simple midpoint of a left–right scale, then, in our data, eighteen out of forty-two governments were split in these terms.

high inflation, for example, right-leaning members of a government might suffer electorally but not left-leaning members.

It is at this junction that we should also distinguish between prospective and retrospective patterns of economic voting. Retrospective patterns of voting in this context would imply that support for left-wing parties would suffer in times of high unemployment, particularly when they are government parties or large parties. Likewise, retrospective voting would imply that (large, governing) right-wing parties would suffer in times of high inflation. Prospectively, however, we would expect support for left-wing parties to rise in times of high unemployment, not so much as a reward for their contribution to policies that brought this condition about, but rather in response to the expectation that left-leaning parties will consider unemployment (and its consequences) a more important problem for government policymaking than right-leaning parties would. The same thing might be observed in the case of right-leaning parties at times of inflation. Our fifth hypothesis is thus:

H5: Effects of unemployment on party support will be strongest for left parties, whereas effects of inflation will be strongest for right parties. The signs of these effects will indicate whether economic voting is retrospective (negative) or prospective (positive).

In regard to H5, and taking account of our earlier comment regarding party size, if there do prove to be circumstances in which voters take account of a party's size rather than its government–opposition status, those might be situations in which prospective voting would be particularly prevalent. To the extent that government status is not helpful to voters in apportioning credit or blame for economic conditions, retrospective voting would make little sense. Large parties might be generally understood to bear primary responsibility for a poor economy, but voters would be unlikely to use this knowledge to shift their votes to small parties (the result would be that erstwhile small parties immediately become large ones, but we know that empirically this does not happen). Instead, what would make more sense in such circumstances is that voters would distinguish between large parties on the basis of their prospective concerns, increasing their support for parties whose policies are most relevant to the problem (be it unemployment, inflation, or low growth) at hand. To a political scientist (who would

know as a matter of course which parties are in government and which
ones influence policy), such circumstances might appear farfetched, but
they are not at all unrealistic for people who operate with lower levels
of information.

Turning to contextual effects, past research has suggested a number of such effects that need to be taken into account in any well-
specified model. In particular, the extent to which political systems
allow a clear identification of responsibility for policy has been found
to play an important role in moderating the effects of economic conditions. This variable rates countries according to how strongly responsibility for policymaking is concentrated or, conversely, fragmented and
divided. Countries such as the United States, where separated powers
and frequent episodes of divided government stand in the way of clear
accountability, get low scores. Countries like Britain get high scores.
Past research using this variable has found that high-clarity contexts
show greater evidence of economic voting than do low-clarity contexts (Powell and Whitten 1993; Whitten and Palmer 1999). In countries where responsibility for government policies is spread across large
numbers of actors, it becomes very difficult for voters to determine
who should be held responsible for the state of the economy. In such
circumstances, many voters may not weigh the state of the economy
at all, so that the effects of economic conditions become weaker in
general. Consequently, the hypotheses presented earlier may be more
or less strongly supported in countries that score differently in this
respect. Specifically, we expect all of the effects hypothesized earlier to
be stronger in systems with high clarity of responsibility.

A similar logic can be applied to systemic classifications made by
Lijphart (1999) and by Esping-Andersen (1990, 1999). Both of these
authors have proposed typologies of political systems that differ in
ways that would be relevant to economic voting. Lijphart's classification distinguishes consensual from majoritarian systems. Only in
majoritarian systems would the distinction between governing and
opposition parties be particularly relevant. Esping-Andersen's typology distinguishes countries with strong social protection from other
countries. Where social protection against the consequences of economic conditions is weak, we expect voters to focus more strongly on
economic conditions as a basis for party support. The two classification
schemes pick out generally the same countries as the Powell and
Whitten classification, making it possibly quite hard in practice to

distinguish between these different reasons why certain countries would find muted reactions to changes in the economy. So, these considerations give rise to three linked hypotheses:

H6a: All of H1 to H6 will be more strongly supported in systems of high clarity;

H6b: All of H1 to H6 will be more strongly supported in majoritarian political systems;

H6c: All of H1 to H6 will be more strongly supported in systems with liberal welfare states.

Most of the literature from which these hypotheses derive implicitly assumes that economic conditions impinge equally on all classes and conditions of voters. Indeed, the assumption that changes in economic conditions are widely felt is one of the reasons for academic interest in the subject of economic voting. However, some scholars have suggested that different groups of voters react differently to economic conditions (Sniderman, Brody, and Tetlock 1991; Bartle 1997; Krause 1997; Pattie and Johnston 2001; Dorussen and Taylor 2002; Kroh 2003; Zaller 2005). Differential reactions could provide evidence of pocketbook voting (Dorussen and Taylor 2002) if the voters most likely to be adversely affected by unemployment or inflation are the ones who react most strongly to those economic conditions. It also could provide evidence of people's reactions to economic conditions being moderated by different values or different skills. It has, for example, been proposed that the way in which voters respond to the conditions they experience is dependent on their political sophistication, with voters of intermediate sophistication being most likely to react to certain types of news, presumably including news about the economy (Ansolabehere and Iyengar 1995: 189). Alternatively, it has been argued that less sophisticated voters would be relatively more responsive to short-term factors such as economic conditions because of their lack of long-term party attachments or ideological orientations (Zaller 2005). Any such heterogeneity would make it harder to detect effects of economic conditions, especially if these effects are small. However, on the basis of the existing evidence, our seventh hypothesis is:

H7: Reactions to economic conditions are heterogeneous among voters, with the most sophisticated voters responding least strongly to economic conditions, and with those dependent on welfare being more sensitive to unemployment and pensioners being more sensitive to inflation.

When it comes to translating the propensity to support parties into votes (and hence into election outcomes), our expectations are highly contingent on circumstance, and in particular on the existing structure of electoral competition between parties. The party with the highest support propensity is first in a voter's preference ordering and gets that person's actual vote. Therefore, economic conditions matter for actual choice only to the extent that they change which party is first in each voter's order of preferences. The implication for party fortunes is that changes in economic conditions will lead a party to gain or lose votes only to the extent that it can acquire or lose first place in large numbers of voters' preferences. A party that has received the votes of virtually all of its potential supporters can hardly do better, and a party that has been reduced to its bedrock of support can hardly do worse, placing a ceiling on the gains (and a floor under the losses) that certain parties can enjoy or suffer. More generally, except when parties are doing neither well nor badly in relation to their electoral potential, these boundaries will create asymmetries in the effects of economic conditions on voters' party choices even when there are no such asymmetries in the effects of economic conditions on the strength of party support. The distinction between support for parties and actual choice may well permit us to account for a phenomenon observed in past studies that is known as the "asymmetric loss curve" (Bloom and Price 1975; Claggett 1986) and that past researchers have ascribed to a psychological mechanism known as "grievance asymmetry" (e.g., Bloom and Price 1975; Price and Sanders 1994; Nannestad and Paldam 1997, 2002). But such an asymmetry has only been found at the aggregate level. Attempts to substantiate the asymmetry with individual-level data have not been successful (Kiewiet 1983; Lewis-Beck 1988; Nannestad and Paldam 1997), creating something of a puzzle for many scholars (see, e.g., Stevenson 2002: 46). We believe that this inconsistency can be resolved if we look separately at preference formation and party choice. At the party choice stage we expect to find:

H8: Deteriorating economic conditions generally have different consequences for actual choice and for parties' vote shares than economic improvements of the same magnitude have for the same parties

H3 to H6 assume that supporters of different parties react differently (in terms of actual choice) to economic conditions because of features of those parties that go beyond the simple question of whether they are government or opposition parties (the prevalent assumption made in past research). If these hypotheses are confirmed, it will follow that this basic assumption of past research cannot be sustained, calling into question fundamental aspects of the research designs employed in past studies.

Finally, our models should take account of a number of considerations that have nothing to do with economic voting per se but that would nevertheless affect the level of support for government parties, presenting the possibility of omitted variable bias if they are not taken into account. The most important of these relate to the characteristics and concerns of individual voters, which are known to explain considerable variance in party support, quite apart from any effects on party support of economic conditions. We do not propose any specific hypotheses with regard to these effects, but we expect them to be similar to those obtained in past research. Indeed, finding such expected effects will help to confirm that our model is well specified.

With regard to parties, various studies have observed a systematic pattern of vote loss for incumbent government parties at elections, irrespective of economic conditions. This loss has been estimated at about 2.5 percent of the votes for government parties over the course of an electoral cycle (Powell and Whitten 1993; Nannestad and Paldam 1994, 2002; Paldam 1991). This "cost of governing" had been predicted by Downs (1957) and is commonly interpreted as the consequence of governments' inability to satisfy conflicting policy demands of different groups of voters, a problem that is not relevant to opposition parties. An auxiliary interpretation (Wlezien 1995, 2004; Franklin and Wlezien 1997; Franklin and Hughes 1999) attributes this declining support to government policy satisfying demand that helped bring parties into office. This explanation has the advantage of helping to account for the fact that government popularity tends to improve during the second half of a term of office. This would be the period during which governing parties try to formulate the policies that they will propose and defend at the following election. To the extent that these policies are attractive to party supporters, they supplant the policies that have been (successfully or otherwise) implemented during the current parliamentary session and provide a reason for voters to support a governing party for another term in office. Various scholars (Reif 1984;

Marsh and Franklin 1996; Marsh 1998; Schmitt and Reif 2003) have found that this pattern exists in the case of elections to the European Parliament.[4] Governing parties tend to lose most votes when European Parliament elections are held about two years after national elections.

This literature thus leads us to expect two effects on support for government parties that are not connected with economic conditions or with individual-level effects on party support, as follows:

H9a: We expect to find a cost of governing that will manifest as a negative effect on all parties that are members of the government;

H9b: We expect to find a loss and recovery of support for governing parties over the course of the (national) electoral cycle, such that support for government parties depends on precisely when in that cycle for each country our data are collected.

Most of these hypotheses will be tested in Chapter 4 by means of regression analysis, using party support as the dependent variable, as explained in Chapter 2. However, H8 cannot be tested by regression analysis but requires an estimation procedure that will be elaborated in Chapter 6, where we focus on election outcomes.

Data

As explained at length in the first two chapters of this book, we believe that in order to make progress in the study of economic voting, we need survey data that meet a number of important criteria. First of all, we need to combine data across a large number of political systems to generate a sufficiently large variation in political and economic contexts. Second, we need data in which – in addition to actual or intended party choice – the propensity to support is measured for a range of political parties, small and large ones, government parties as well as opposition parties, left- and right-leaning parties, parties that have only recently become members of governing coalitions, as well as parties that have governed for decades. Finally, the data need to include the most important control variables, which (in addition to standard demographics

---

[4] These elections occur at different times in the national electoral cycles of most countries (Luxembourg is the only country whose national elections have been synchronized to the same cycle as elections to the European Parliament).

such as class, religion, and age) include issue preferences and left–right distances from parties.

For the analyses in this book, we employ three large-scale surveys of the electorates of member countries of the EC/EU conducted in mid-1989, mid-1994, and mid-1999 (see Appendix A). These provide us with a total of forty-two political contexts for which distinct readings of economic conditions are available and within which we can evaluate individual-level political preferences (and the consequences of those preferences for party choice). The occasions for these surveys were the five-yearly elections to the European Parliament, but it is important to stress that none of the survey items used in this book relate specifically to the European Parliament elections. All of the items we employ relate either to the national political environments within member countries or to politics in general. From the perspective of our interests here, the surveys are convenient, equally-spaced sources of survey data that meet the requirements for an analysis of economic voting as set out in Chapters 1 and 2. In the remainder of this chapter, we will first discuss the possible consequences of the fact that the data collection took place following elections to the European Parliament. Then we will discuss the political and economic contexts in which the data were collected.

European Elections Studies

Our data come from a series of independent cross-section surveys fielded immediately after elections to the European Parliament held in all countries of the EU in 1989, 1994, and 1999. In 1989 and 1994 the questionnaires, administered in the language of each country, were contained in the European Omnibus Surveys, which also contained the regular Eurobarometer surveys of the Commission of the European Communities. Because of their great potential for cross-country comparative research, Eurobarometers have been used successfully in prior studies of economic voting (e.g., Lewis-Beck 1988). The 1989 and 1994 studies both involved interviews with some 12,500 respondents divided into independent national samples of some 1,000 respondents each. This number was smaller for Luxembourg (about 300). In 1999 the study was based on a stand-alone survey conducted by telephone interviewing. The number of interviews carried out in 1999 varied between the countries, with some 1,000 interviews in Denmark,

France, Germany, the Netherlands, Spain, and Britain and some 500 interviews in each of the remaining countries except Luxembourg and Italy. In Luxembourg, 300 interviews were felt sufficient. In Italy, the questionnaire was administered to a telepanel, and some 3,700 interviews were realized.

The studies provide three convenient sources of data regarding citizen preferences for the political parties that compete for their support – data that are readily linked to measures of economic conditions in all countries of the EU. In 1989 and 1994 the twelve member states were Belgium, Denmark, France, Germany, Britain, Greece, Ireland, Italy, Luxembourg, the Netherlands, Portugal, and Spain. In 1999 three new members joined the EU: Austria, Finland, and Sweden. Because of the federal structure of the Belgian state, Flanders and Wallonia have separate party systems. This means that Flemish parties compete for the support of Flemish voters, while Wallonian parties compete for the support of Wallonian voters. We therefore treat these Belgian regions as two separate political systems.[5] The combination of three sets of surveys thus yields variation over forty-two economic and political contexts (thirteen in 1989, thirteen in 1994, and sixteen in 1999).[6] Within our forty-two contexts, we investigate preferences for a total of 295 parties across 32,950 individuals.[7]

---

[5] We treat the two Belgian regions as separate contexts because our dependent variable – the propensity to vote for each of the parties in a political system – is context specific. Flemish voters can vote only for Flemish parties, which are entirely different from those that vie for the votes of Walloon voters. As we explained in Chapter 2, this allows us to take party competition into account when analyzing the impact of economic conditions. However, two of our indicators of economic conditions – economic growth and inflation – have the same value in Flanders and Wallonia. Change in unemployment was measured separately for these two contexts.

[6] Respondents from Northern Ireland, as well as respondents from East Germany in 1994 (soon after German reunification), were excluded from our analyses, because normal patterns of credit and blame were not expected to operate in the same way in these contexts as elsewhere.

[7] In this book we focus on data from the postelection wave of each study (where there was more than one wave), which, in 1989, was largely funded by a grant to Mark Franklin from the British Economic and Social Research Council and in 1994 by grants to Hermann Schmitt and Cees van der Eijk from the German and Dutch National Science Foundations. The 1999 study was funded largely by the University of Amsterdam, with important additional contributions from the Dutch National Science Foundation, the Centro de Investigaciones Sociológicas (CIS) (Madrid), the University of Mannheim, and Trinity College, Connecticut. The studies are available for secondary analysis from Steinmetz Archives (Amsterdam) and the Zentral Archive (Cologne), as well as from the Inter-university Consortium for Political and Social Research

This book investigates the effect of national economic conditions on propensities to support national parties and on (intended) national party choice; and it is far from obvious that European elections would provide the kind of political context in which citizens would hold national governing parties accountable for their management of national economies. There are, however, two reasons why the fact that the surveys were originally conceived as European election studies is irrelevant. The first reason is that the crucial dependent variable, party support propensities, is derived from a survey item that does not refer to European elections and that is, indeed, designed to tap orientations toward national political parties (we discussed this survey item at length in Chapter 2). The dependent variable in our study is found to be almost perfectly linked to (intended) votes in national elections on the basis of the Downsean support maximization decision rule (see Chapter 1 and Figure 1.1). Indeed, the link to national elections is closer than the link to the European Parliament elections that are the ostensible object of these studies. EU-wide, only 87 percent of respondents voted in those elections for the party to which they gave the highest utility in 1999, 6 percent less than the 93 percent who gave the highest utility to the party they said they would have voted for in a national election held on the day of the interview (van der Brug, van der Eijk, and Franklin, forthcoming).

A second reason we feel justified in using European Elections Studies to study economic voting is that European elections have been found to have the character of second-order *national* elections (Reif and Schmitt 1980). This means that party choice in these elections is overwhelmingly motivated by factors that derive from the national political arena in each country. Other research (van der Eijk and Franklin 1996; van der Eijk, Franklin, and Marsh 1996; Schmitt and Thomassen 1999; van der Brug and van der Eijk forthcoming) has shown that elections to the European Parliament do not provide stimuli that divert citizens from the concerns that characterize their national political circumstances.

(ICPSR) at the University of Michigan. The studies are extensively documented on the European Elections Studies Web site (http://www.europeanelectionstudies.net, which also includes a bibliography of publications emanating from these studies). Altogether 36,002 respondents were interviewed. When pooled and stripped of cases that were lacking essential data on the dependent variable, they give us an overall total of 32,950 usable cases for analysis.

The reasoning just outlined can be checked in a straightforward and rather definitive fashion. Though European elections are generally conducted separately from national elections, because the two election cycles are usually of different lengths there have always been a few instances of national elections occurring on the same day as European elections (three in 1989, one in 1994, and two in 1999).[8] These six cases provide us with a means of checking our reasoning.[9] If the basis for national party choice at the time of a real national election were to differ from the basis for the hypothetical choices given by respondents asked how they would vote if a national election were held that day, then we should be able to detect such differences by using appropriate interactions with a dummy variable indicating whether a real (concurrent) national election was held at the same time as the European election. In past analyses (Oppenhuis 1995; van der Eijk and Franklin 1996), the use of such dummy variables did not succeed in demonstrating anything special about support for political parties at the time of concurrent national elections. By implication, the findings of those studies were no different from findings that would have been obtained had the dependent variable related to real rather than hypothetical national elections. In Chapter 7 we will show that the same is true of the analyses conducted in this book.

For these reasons, European election studies provide data sources that appear not at all unsuited to an analysis of economic voting. Indeed, we have argued elsewhere that there can be considerable advantages to employing studies of nationwide elections that are not national elections (van der Eijk and Franklin 1996). National executive office-holding is not at stake in these elections. No government stands to be dismissed or affirmed in office. For that reason, we will see baseline forces at work unclouded by the idiosyncrasies of high-profile campaigns. If ever economic conditions are to show their power to affect voter preferences, it will be at elections such as these, as already argued in the Introduction to this volume.

The studies offer several other major advantages. First, these are very-large-scale surveys of some 13,000 respondents each. Surveys of

---

[8] Luxembourg has chosen to have the two cycles coincide so that national and European elections are always conducted concurrently in that country.

[9] Since European Parliament elections have virtually no public visibility, the occurrence of a national election on the same day will cause the EP election to be completely overshadowed by its more salient counterpart.

such magnitude are rare and provide unique power to detect quite small effects that might not be statistically significant in surveys of more typical size (cf. Zaller 2002). Second, these are surveys that were based on separate probability samples within each electoral context, maximizing our ability to detect effects of variables whose variation occurs between these contexts, as is the case for our measures of economic conditions (Stoker and Bowers 2002).[10] Third, though separate samples were drawn from each of the included countries, the questions in these surveys were posed simultaneously and were identical in wording (apart from being translated into ten different languages – twelve in 1999). These are not datasets built up from separate studies by finding similar questions asked not too far apart in time and recoding their categories to match as far as possible (as was done, for example, by Franklin, Mackie, and Valen, et al. 1992 and by Duch and Stevenson 2003). Rather, the same questions were asked of all respondents, in every country, providing us with rich and comparable individual-level data regarding left–right positions (both of individuals and of parties), general political orientations, preferences regarding important issues, and the standard demographic variables relating to education, gender, age, class, religion, and income.

Finally, of the few datasets that are truly comparative in this way, these are the only ones that contain the measures of respondents' propensities to support each political party, whose importance we have stressed so strongly in earlier chapters. As discussed at length in Chapters 1 and 2, these measures enable us to overcome a number of problems that beset the use of party choice as a dependent variable in cross-national comparative research.

So much for the individual-level variables. What of the party-level and systemic variables that we have made so much of in past chapters? And, above all, what of the measures of economic conditions?

Measuring the State of the Economy

In this study, we employ as measures of the state of the economy three indicators: unemployment, inflation, and economic growth, which are official statistics that we obtained from the OECD. These are not the

[10] This is no small matter. The American National Election Study acquired a sampling frame of this type only for its study of the 2004 American presidential election.

only indicators available, but for three reasons they are the obvious ones to use. In combination, these three measures provide a good indication of how an economy as a whole is doing. Moreover, they are measured in a rather standard fashion to ensure comparability across countries. Above all, these measures are surely the ones that are most visible to the public and thus most likely to play a role in helping citizens to form their judgments of how the economy is doing. It is not surprising, therefore, that most studies of economic voting use these three measures. By using them ourselves, we maximize comparability with past research.

More difficult questions arise from the need to decide whether we should focus on levels of unemployment, inflation, and growth, or on changes in these three indicators, and from the need to decide on a baseline that we would expect voters to employ when assessing the economy. By defining the variables in one way or the other, we implicitly make assumptions about voters' criteria in judging the state of the economy. Much of the research on economic voting consists of time series models in the context of a single country. When measures of economic conditions are then linked to the popularity of government parties, the variation in the time series describes deviations from a long-term average. Implicitly, these single-country studies assume that voters apply *national* criteria to evaluate the state of the economy. Even when the independent variables relating to economic conditions are measured in terms of change over time (which is inherently the case when investigating economic growth and inflation), the variation in the time series describes relative change in comparison to the average change in the time series. With such country-specific data, there is no clear reason for preferring to focus on change rather than on levels of economic conditions.

In cross-country comparative research we are confronted with a different situation. In such a study, variations in economic conditions pertain to deviations from a cross-country average. The consequences could be rather bizarre if we then used levels of unemployment (for example) as our predictor. Between 1994 and 1999 unemployment figures in Spain were brought down from 24 percent to 16 percent. However, in 1999, Spain had the highest unemployment rate of all EU countries. The question is whether the 16 percent would be interpreted by Spaniards to mean that the government's economic policies had failed

(Spain still had the highest unemployment rate in the EU) or whether it would be an indication of success (the government had succeeded in bringing Spanish unemployment down quite substantially). We decided that a change variable would be more meaningful in the comparative context than a variable that describes the level of unemployment. We therefore decided to employ change measures for all three economic indicators: percentage change in annual rate of unemployment, percentage change in prices (inflation), and percentage change in gross national product (economic growth), as has been done in other similar research (see, e.g., Stevenson 2002).

The Political and Economic Settings in 1989, 1994, and 1999

The first of our three studies was fielded immediately after the European elections of June 1989. This was five months before the Berlin Wall came down, a historical development that very few would have anticipated even in June of the same year. In terms of the psychological situation, people might have felt that the cold war was winding down, especially since Gorbachov was a very popular figure in Europe, but no one would have said that it was over. Five years later, in 1994, the fall of the Berlin Wall was clearly in the past, but the ultimate effects in terms of the transformations of past members of the Warsaw Pact (and thus for peace and stability in Europe) were still quite uncertain. By 1999 it had become clear that the transition to democracy of previously Communist European countries was going to be successful, and that many of these countries would join the North Atlantic Treaty Organization (NATO) and the EU. At the same time, the wars of secession and civil wars in the former Yugoslavia had brought large-scale violence to the doorstep of the EU. So, the studies span a period of significant historical development in Europe. Nevertheless, except for the addition of Austria, Finland, and Sweden in our 1999 study, and of East Germany to the German state (the additional *Länder* were included in our survey of 1999, though not in our survey of 1994, so soon after reunification), we study the same countries with the same political systems over the entire period. Arguably, a much longer period would have brought about changes (such as had occurred in the Belgian party system during the 1980s) that might cause problems of comparability.

Though manifestly unchanging in certain important respects, what is particularly relevant for the study at hand is that the forty-two contexts provide substantial variation in other critical respects. A first requirement is that economic conditions should have varied substantially between different countries and over the ten-year period of our study. To a large extent, during this period the member states of the EU were pursuing very similar economic policies, which aimed at stability of prices and exchange rates. One might therefore question whether a study within the EU yields sufficient variation in economic contexts to estimate effects of economic circumstances. Table 3.1 shows how our three indicators of economic circumstances – change in unemployment, change in the cost of living, and change in gross domestic product (GDP) – varied over the forty-two contexts that we study. Unemployment change ranges from a 2.9 percent decrease in Spain in 1999 to a 1.4 percent increase, also in Spain, in 1994; inflation ranges from 0.3 percent in Sweden in 1999 to 13.7 percent in Greece in 1989; and economic growth ranges from 0.8 percent in Denmark in 1989 to 8.6 percent in Ireland in 1999. Evidently, our data contain a large range of economic conditions. This variation should give us sufficient leverage to uncover and estimate any effects of the economy on voters. If higher economic growth is good for government parties, and if higher inflation and rising unemployment are bad, this should be apparent in our survey data.

It should be noted in passing that, as a consequence of economic and political integration, the economies of EC/EU countries are becoming more similar over time. The attempts by EU member states to meet the convergence criteria that would eventually determine whether they could become part of the Euro zone is most visible in levels of inflation, which had become very similar by 1999. Nevertheless, over our period as a whole, the range of variation across countries and years provides us with quite adequate leverage for the analyses to be performed in this book.

A second requirement for our study is that different parties should have been in power during different portions of this period. If we had studied countries where the same party was always in office, we would have run the risk of finding all sorts of spurious relationships between the state of the economy and support for the various political parties. When different parties are responsible for managing the economy at

TABLE 3.1. *Aggregate Economic Statistics*

	1989			1994			1999		
	% Change in Unemployment	% Inflation	% Growth in GDP	% Change in Unemployment	% Inflation	% Growth in GDP	% Change in Unemployment	% Inflation	% Growth in GDP
Flanders	-2.4	3.1	3.9	0.9	2.3	2.2	-0.7	1.1	1.8
Wallonia	-1.7	3.1	3.9	0.8	2.3	2.2	-0.7	1.1	1.8
Denmark	0.0	4.8	0.8	-2.0	1.9	4.4	-0.6	2.5	1.3
France	-0.6	3.7	3.8	0.6	1.8	2.6	-0.5	0.6	2.4
Germany	-0.6	2.8	3.4	0.6	2.9	2.8	-0.6	0.6	1.5
Britain	-2.0	7.8	2.1	-0.9	2.4	3.8	-0.2	1.6	1.7
Greece	-0.8	13.7	3.5	0.3	11.1	1.5	0.8	2.7	3.3
Ireland	-0.6	4.1	6.5	-1.3	2.3	6.8	-1.9	1.6	8.6
Italy	0.3	6.3	2.9	0.9	4.0	2.2	-0.5	1.7	1.0
Luxembourg	-0.3	3.3	6.7	0.6	2.2	3.8	-0.4	1.1	5.1
The Netherlands	-0.2	1.1	4.6	0.6	2.5	2.7	-0.7	2.2	3.0
Portugal	-0.7	12.6	5.2	1.2	5.2	1.1	-0.7	2.3	3.1
Spain	-2.6	6.8	4.7	1.4	4.7	2.1	-2.9	2.3	3.7
Finland							-0.5	1.2	3.7
Sweden							-0.9	0.3	3.9
Austria							-0.7	0.6	2.2
EU average	-0.9	5.6	4.0	0.3	3.5	2.9	-0.7	1.5	3.0

Source: Eurostat Series: *Basic Statistics of the European Union.* See also OECD, *Main Economic Indicators,* http://www.oecd.org/std.

different points in time for each of these countries, this risk is considerably diminished. Fortunately, our data meet this requirement. Of the countries that were included in all three surveys, changes in government composition took place everywhere except in Belgium and Luxembourg.

In addition to deciding whether we have adequate variation within each country in the composition of governments, we should assess the degree of variation in other party characteristics. Let us, first of all, see what the variation is in the left- and right-wing leaning of government and opposition parties. For each party in the dataset, respondents were asked to indicate where that party was located on a 10-point left–right scale on which the value 1 was labeled "left" and the value 10 was labeled "right." We characterized the ideological complexion of parties from their median placement by the survey respondents.[11] The average of these positions for government parties was 5.49, which is almost perfectly in the center of the 10-point scale, with a standard deviation of 1.69. Obviously, most government parties are situated not very far from the center of the left–right spectrum. However, some governments contained radical left-wing parties, notably in France, where the Communist Party (located at 1.95 on the left–right dimension) was a member of the government in 1999; in Finland, where, in 1999, the Finnish Left Alliance (at 1.87 on the left–right dimension) was part of the coalition government; and in Germany in 1999, where the Greens (at 3.28) were in a coalition with the SPD. The most right-wing party included in any government was the Italian Alleanza Nazionale in 1994 (with a score of 9.48). Table 3.2 shows the variation in left–right complexion of parties that were government members, and of those in opposition, over the years in countries that we investigate.

The most striking development evident in Table 3.2 is that, by 1999, governing parties had become more left-leaning than they had been in

---

[11] In view of the fact that parties' (perceived) ideological positions contribute to our explanation of the propensity to support such parties, one might wonder whether these perceived positions are actually endogenous in relation to party preferences. Fortunately, the risk of endogeneity is minimal, as parties' positions are not derived from the perceptions of those who voted for them (or who had high propensities to do so), but rather from the perceptions of all respondents, including those with low levels of support for the party in question.

TABLE 3.2. *Left–Right Positions of Government and Opposition Parties*[a]

	1989	1994	1999	All years
Left opposition parties	43.8%	40.5%	37.4%	40.3%
Right opposition parties	29.2%	28.6%	33.0%	30.5%
Left government parties	11.5%	10.7%	23.5%	15.9%
Right government parties	15.6%	20.2%	6.1%	13.2%
All parties	96	84	115	295

[a] Cell entries are percentages of all parties that fall in each category in each year.

earlier years. In 1989 and 1994, most government parties had been right-leaning, whereas the reverse occurred in 1999. So, the ideological variation in our data exists not only between countries but also over time, giving us confidence that our data contain sufficiently diverse combinations of parties inside and outside governments of sufficiently diverse ideological complexions. So, if left parties are indeed held more responsible for unemployment and right parties for inflation, this can be readily determined from the available data.

Yet another party characteristic whose importance we have stressed is party size. It will come as no surprise to discover that parties in the countries that we study differ markedly in size, with considerable differences between countries both in the number of parties and in the sizes of the largest parties (see Table 3.3). If large parties are indeed held more responsible by voters for economic conditions than small parties, this should be apparent in the data we employ.

Party control of the prime ministry and the ministry of finance was a further party characteristic we suggested as possibly playing a role in the attribution of credit or blame for economic conditions. Table 3.4 documents the fact that most governments see these two ministries controlled by the same (largest) party. Occasionally, however, the table shows a split in party control, with the finance ministry going to a different party than the prime ministership. This happened in the Netherlands in 1994 and 1999, in Belgium in 1989 and 1994, and in Italy in 1989. In addition, there are two instances where the finance minister was an independent. If voters take account of such particularities of party control, we should be able to discover this.

Moving up from the party level to the level of the election, we have mentioned that time since the previous election might be important

TABLE 3.3. *Number of Parties Included in the Analyses and Summary Statistics of Parties' Sizes (in Proportion of Seats in the National Parliaments)*

	1989			1994			1999		
	Number of Parties	Minimum Size	Maximum Size	Number of Parties	Minimum Size	Maximum Size	Number of Parties	Minimum Size	Maximum Size
Flanders	5	0.03	0.20	6	0.03	0.18	6	0.03	0.19
Wallonia	6	0.00	0.19	5	0.00	0.16	5	0.01	0.14
Denmark	7	0.05	0.31	8	0.02	0.39	10	0.02	0.35
France	10	0.00	0.47	8	0.00	0.48	9	0.00	0.43
Germany	5	0.00	0.45	6	0.00	0.48	9	0.00	0.45
Britain	6	0.00	0.59	6	0.00	0.53	6	0.00	0.63
Greece	6	0.00	0.54	5	0.00	0.57	7	0.00	0.54
Ireland	7	0.00	0.49	7	0.01	0.41	7	0.01	0.46
Italy	10	0.01	0.37	7	0.00	0.24	9	0.00	0.27
Luxembourg	7	0.00	0.39	6	0.00	0.37	7	0.00	0.35
The Netherlands	9	0.01	0.36	9	0.01	0.25	10	0.00	0.30
Portugal	10	0.00	0.59	5	0.00	0.59	5	0.00	0.49
Spain	8	0.01	0.53	6	0.00	0.45	6	0.01	0.45
Finland							8	0.01	0.26
Sweden							7	0.05	0.38
Austria							6	0.00	0.39

TABLE 3.4. *Party Control Over Prime Ministership and Over Ministry of Finance*

	1989		1994		1999	
	Prime Ministership	Finance Ministry	Prime Ministership	Finance Ministry	Prime Ministership	Finance Ministry
Austria					SPÖ	SPÖ
Belgium: Flanders	CVP	PSC	CVP	PSC	CVP	CVP
Belgium: Wallonia	CVP	PSC	CVP	PSC	CVP	CVP
Britain	Conservatives	Conservatives	Conservatives	Conservatives	Labour	Labour
Denmark	KF	KF	SD	SD	SD	SD
Finland					SDP	KOK
France	PS	PS	RPR	RPR	PS	PS
Germany	CDU	CSU	CDU	CSU	SPD	SPD
Greece	Pasok	Pasok	Pasok	Pasok	Pasok	Pasok
Ireland	FF	FF	FF	FF	FF	FF
Italy	DC	PSI	FI	Independent	DS	DS
Luxembourg	CSP	CSP	CSV	CSV	CSV	CSV
The Netherlands	CDA	CDA	CDA	PvdA	PvdA	VVD
Portugal	PSD	PSD	PSD	PSD	PS	Independent
Spain	PSOE	PSOE	PSOE	PSOE	PP	PP
Sweden					SAP	SAP

TABLE 3.5. *Time That the Current Government Has Been in Office (Months)*

	1989	1994	1999
Belgium: Flanders	13[a]	32	48[a]
Belgium: Wallonia	13[a]	32	48[a]
Denmark	12	17	15
France	13	15	24
Germany	33	41	8
Britain	24	25	25
Greece	48[a]	8	32
Ireland	27[a]	28	24
Italy	23	1	8
Luxembourg	60[a]	60[a]	60[a]
The Netherlands	37	55	10
Portugal	22	32	44
Spain	36	11	37
Finland			50
Sweden			8
Austria			29

[a] National election held concurrently with European Parliament election.

in determining support for government and opposition parties and perhaps in moderating the effects of economic conditions. Not surprisingly, our data show considerable variation in how long each government had been in office. Our surveys of individual countries are conducted simultaneously at three points in time whereas national elections occur fairly randomly over time across the countries concerned. Table 3.5 shows the results in terms of the number of months elapsed, at the points in time that our surveys were conducted, since the current government took office in each country. The values run from one to sixty months, which covers the entire range of logical possibilities.[12]

The last political variable that we investigate in this book is the index of "clarity of responsibility" proposed by Powell and Whitten (1993) and elaborated in Whitten and Palmer (1999). Whitten and Palmer (1999: 56) construct this index from four indicators: the existence of

---

[12] In the Netherlands, an election had been held only one month before our 1994 survey was fielded. However, coalition negotiations were still underway, and the government in office was the caretaker government that had called the elections. It had been in office for fifty-five months by the time of our 1994 survey.

TABLE 3.6. *Dichotomy of High- and Low-Clarity Contexts*

Low-Clarity Contexts	High-Clarity Contexts
Austria (1999)	Britain (1989, 1994, 1999)
Belgium: Flanders (1989, 1994, 1999)	Greece (1989, 1994, 1999)
Belgium: Wallonia (1989, 1994, 1999)	Finland (1999)
Denmark (1989, 1994, 1999)	Ireland (1994)
France (1989, 1994, 1999)	Luxembourg (1989, 1994, 1999)
Germany (1989, 1994, 1999)	Portugal (1989, 1994, 1999)
Ireland (1989, 1999)	Spain (1989, 1994, 1999)
Italy (1989, 1994, 1999)	
Netherlands (1989, 1994, 1999)	
Sweden (1999)	
$N = 25$	$N = 17$

bicameral opposition, whether opposition parties chair legislative committees, whether there is a minority government, and whether there is weak party cohesion.[13] If all of these characteristics are present, there is little clarity of responsibility. Whitten and Palmer (1999) divide the remaining electoral contexts into two groups: a high-clarity group and an intermediate group. Within our data set, only four of the forty-two contexts were classified as having a very low level of clarity, so we combined this group with the intermediate group, giving us two groups of electoral contexts: those with high levels of clarity and those with low levels of clarity.[14]

Table 3.6 provides some descriptive information about the distribution of this variable across the forty-two contexts. Evidently, the index of clarity of responsibility not only differentiates between countries,

[13] Royed, Leyden, and Borrelli (2000) replicated the model of Powell and Whitten and tested a number of alternative system characteristics, such as the distinction between single-party governments and coalition cabinets. They show that this leads to different results, but they are not quite able to interpret them, and they end their contribution with the open-ended conclusion that "political context defined differently may indeed matter for economic voting" (p. 683). We chose to employ the index of Whitten and Palmer, which is the improved version of the Powell and Whitten index, for two reasons. First, it has been shown to yield meaningful results; second, within the group of countries that we study, there are too few single-party governments for us to make a meaningful distinction on that basis.

[14] As a check on our findings, we tried excluding the four low-clarity countries and reran all of our analyses without them. The findings were not significantly different from the findings made when these countries were included in the group with less clarity.

but can also vary also between elections in the same country. However, only in the case of Ireland is a country in one year (1994) classified differently than in the other years (1989 and 1999). In all other systems, the classification that we employ is constant over the period we investigate. More importantly, we can make a rather even distinction between seventeen contexts with high clarity of government responsibility and twenty-five contexts in which responsibility is not so clear.

Operationalizing the Variables

As explained in Chapter 2, in order to analyze party support – the first stage of our two-stage model – across all parties and electoral contexts simultaneously, we need to reorder the data into a stacked data matrix where the respondent * party combination is the unit of analysis (see Figure 2.1). Propensities to support each party are placed "on top of each other" to constitute a single variable ranging across parties for each individual and across individuals for each party, and ranging equally across electoral contexts. The independent variables are reconceived for the analysis of stacked data along the lines explained in detail in Chapter 2.

A Caveat

In this chapter, we have listed the hypotheses we intend to test and described the data that we will use to test them with, explained why we think these data are appropriate for studying the effects of economic conditions on party choice, and detailed the wide range of contextual variation that they contain. There is one caveat, however, that deserves to be stated.

As is the case in all studies of economic voting, we should bear in mind that we do not have a random sample of economic contexts. Our range of economic conditions does not contain cases of hyperinflation, such as those found in Turkey and Argentina in the late 1990s, when large numbers of people lost most of their life savings over the course of one or two years. Also, we do not analyze circumstances in which economic growth was strongly negative, as happened in Russia and Turkey during the 1990s. Obviously, dramatic economic developments such as these may well lead to effects on party support and election outcomes that are much larger, and conceivably even of a different character, than those that we are able to observe within the dataset we analyze here. In that respect, the conclusions that we will be able to draw from our study will be limited to situations in which economic circumstances are rather stable. Nevertheless, this caveat is no different from that which applies to virtually all extant investigations of economic voting. Indeed, these are the situations that typically do pertain in advanced industrial democracies in the contemporary era, and those are the countries to which we expect to be able to generalize our findings.

4

Effects of the Economy on Party Support

In this chapter, we will develop and test a model of the effect of objective economic circumstances on individual-level support for political parties. Most of the evidence previously found for effects of the objective state of the economy on party support has been found at the aggregate level (e.g., Hibbs 1977; Tufte 1978; Chrystal and Alt 1981; Fair 1988; Lewis-Beck 1988; Markus 1988, 1992; Erikson 1989; Clarke and Whiteley 1990; Mackuen, Erikson, and Stimson 1992; Powell and Whitten 1993; Price and Sanders 1993; Clarke and Stewart, 1995; Norpoth 1996; Sanders 1996; Clarke, Stewart, and Whiteley 1998; Whitten and Palmer 1999; Campbell and Garand 2000). It has been suggested (e.g., Jacobson 1983; Lewis-Beck 1988: 29–31) that these results may have reflected the ecological fallacy first identified by Robinson (1950), making it problematic to draw inferences from aggregate data about the behavior of individuals. More to the point, in our opinion, even assuming that effects found at the aggregate level are not spurious, aggregate analyses do not allow us to assess the importance of economic circumstances relative to other considerations that affect individuals' electoral choices, such as ideological predispositions or issue preferences, and give us no way of knowing under what circumstances these other considerations might trump the effects of economic conditions.

We will start by replicating with our data models of economic voting used in aggregate analyses, in which party choice is typically predicted only by the previous vote share of government parties (to control for time-serial dependencies) and by interactions of a government party dummy variable with measures of the state of the economy.[1] After that, we will introduce various control variables shown in previous individual-level studies to be the most important determinants of party choice. Given the structure of the data matrix, we are not restricted to employing just individual-level controls, but can also take account of variables at the party and systemic levels that may (regardless of the state of the economy) also affect party support. The most important independent variable, based on our own and previous theorizing, is whether a party is a government party or an opposition party. Not only do we need this variable in order to see whether voters are particularly prone to hold government parties accountable for economic conditions, and how they treat opposition parties (in order to test H1 and H2 from Chapter 3). In addition, this variable is required in order to test ideas relating to time in office and the timing of our surveys in the national electoral cycles of the countries we study (H3 and the two versions of H9). Also at the systemic level, we include a measure of system clarity, derived from Whitten and Palmer (1999), and other classifying variables needed to test the different versions of H6. Additional party-level control variables include party size (to test H4a), standing in terms of ministerial portfolios (H4b), and ideology (H5). The test of H5 will also inform us about the prospective or retrospective orientations of voters in different circumstances, which does not require any separate independent variables but relies on inspection of patterns of voter response to economic conditions in relation to parties of different ideological types. The remaining two hypotheses (H7 and H8, which relate to voter heterogeneity and to asymmetric effects of improving and worsening economic conditions) will be assessed in later chapters.

Before moving on to more elaborate models, we start with the simplest one, in which all government parties are held equally accountable for the state of the economy.

---

[1] Taking models defined at the aggregate level and replicating them at the level of the units in our stacked data matrix (respondent*party combinations) is not totally straightforward. To test the same hypotheses, one needs models that look somewhat different. Vote shares at the aggregate level are replaced by the propensitiy of individuals to support political parties, effects of the economy by interactions with the party attributes that are expected to be relevant, and previous vote shares of parties by previous choice of the respondent, as we will see.

TABLE 4.1. *Three 'Naïve' Models Predicting Propensities to Support Political Parties*

	Model A		Model B		Model C	
	B	SE	B	SE	B	SE
Previous national vote			1.022	0.009**	1.024	0.008**
Party size					6.123	0.103**
Government party	1.044	0.038**	1.077	0.032**	−0.001	0.035
GDP	0.021	0.013	0.015	0.011	0.034	0.010**
Unemployment	0.050	0.022	0.053	0.019	0.062	0.018**
Inflation	−0.053	0.006**	−0.058	0.005**	−0.055	0.005**
Government party * GDP	0.196	0.025**	0.224	0.021**	0.093	0.020**
Government party * unemployment	0.128	0.040*	0.124	0.034**	0.043	0.032
Government party * inflation	0.051	0.014**	0.079	0.012**	−0.078	0.012**
Weighted N	32,950		32,950		32,950	
Adjusted R²	0.027		0.315		0.382	

Note: Significant at *0.01, **0.001.

Economic Voting and Government Status

Table 4.1 presents three regression models of economic voting (Models A, B, and C). In each model the dependent variable is the propensity of respondents to support a political party – with the data arranged in the form of a stacked and pooled data matrix (see Chapter 2). We report effects (b's) and the standard errors of those effects, flagging with asterisks any relationships significant at the 0.01 level or better.[2]

Our first model (Model A) is a "naive" model, in which party preferences are only based on parties' government or opposition status and on the state of the economy.[3] The parameter estimates of Model A clearly suggest that this model is not properly specified. The large positive effect for the dummy variable "government party" suggests

---

[2] In Chapter 2 we specified our strategy for assessing significance (see the section on 'Operationalizing the Two-Stage Model of Party Choice."

[3] Our data yield no serious problems of multicollinearity between the economic variables that are at the core of our interest. Economic growth and inflation are correlated −0.42, while change in unemployment is not related to either of the other two economic conditions.

that after we control for effects of the economy, all government parties are preferred simply as a result of being government parties. This runs counter to all previous findings. Effects of economic growth, with government parties gaining from economic growth and other parties not (the significant effect for government parties has to be added to the not quite significant effect for all parties), are quite sensible.[4] The same cannot be said for effects of unemployment and inflation.

Indeed, coefficients for unemployment and inflation are quite counter to expectations. They suggest that government parties would benefit from increases in unemployment (where the coefficients echo those for economic growth) and would not be hurt by inflation (where the positive effect for government parties almost exactly cancels out the negative effect for all parties). Worse, the implication of the two coefficients involving inflation is that opposition parties are hurt by inflation, as shown by the negative and significant effect of this variable when not interacted with government party. Even though previous studies have sometimes found counterintuitive results for the effects of inflation (e.g., Paldam 1991), these findings would be hard to accept even in a model that was believed to be properly specified. Since we do not believe this model to be properly specified, the findings lend support to this assumption.[5] Note in passing the very low variance explained by objective economic conditions in Model A – less than 3 percent – when these are taken with government status as the sole predictors of party preferences at the individual level.

Model B shows what happens if we include previous vote, as almost all aggregate-level models do.[6] This variable emulates what in

---

[4] Note that assessing the impact of different effects involving interactions is not straightforward. There are two effects of each economic variable, one for government parties and one for nongovernment (i.e., opposition) parties. Government parties gain $(0.021 + 0.196) = 0.217$ of a point on the dependent variable from the effects of a 1-point change in GDP growth, while nongovernment parties gain only an insignificant 0.021 from a similar 1-point change. The dependent variable is measured on a 10-point scale (see Chapter 2).

[5] Our discussions in Chapters 1 and 2 lead us to be suspicious of models that do not involve all the controls that we proposed at the individual, party, and context levels.

[6] It is not customary in cross-sectional research designs to include this variable. We have, however, included it because it controls for the effects of stable but otherwise unspecified individual-level characteristics impinging on party preferences in each country (such as postmaterialism). Another advantage of including it is that this gives us maximum comparability with aggregate-level studies in which the popularity of governing parties is customarily predicted by their popularity at some earlier point in time. As it

aggregate-level models would have been a party's lagged vote share, controlling for time serial dependency. At the individual level, this variable also picks up individual-level attributes that affect current as well as previous party support.[7] This variable hugely increases the variance explained, as is only to be expected, but hardly changes any of the parameter estimates from those seen in Model A. In view of the lack of relevant controls that we discussed in earlier chapters, Model B is also a naive model that is no easier to accept than Model A. In Model C we introduce one of our most important control variables, party size. Although this addition increases the model's sophistication, it still omits most of the control variables that we discussed earlier as necessary for proper specification. Nevertheless, by adding this control variable we get somewhat more sensible results. In this model, government parties no longer appear to gain (in terms of their level of support) from being in office, though the "cost of governing" losses seen in other studies (Powell and Whitten 1993; Nannestad and Paldam 1994, 2002; Paldam 1991) are still not apparent. The effects of not only economic growth but also inflation are now consistent with the basic idea of economic voting. In contrast to what was shown in Models A and B, government parties lose more support in Model C than opposition parties do as a consequence of higher inflation. As regards unemployment, government parties no longer benefit more than opposition parties do from higher unemployment. However, the effect of unemployment in Model C nevertheless remains inconsistent with theories of economic voting since this model shows all parties benefiting from greater unemployment.

The models presented in Table 4.1 are a mixed bag, though the findings do accord with those of past studies of party support propensities in demonstrating the importance of including party size in an individual-level analysis of party preferences (Oppenhuis 1995; van der

happens, we find that its presence or absence makes little difference to the effects of economic variables (compare Models A and B in Table 4.1).

[7] This control for time serial dependency is not quite what we would have wished in terms of matching the information we have for current party support. Our data contain information about current support for each of a series of parties, but as far as the past is concerned, our information does not stretch beyond party choice at the past national election. In the design of the stacked data matrix, this variable is coded 0 for each party that a respondent did not vote for at that election and 1 for the single party that was chosen.

Eijk and Franklin 1996; van der Eijk, Franklin, and van der Brug 1999). Though the findings in Model C, which includes party size, are not quite what we expect theoretically, they do not do violence to most of our ideas (and to the most frequently reported findings in the literature) about economic voting (as do the findings of Models A and B). The unexpected aspects of Model C's findings are in keeping with the common set of inconsistencies and instabilities that aggregate-level studies display. Model C also explains considerably more variance than Model B, confirming our earlier argument that party size plays an important role in the formation of party preferences. Still, we need to see whether we can improve on this model by including as additional control variables independent variables found in past research to be important determinants of individual-level party preference.

In Table 4.2 we thus include individual-level controls and, in the later models, additional controls for party and contextual characteristics. Table 4.2 starts with Model D, which contains no economic variables, just variables found in past research to explain party preferences at the individual level. It is included mainly to demonstrate the far greater variance explained that occurs (compared with the models in Table 4.1) with a more properly specified model of individual-level party support. Adding economic variables to this model yields Model E, which raises the variance explained by less than half of 1 percent. The effects of economic conditions in Model E are, however, almost indistinguishable from those in Model C. Adding individual-level control variables does not give us more (or less) plausible effects of economic conditions, though Model E does show parties in government paying a small electoral cost of governing (consistent with past findings), which Model C did not. Model F adds time since the last election together with the quadratic term that is expected to show the workings of midterm loss. Adding these variables does not increase the variance explained, but it does yield an effect for the cost of governing whose magnitude is consistent with estimates made in past research. Model F hardly changes the effects of economic variables, except that the effect of unemployment, on support for government parties at last has the correct sign, though it is still not statistically significant. In combination with the main effect of unemployment this reiterates the counterintuitive effects of unemployment found in previous models: all parties gain from unemployment, government parties almost as much

TABLE 4.2. *Elaborated Models Predicting Propensities to Support Political Parties*

	Model D		Model E		Model F	
	B	SE	B	SE	B	SE
Previous national vote	0.762	0.009**	0.764	0.009**	0.765	0.009**
Party size	5.417	0.102**	5.646	0.106**	5.714	0.107**
Government party * time since last election					−0.005	0.002*
Government party * time since last election squared					0.001	0.000**
Class	0.354	0.027**	0.355	0.027**	0.355	0.027**
Religion	0.304	0.026**	0.306	0.026**	0.306	0.025**
Left–Right distance	−0.333	0.007**	−0.328	0.007**	−0.327	0.007**
Issues	0.469	0.020**	0.470	0.020**	0.470	0.020**
EU approval	0.268	0.031**	0.271	0.030**	0.271	0.030**
Issues * perceptual agreement	−1.211	0.175**	−1.204	0.174**	−1.205	0.174**
Government party	−0.025	0.035	−0.105	0.036*	−0.286	0.046**
GDP			0.034	0.011*	0.034	0.011*
Unemployment			0.071	0.018**	0.071	0.018**
Inflation			−0.041	0.005**	−0.041	0.005**
Government party * GDP			0.074	0.021**	0.071	0.022**
Government party * unemployment			0.029	0.033	−0.004	0.034
Government party * inflation			−0.082	0.012**	−0.083	0.012**
Weighted N	27,505		27,505		27,505	
Adjusted R^2	0.458		0.462		0.462	

Note: Significant at *0.01, **0.001.

as others. Still, the model lends some support to H1 and H2 from Chapter 3.

The effects of the individual-level control variables will be discussed in detail in Chapter 5. However, a few observations can be made at this point. First of all, it should be mentioned that explaining 45 percent of the variance in an individual-level model is very respectable. Moreover, this is not actually an individual-level model but rather a model disaggregated to the level of the respondent's support for each political party.

Disaggregation generally increases total variance without commensurately increasing our ability to explain that variance.[8] We should also mention that the effects of various determinants of party choice are of the same general magnitude as found in previous studies (Oppenhuis 1995; van der Eijk and Franklin 1996; van der Eijk, Franklin, and van der Brug 1999). All these attributes of Model F reassure us that it is a properly specified model of party support.

At the party level, we find a highly significant and positive effect on the support for government parties of the quadratic term measuring time since the last election.[9] This supports the findings of various previous studies, which show that the loss of government popularity tends to be highest at midterm. The same is true for the highly significant negative effect for government parties, which is also a regularity that has often been observed empirically. Parties cannot remain in office indefinitely because they almost invariably lose support with the passage of time. We also find significant effects of the interaction of issue proximity with perceptual agreement of party positions, which replicates earlier findings.[10]

---

[8] We believe that the disaggregation is necessary in order to properly specify the processes at work, but that does not mean that we expect to explain as much variance as we would in an individual-level analysis. The fact that we do explain so much variance is consequently quite satisfying.

[9] The measure of time since the previous election has been centered on its average value in our data (twenty-eight months), so this variable starts negative and becomes positive after twenty-eight months. Added to the (negative) popularity of government parties lower down in the table, we find that government popularity starts out slightly positive at 0.04, drops to a highly negative −0.304 exactly two years after an election occurs, and then starts to rise, ending (for countries with four-year terms of office) somewhat below the point at which it started, at 0.004. The average country in our data holds European elections twenty-eight months after national elections, at which point government parties suffer a hit of −0.286 to their popularity – the coefficient seen for government parties when the two "time since" variables (which have been centered on their mean values) are 0.

[10] Perceptual agreement of party positions is a measure of the extent to which respondents in each country agree on the location of their political parties in left–right terms (van der Eijk 2001). In earlier research we found that the effect of left–right proximity varies across political systems, and that this variation can be accounted for by the extent of perceptual agreement (Oppenhuis 1995). In this research the effect of this interaction, while significant until the previous vote is included in the equation, drops out in the presence of this additional control and so is excluded from the tables presented in this book, along with other individual-level predictors of party preference that did not prove significant.

When Powell and Whitten (1993: 396) estimated their aggregate-level model of economic effects on election outcomes, in which they took account only of the government status of parties (and not of contextual effects or of the ideological complexion of the governing parties), they found three insignificant effects: negative in the case of unemployment and inflation, positive in the case of economic growth. It seems that we have obtained with Model F very similar findings at the individual level. Though some of our coefficients are significant because of the much larger N available to us in an individual-level study, nevertheless, the individual-level effects of the economy that we find are very minor (as were the aggregate effects found by Powell and Whitten), compared to the effects of other predictors of party choice. For instance, when a country has 1 percent more economic growth, the model predicts that, ceteris paribus, the propensity of voters to support opposition parties increases by 0.034 of a point, while their propensity to support government parties increases by 0.105 of a point (0.034 + 0.071) on a 10-point scale. We have already mentioned the tiny increase in variance explained that occurs when economic conditions are taken into account.

Nevertheless, as far as we are aware, this is the first time that aggregate-level findings (in this case, widely respected benchmark findings) have been replicated at the individual level. Like Powell and Whitten, we will move on to assess the ways in which different kinds of parties are affected differently by economic conditions. But first, we should draw attention to an intriguing implication of Model F.

The unexpected effect of unemployment in Model F looks like an anomaly, but it might not be. At this point in our argument we are still dealing with party support rather than party choice, but the findings regarding support have implications for preferences (and hence for choice). Since party preferences were measured separately for each party, our method enables us to assess preferences that can increase or decrease for all parties simultaneously as a consequence of economic conditions. Obviously, measures of party choice could not have yielded these results, because a gain in popularity of one party necessitates a drop for other parties.

Suppose it is true that, during the period and over the countries that we study, unemployment did not hurt government parties. What would that mean? Most straightforwardly it would mirror the fact, observed in the Introduction to this volume, that when (in the countries and period that we study) governments were voted out of office, this generally was not regarded as being the result of high unemployment, not even in those cases where unemployment was endemically high. In Model F we see an apparent concomitant of that observation in terms of the party preferences that accompany rising unemployment. All of these coefficients are positive except for one very small and insignificant negative effect that could never overcome the positive balance for any specific group of parties: all parties seem to gain support under conditions of rising unemployment. In terms of the basic theory of economic voting, which is that government parties are punished electorally for poor economic performance, it would mean that electoral incentives to control unemployment were absent in these countries at these times. Such an interpretation of our findings would run counter to the common observation that government parties of all ideological complexions do in fact pay considerable attention to unemployment and to the crafting (and selling) of policies designed to tackle unemployment. Yet, as Dr. Johnson once observed, "nothing concentrates a man's mind so much as the prospect of being hanged." Perhaps stronger electoral incentives would have engendered greater focus, and the greater focus might in turn have brought the sort of results in the fight against unemployment that were seen with the successful tackling of inflation in these same countries at an earlier period.

Such an interpretation of our findings would give rise to a puzzle, of course. Why should unemployment have such anomalous effects on party support propensities? Why would voters not reduce their support for parties that permitted unemployment to rise? We will return to this question at various points in this and later chapters.

Time in Office and Control of Economic Ministries

In Chapters 1 and 3, we suggested that among the variables that might be needed in a properly specified model of economic voting, we should consider including variables that might reflect on the responsibility of particular government parties for economic conditions – especially how long they had been occupying the seats of power and whether they controlled the prime ministership or ministry of finance. Time in office in our data ranges from one month (the 1994 Berlusconi government in Italy) to fifty-five years (the Belgian Christian Democrats), yet none of the three ways in which time in office could be operationalized yielded significant findings (for details see Appendix B).[11] A variety of models operationalizing the role of the prime minister and minister of finance similarly failed to demonstrate the need to elaborate Model F (see Appendix B, Tables B.1 and B.2).[12] So, our findings fail to support H3 or 4b from Chapter 3. It appears that any mis-specification of previous models through the omission of these effects was not grave.

Economic Voting and the Effect of Party Size

Even though government parties will try to take the credit for good economic circumstances, and even though opposition parties will often try to blame the government when the economy does badly, responsibility for the state of the economy is not always so clear-cut, as was discussed at length in Chapter 3. In particular, we argued that party size may serve as a proxy for voters, telling them which parties are players in the policymaking process. We should therefore control for party size as a moderator of the effect of economic conditions on party support.

An additional reason for controlling for party size is that large government parties are in a much better position to affect government policies than small government parties are. We have already pointed out that, in our data, the largest party always controls the prime ministership (and often the ministry of finance as well). Moreover, such parties attract more media attention, and consequently their responsibility is more visible to the public. To test the hypothesis that effects of

[11] Voters might assign responsibility to parties based on total length of time in office, even with different coalition partners, on the length of time a specific coalition had been in office, or on the length of time since the most recent election. None of these formulations produced significant findings.
[12] The party of the prime minister and that of the minister of finance was identified in each context, and dummy variables indicating each ministry were added to Model F. In alternative specifications, these variables were substituted for government party in Model F, as was a dummy variable indicating control of either ministry. None of these models added significantly to the variance explained or produced more substantively interpretable findings.

TABLE 4.3. *Interacting Economic Voting with Party Size*[a]

Independent Variables	Model G		Model H	
	B	SE	B	SE
Government party	−0.213	0.050**	−0.167	0.048**
Party size	6.659	0.147**	6.644	0.144**
Government party * party size	−2.047	0.216**	−2.056	0.213**
GDP	0.026	0.012	0.037	0.011**
Unemployment	0.058	0.020*	0.065	0.019*
Inflation	−0.042	0.006**	−0.040	0.005**
Government party * GDP	0.105	0.027**	0.084	0.021**
Government party * unemployment	0.164	0.041**	0.116	0.037*
Government party * inflation	−0.126	0.023**	−0.061	0.013**
Party size * GDP	−0.199	0.100		
Party size * unemployment	−0.293	0.150	−0.164	0.135
Party size * inflation	−0.024	0.040		
Gov. party * party size * GDP	0.210	0.142		
Gov. party * party size * unemployment	−0.710	0.214**	−0.754	0.187**
Gov. party * party size * inflation	0.241	0.074*		
Weighted N	27,505		27,505	
Adjusted R²	0.466		0.466	

Note: Significant at *0.01, **0.001.
[a] The estimated model includes all control variables in Model F (see Table 4.2). Since the effects of the control variables are not relevant to the topic of this study, these effects are not presented here.

economic conditions are moderated by party size (not just for government parties but for opposition parties also), we interacted all variables pertaining to the economy with party size.[13]

Each of the interaction terms presented in Table 4.3 can only be understood in relation to the other relevant coefficients. This makes them very difficult to interpret in a straightforward fashion. One of the few things that is immediately clear from Model G is that it yields at least one strong and theoretically very meaningful higher-order interaction: the interaction between government parties, party size, and unemployment. This effect is strong, significant, and (as expected theoretically) negative. This indicates that especially large government

[13] Party size is measured by the proportion of seats held by each party in the most important chamber of the legislature at the time the interviews were conducted.

parties are hurt electorally by rising unemployment, whereas smaller government parties are much less affected. Before we elaborate on the implications of this model for different types of political parties, we should consider whether it could (and thus should) be made more parsimonious. This is particularly important because the large number of higher-order interactions leads to considerable multicollinearity in the model, partly due to the fact that the different aspects of the economy are not totally independent of each other. When there is much economic growth, unemployment will normally decrease.[14] Particularly if we interact these variables with a large number of other variables, they are bound to be largely collinear. This decreases the reliability of the estimated coefficients. So, if we omit effects that are not or are barely significant, the resulting model may well contain more reliable estimates of the effects of other variables.

All lower-order interactions with party size and the state of the economy in Model G are insignificant. Yet, we cannot remove these interaction terms without also removing the higher-order ones. As a first step toward making the model more parsimonious, we excluded the two interaction effects involving party size and inflation. The effect of party size interacted with inflation was not significant. Though the higher-order effect (government party * party size * inflation) was significant, its effect was small and in the opposite direction from what was theoretically expected. After we excluded the interaction effects of party size and inflation, the interaction effects of party size and economic growth still failed to attain significance, so we excluded those effects as well.

These exclusions give rise to the second model in Table 4.3, Model H, which is in many respects an improvement over Model F. This model, at last, provides us with a basis for understanding how changes in unemployment affect party choice. The strong negative effect for the interaction of party size * government parties * unemployment suggests that large government parties in particular are held responsible for

---

[14] At the country level ($n = 42$), the correlation between economic growth and change in unemployment is $-.416$, which indeed shows that unemployment tends to decrease if a country experiences high economic growth. The correlations between inflation and economic growth and between inflation and change in unemployment are very small, however: respectively .003 and .000.

TABLE 4.4. *Effects of Economic Conditions on Preferences for Various Prototypical Parties (Based on Model H, Table 4.3)*[a]

		GDP 1% Higher	Unemployment 1% Higher	Inflation 1% Higher
Government party	Large	0.121	−0.062	−0.101
	Small		0.211	
Opposition party	Large	0.037	0.022	−0.040
	Small		0.070	

[a] A large party is a party that occupies 40% of the seats in parliament, a small party has 10% of the seats. The imputed values for party size (in Model H) are 0.2648 (large party) and −0.0352 (small party).

increasing unemployment. Grasping the import of the findings in Table 4.3 is still very difficult, however, because higher-order interactions can only be interpreted in combination with lower-order interactions and main effects.

To make this and subsequent models easier to interpret, we distinguish a small number of prototypical parties and use the findings from our models to assess how support for each of these would be affected by specific economic changes. As Model H focuses on two party attributes (government status, and size of parties), we distinguish large and small government parties and large and small opposition parties. For illustrative purposes, we define a large party as one that holds 40 percent of the seats in the national parliament and a small one as one that holds 10 percent of the seats. For each of the resulting four types of parties, we can add the relevant coefficients from Table 4.3 to arrive at the total effects of economic changes (see also footnote 4). Applying this procedure, we show in Table 4.4 how average preferences for these four prototypical parties would change as a consequence of a 1 percent change in economic conditions (respectively, economic growth, unemployment, and inflation). Since the interactions between party size, on the one hand, and inflation and economic growth, on the other, turned out to be not significant, they were excluded from our final Model H. Table 4.4 therefore does not contain differences between large and small parties in the effects of economic growth and inflation. The findings for these two economic indicators are very straightforward. When there is much economic growth, support for opposition parties increases a little, while support for government parties increases considerably. With inflation the reverse happens. Opposition parties become less attractive as a result of increased inflation but government parties even more so.

The reader should bear in mind that in this chapter we are thinking about party support (the first stage in Downs's two-stage process), upon which effects need not be symmetrical, quite in contrast to effects on party choice (the second stage, which we do not consider until Chapter 6). Support can increase for all parties at the same time (and might do so in boom times), but such increases need not be the same for all parties. Equally, all parties can simultaneously lose support (although again, not necessarily to the same degree). In our opinion, conflating the two stages in Downs's model has tended to contaminate our thinking about effects of economic conditions (and quite possibly about other effects as well). Indeed, we will see in a later section that, for some types of political systems, where it is hard for voters to know which parties to hold responsible for economic conditions, it makes more sense to think of the regime as a whole falling into disfavor in bad economic times.

The effects for unemployment deepen the puzzle we mentioned earlier. Voters' support for large government parties declines when unemployment increases, as anticipated in the literature and in accordance with our hypotheses, but the decline is small and quite overwhelmed by the support that small government parties appear to gain. Opposition parties, by contrast, make consistent if modest gains. This does not come as a surprise because we might expect that, if the government is not doing a good job, opposition parties – which normally propose different economic policies – would gain commensurately.

The surprise in Table 4.4 is that small government parties benefit the most from higher unemployment rates. It is as though these small parties were being rewarded – perhaps for exercising veto power in economic management, standing in the way of reforms that their larger coalition partners would otherwise introduce. In order to evaluate this possibility, we need to further elaborate our model by taking account of the ideological complexions of parties. It could be the case that small government parties happen to be of a different ideological type than large government parties, accounting for the surprising effects of unemployment for small government parties. This is what we turn to next.

Economic Voting and Parties' Ideological Positions

It has been suggested several times that left-wing governments will particularly be held responsible for rising unemployment, while right-wing governments will particularly be held responsible for rising inflation (Hibbs 1977, 1982; Powell and Whitten 1993; Whitten and Palmer 1999). Governments of both ideological complexions are expected to be held equally responsible for economic growth. In this research, we focus on parties rather than governments and, to the extent that voters hold government parties responsible for the state of the economy, we might expect support for right-leaning government parties to be more affected by levels of inflation than support for left-leaning government parties, which, by contrast, would respond more strongly to changes in unemployment. Parties of all ideological complexions would be expected to promote economic growth, so levels of growth should affect support for all government parties equally (albeit in proportion to their size).

Previous aggregate-level analyses by Powell and Whitten (1993) suggest that this is what happens. The contribution of these authors to the field of economic voting was important because they showed that the aggregate success of left-leaning governments depended particularly on unemployment, whereas voters held right-leaning governments much more responsible for inflation. Our design allows us to distinguish between different parties and to test these effects at the individual level. We do, however, expect to find similar patterns.

In order to test these expectations, we classified all parties in our sample as left- or right-leaning. For this purpose, a survey question was used in which respondents were asked, for each of the parties in their country, to indicate what its position was on a 10-point scale of which the extremes were labeled "left" (1) and "right" (10). If the median of the voters' perceptions was at the positions 1 through 5.5 on this 10-point scale, a party was classified as left-leaning. If the median perception was higher than 5.5, a party was classified as right-leaning. In the analyses to be presented in this section, indicators of economic voting will be interacted with this variable.[15]

---

[15] We dichotomize the left–right location of parties partly to simplify the exposition and partly to avoid any problems of intersystem differences in the way the scale is used. By dichotomizing the scale in each system at its midpoint, we make the least demanding

TABLE 4.5. *Effects of Economic Conditions on the Propensity to Support Various Prototypical Parties (Based on Model I, Appendix B)*[a]

			GDP 1% Higher	Unemployment 1% Higher	Inflation 1% Higher
Government parties	Left parties	Large	0.063	−0.291	−0.099
		Small	0.185	0.254	
	Right parties	Large	0.055	0.032	−0.125
		Small	−0.286	0.004	
Opposition parties	Left parties	Large	0.033	0.069	−0.029
		Small	0.070	0.146	
	Right parties	Large	−0.111	−0.326	−0.055
		Small	−0.187	−0.323	

[a] A large party is a party that occupies 40% of the seats in parliament, a small party has 10% of the seats. The imputed values for party size (in Model I) are 0.2648 (large party) and −0.0352 (small party).

We start with the full model, in which we interacted the three indicators of the economy with dummy variables for government party and left–right position of parties, as well as with party size. The resulting model contained many insignificant effects, particularly those involving the combination of party size and inflation. After excluding the insignificant effects, we obtained results that are summarized in Table 4.5. Here again, we focus on the consequences of a 1 percent change in unemployment, inflation, and economic growth. The full model (Model I) from which this table is derived can be found in Appendix B (Table B.3) and will be presented in more detail in Chapter 5.

Since none of the interactions with party size and inflation is significant, these effects are not reported in Model I (see Appendix B). Thus, small and large parties are not distinguished in Table 4.5 when it comes to the effects of inflation. The findings for inflation are thus particularly straightforward, affecting preferences for all parties negatively, right-leaning government parties most of all. Effects on support fall off as we consider in turn left government parties and right opposition parties, and are weakest of all for left opposition parties. Left-leaning

assumptions regarding comparability. The same variable used at the individual level does not raise the same problem because we standardize each variable in each country by viewing it in terms of its predictions (y-hats), as explained in Chapter 2. We could do something similar at the aggregate level, but the results would be hard to interpret and discuss.

opposition parties are thus the relative beneficiaries of inflation, losing less support than other parties.

The effects of unemployment on different types of parties are much more complex. Large left-leaning government parties are badly hurt by higher unemployment. This is very much in line with theoretical notions put forward in the literature, which propose that left-wing parties are expected to proactively do anything in their power to keep unemployment low. When they fail to do so, they will be punished. The positive effect of unemployment on support for small left government parties seems rather anomalous, however. We will return to this anomaly a little later. For the moment, it suffices to say that the anomaly would not be noticed in conventional approaches to the study of economic voting, since few voters support small parties and the increase in such support would be swamped by large changes in support for their larger coalition partners. Right-leaning government parties are hardly affected by changes in unemployment, as would be expected on the basis of past theorizing.

Prospective Economic Voting?

It is when we turn to opposition parties that we see really unexpected findings. Conventional wisdom would suggest that opposition parties benefit in terms of votes from rising unemployment. In terms of party support, we find indeed that left-leaning opposition parties gain in these circumstances; however, right-leaning opposition parties (both small and large) do not benefit from higher levels of unemployment. When unemployment increases, they even lose support. The anomalous findings regarding both right-leaning opposition parties and small left government parties suggest a form of issue voting that prospectively takes into account expectations about the future actions of parties. What our findings seem to show is that, whereas government parties are evaluated on the basis of a mixture of prospective and retrospective assessments (consistent with H5 from Chapter 3), opposition parties are judged primarily on prospective grounds,

When unemployment increases, people become more likely to support a party that can plausibly promise to bring unemployment down while being willing to defend welfare arrangements that guard citizens against the consequences of unemployment. This readily explains the failure of right-wing opposition parties to gain from unemployment. Voters anticipate that if these parties are elected, unemployment will not be as high on their agenda as it would be on left-wing parties' agenda, and these are also the parties least likely to defend welfare arrangements. This reasoning would explain why right-leaning opposition parties lose, while left-leaning opposition parties gain, when unemployment increases. It would also explain why small left-wing opposition parties gain more than larger ones. Small left-wing parties tend to be more radical and tend to be firmer defenders of welfare arrangements. So, the patterns of support for opposition parties in the face of increased unemployment are understandable if one assumes that voters are judging such parties prospectively.

The pattern in support for government parties can similarly be explained if we are willing to accept the idea that voters evaluate these parties by a mixture of prospective and retrospective considerations. Large left-leaning parties are normally expected to give priority to unemployment problems, but in the circumstance of increasing unemployment, if they are in government, they lose credibility in that regard. So, they lose support. But small left parties are situated rather differently. It is very rare for small left-leaning parties to be in a coalition with only right-leaning parties. Normally, they can only enter a coalition with a larger (often more moderate) left party. When unemployment increases, the small left government parties are, on the one hand, in a position to serve as defenders of welfare arrangements; and on the other hand, they can blame the larger left government party for not having done enough to keep unemployment down. The gain by small left government parties in conditions of rising unemployment is larger than the gain by small left opposition parties, suggesting a degree of pragmatism among voters who may expect the experience of governing to have given these parties a better chance of implementing their programs than (possibly inexperienced) opposition parties. Alternatively, voters may be rewarding these parties for having "fought the good fight" against coalition partners bent on reducing benefits and entitlements in the hope of reducing unemployment. In either case, voters are not reaching blindly for any radical solution to the unemployment problem: their reactions appear to be quite pragmatic, being closely tied to the realities of the political situation.

Why are right-leaning government parties hardly affected by rising unemployment, while right-leaning opposition parties are badly hurt? To the extent that voters evaluate government parties retrospectively, they may not have expected right-leaning government parties to do much about unemployment, so rising unemployment would not much affect their support. Such parties were evidently elected for other reasons than tackling unemployment, and whether they have satisfied their supporters in terms of those other concerns will be unconnected with the unemployment situation. This is the reasoning put forward by Powell and Whitten (1993) that is appropriate to retrospective voting. When it comes to opposition parties, however, we suggest that voters are not reacting retrospectively to the state of the economy. Instead, what matters where opposition parties are concerned are prospective considerations. Prospectively, right-leaning opposition parties do not benefit from unemployment for exactly the same reason that right-leaning government parties are not hurt: they are not expected to do anything about the problem. The negative effects for right-leaning opposition parties are thus a signal that prospective considerations are paramount for potential supporters of these parties where unemployment is concerned.[16]

If we now turn to levels of economic growth, we again find it hard to interpret the findings without assuming a prospective orientation on the part of voters. In the first place, we can see that large government parties are hardly affected by growth (or by lack thereof). But economic growth does make right-leaning opposition parties less attractive, and it is even more hurtful to small right-wing government parties. It seems that right-wing parties appear most attractive when growth is low, as though voters were focusing on the ability of such parties to correct the low-growth situation – a reaction very much in line with voters' apparent reactions to unemployment. By contrast, when growth is high, it is small left-wing parties that benefit. This finding would make no sense in a retrospective world. But perhaps what we are seeing here is further evidence that voters also have prospective economic concerns.

---

[16] The larger magnitude of so many of the coefficients where unemployment is concerned could be due to the high salience of unemployment in the countries that we study. We mentioned in the Introduction that opinion polls regularly show unemployment as being viewed as the most important problem facing these countries.

Smaller left-wing parties often emphasize not only materialist but also postmaterialist values such as environmental protection and equality of opportunity for different groups of citizens. Citizens may be more willing to support these kinds of platforms when the economy is booming than in periods of malaise. This interpretation of our findings would thus support the "luxury goods" hypothesis put forward by Stevenson (2002). Moreover, the apparent preference of voters for small government parties of this type over small opposition parties hints at the same type of pragmatism that we suggested might be reflected in responses to higher unemployment. When choosing a more radical alternative, voters prefer radical parties with government experience to those with no (recent) government experience.

The evidence for prospective economic voting that we derive from Table 4.5 is only indirect, yet our findings do lend support to H5 in Chapter 3. Left parties do appear to be held more accountable for unemployment, while right parties appear to be held more accountable for inflation. Moreover, opposition parties are evaluated primarily on prospective grounds, whereas for government parties, both prospective and retrospective considerations appear to play a role.

Though we have presented our interpretation of the coefficients in Table 4.5 as though the different behavior patterns might all be observed in the same political system, in practice it is quite likely that different patterns of behavior are more typical of different political systems (retrospective behavior in some and prospective behavior in others). In a later section we will find that this is indeed the case – a finding that both validates the variety of patterns we have just distinguished and makes them more comprehensible.

The "European Malaise"?

The puzzle over effects of unemployment in Europe's recent history can be almost entirely resolved in light of the ideological complexions of parties of different sizes. We have seen that when we distinguish parties according to their size and ideological complexion, the propensity of voters to support (or not) different parties during times of increasing unemployment appears quite interpretable. Yet, the overall impression of the effects of unemployment that we see for different parties is one of inconsistency. Some government parties are positively affected, some negatively. The effects are also inconsistent for parties of particular ideological complexions and sizes. This mixed bag of effects seen in Table 4.5 is apparently due to internal battles waged within governing coalitions on the left of the political spectrum that pit small (and generally more ideologically extreme) parties against large (and more moderate) ones. The result is to dilute the negative effects of unemployment on governing parties taken as a whole.[17] These findings help us to make sense of the apparently positive effects of unemployment on all parties taken together that we pointed out as being an apparent implication of Model F. Those findings were biased as a consequence of the omission of party size and ideology as independent variables.[18] Model I does not, as Model F seemed to do, imply that all parties gain as a consequence of rising unemployment. To the contrary, some gain, some suffer, and some are hardly affected. As a consequence of this mixture of effects, it is not possible, in the context of this model, to talk about an overall balance of effects (whether positive or negative), as was possible with Model F.[19]

These effects are compatible with neo-liberal descriptions of what is often referred to as the "European economic malaise" in publications such as *The Economist*. According to this perspective, necessary economic restructuring – mainly in terms of privatization, deregulation and the trimming of welfare arrangements – is seen to have been obstructed or frustrated by left-wing parties and their electoral support coalitions. The consequence would be relatively high unemployment

[17] According to this argument, the fall from grace of the left-leaning German government under Gerhard Schroeder, which led to early elections being called in Germany during 2005 (outside the period that we study), would be due to the fact that there was no small left coalition partner to "fight the good fight" against economic restructuring. The SPD's Green partner had other political concerns. Consequently, this is a clear case (such as does not exist during the period that we study) of a left-leaning government being voted out of office because of high unemployment, which had risen to record levels despite a number of policies intended to restructure the economy in a neo-liberal fashion. As predicted by our model, the right-wing opposition parties were unable to benefit from rising unemployment. Rather, it was the radical left (the Linke Partei) that won support at the expense of the more moderate left-wing parties.

[18] These omitted variables are, of course, correlated with other independent variables in the model, implying that their inclusion has the effect of changing certain other coefficients as well.

[19] Were we to be interested in the overall balance of effects, it would be necessary to evaluate the implications of Model I separately for each party and then average the results. An overall accounting of this type will be conducted in Chapter 6.

and the lack of electoral incentives to deal with this, precisely what our findings show. Of course, these findings are equally compatible with a different interpretation of economic developments. The voters who object to economic restructuring may be quite correct in being skeptical of privatization and deregulation as panaceas for reducing unemployment and stimulating growth, particularly when, during the period that we study, some countries appeared to enjoy unusually successful economies because of corporatist and statist arrangements that are anathema to the neo-liberal view – the often-touted "Dutch miracle" (Visser and Hemerijck 1997; Haverland 2001).[20] Either interpretation can quite adequately explain the seeming lack of electoral consequences referred to in this book's Introduction. The important point in this regard is that propensities to support right-leaning and left-leaning government parties are not hurt as much by unemployment as could have been expected on the basis of conventional theorizing about economic voting – parties of the right because they are not held accountable for unemployment and parties of the left because of conflicting priorities.

Of course, as already mentioned, the findings in this chapter relate to party support propensities, not to actual votes. In Chapter 7 we will return to the theme of European unemployment levels when we translate support into votes at the second stage of our two-stage approach to understanding economic voting.

System Characteristics and Economic Voting

According to the logic introduced in Chapter 1, we ought to look not only at party but also at system characteristics. There are all sorts of reasons why we should suppose that economic voting does not unfold in the same way in different countries. Powell and Whitten

[20] Much in contrast to the neo-liberal view of a European malaise, a different strand of literature emphasizes for the period that we study extraordinarily successful economic performances in some European countries, attributed to corporatism and social concertation mitigating market forces. Nickell and van Ours (1999) refer to a "European unemployment miracle," van Ark and de Haan (2000) to a successful "Delta model." See also Hemerijck (2003). After the turn of the millennium, economic conditions in these countries deteriorated markedly, and the discussion continues over the extent to which the economically successful 1990s are to be explained by social concertation or the meager years since 2000 by insufficient neo-liberal restructuring.

(1993) have suggested that economic voting would be more apparent in countries where responsibility for economic management can be more clearly attributed to governments than in countries with lower clarity of responsibility.[21] Whitten and Palmer (1999) have suggested that clarity of responsibility is not just a country attribute, but also a feature that could vary in the same country between one election and the next. Even though other systemic factors have never been suggested as possibly affecting economic voting, we should consider this possibility too. As argued in Chapter 3, it is not implausible to suppose that systemic characteristics such as consensual government or strong social protection could weaken the impact of economic conditions in much the same way that lack of system clarity does, perhaps even accounting for Powell and Whitten's findings.

Implementing any test for additional factors over and above those we have already investigated in Model I, Appendix B, and reported in Table 4.5 runs into problems of a mundane technical nature. Model I contains twenty interaction terms out of a rather larger potential number (some of which are not included in Model I because they proved not significant) that would have to be assessed as soon as system characteristics were added. And adding system characteristics would at least double the number of required interactions. Though we have derived our economic data from forty-two different contexts, it is evident that by the time we have implemented forty or more interaction terms, we will have spread our data very thinly over the available contexts so that the values of many parameters could end up depending on one or a very few cases at the system level. This would result in unstable and possibly misleading results.[22] So, system characteristics can only be included in a simpler model.

There are basically two ways in which we can simplify the model. The first would be to exclude all interactions with party size. This is unattractive because we demonstrated in the previous chapter that we

---

[21] Powell later elaborated this idea (2000) to distinguish countries that followed what he called a "majoritarian vision" of democracy from those that followed a "proportional vision."

[22] We checked for multicollinearity in all of our analyses. The tolerance levels of the parameters in Model I are still acceptable, but when all possible interactions with system characteristics are included, the tolerance levels in several instances are below 0.05, which means that such estimates lack robustness.

needed the interactions with party size to obtain meaningful results. However, Powell and Whitten (1993) and Whitten and Palmer (1999) arrived at sensible results in high-clarity elections on the basis of the distinction between government and opposition parties without taking the relative strength of the parties into account. It is true that in our data most elections are held under less clear circumstances and that their model provides no good explanation for economic voting in such circumstances; but when we exclude the interactions with party size, our approach does enable us to replicate Whitten and Palmer's (1999) model at the individual level. At the very least, we could expect this simplified model to generate sensible results in the high-clarity contexts.

The second way in which Model I could be simplified would be by excluding the government party status of parties from the model altogether, thus distinguish parties only according to their size and ideological complexion. Such a model flies in the face of one of the established "facts" of economic voting, namely, that government parties benefit from economic prosperity, whereas they are hurt by economic recessions. Our earlier findings in this chapter, however, suggest several reasons for supposing that a model that focuses on party size may be at least as appropriate as one that focuses on government status. In the first place, the two variables amount to much the same thing in practice: large parties are government parties more often than not. In the second place, the argument we made earlier about voters perhaps being more aware of a party's size than its government status might provide the reason why Whitten and Palmer's (1999) model does not work in low-clarity countries. A model that focuses on party size might well have more general applicability. In the third place, we have seen that prospective voting plays a large part in explaining differences in voters' party support. To the extent that this is so, it removes the need for voters to identify parties according to whether they are currently members of the government or not.

We will attempt both approaches to simplifying our model and interact these simplified models with Whitten and Palmer's clarity of responsibility index. Because the tables showing interaction effects for these models are very unwieldy, they will not be presented here (they can be found in Appendix B). Instead, we will move directly to summary tables of the sort employed earlier in this chapter to make plain the consequences of stylized changes of 1 percent in economic conditions for the strength of support for a limited number of prototypical parties.

Clarity of Responsibility

The models of economic voting presented so far in this chapter assumed implicitly that voters in all political systems react in the same way to the state of the economy, and that voters in all political systems take account of similar strategic concerns (in terms of whether parties are small or large, government or opposition, left or right). This assumption may, however, not be valid. Though we have managed so far to arrive at sensible effects of economic conditions without taking clarity of responsibility into account, it is possible that the effects we measured only exist in high-clarity countries, as explained in Chapter 3.

We start by replicating as far as possible with our data the tests conducted by Powell and Whitten (1993). Our test of whether government parties are held responsible for economic conditions only in high-clarity countries is conducted in two steps. We first return to the rather basic Model F (Table 4.2) – the model that contained only government/opposition status – and we add high/low-clarity interactions to this model. In the second step we also include ideological complexions of parties (details of both steps are presented in Models J and K, Appendix B, Table B.4). The results after the second step are summarized in Table 4.6. In this table we look, once again, at the consequences of a 1 percent increase in economic growth, unemployment, and inflation for prototypical parties.

The results presented in Table 4.6 demonstrate that effects of economic conditions in high-clarity countries are in line with the findings of Whitten and Palmer (1999) and with our own hypotheses. In high-clarity countries, left-wing government parties lose as a result of higher unemployment, while left-wing opposition parties gain support. Right-wing parties are hardly affected. Inflation hurts all parties, but government parties much more than opposition parties. Economic growth helps all parties, but government parties much more than opposition parties.[23]

---

[23] A test of the different effects of inflation in the high- and low-clarity countries is complicated by the fact that we encountered serious multicollinearity problems with

TABLE 4.6. *Effects of 1% Higher Inflation, Unemployment, and Economic Growth on Preferences for Various Prototypical Parties in Different Electoral Contexts (Based on Model K, Appendix B, Table B.4)*

			Change Because of Unemployment	Change Because of Inflation	Change Because of Economic Growth
High clarity of responsibility	Government party	Left-leaning	−0.136	−0.098	0.203
		Right-leaning	0.000	−0.090	
	Opposition party	Left-leaning	0.223	−0.012	0.028
		Right-leaning	0.080	−0.042	
Low-clarity of responsibility	Government party	Left-leaning	0.039	−0.067	0.117
		Right-leaning	0.238	−0.033	
	Opposition party	Left-leaning	−0.217	0.104	0.012
		Right-leaning	−0.103	−0.094	

In low-clarity countries the patterns are, however, not very sensible, except for those associated with economic growth. Government parties – left-leaning ones in particular – gain support as a result of higher unemployment, whereas the reverse is true for opposition parties, quite contrary to expectations. When it comes to inflation, it is left-leaning opposition parties that gain rather than the right-leaning ones that theory would lead us to expect. So we conclude, as have previous authors (Powell and Whitten 1993; Whitten and Palmer 1999), that the government–opposition dichotomy does not really work in low-clarity contexts.

What of the size attribute? Our next step is to evaluate a model that excludes government–opposition status and instead employs interactions with party size. The results are summarized in Table 4.7, which is based on Model Q presented in Appendix B (Table B.5). Because, as usual, higher-order interactions need to be taken in conjunction with lower-order interactions involving the same variables, the table

these parameters. This is largely due to the fact that high-clarity countries (Greece, Spain, Portugal, and Britain in particular) are countries experiencing relatively high levels of inflation. As a result, four of the effects involving inflation have tolerance levels below 0.10 and two have tolerance levels below 0.05, which indicate strong multicollinearity and unstable results as a consequence. This somewhat reduces our satisfaction with the government–opposition model even in high-clarity contexts.

TABLE 4.7. *Effects of 1% Higher Inflation, Unemployment, and Economic Growth on Preferences for Various Prototypical Parties in Different Electoral Contexts (Based on Model L, Appendix B, Table B.5)*[a]

			Change Because of Unemployment	Change Because of Inflation	Change Because of Economic Growth
High clarity of responsibility	Large party	Left-leaning	−0.105	0.329	0.097
		Right-leaning	0.036	0.316	0.132
	Small party	Left-leaning	0.178	−0.073	0.063
		Right-leaning	−0.059	−0.100	−0.069
Low clarity of responsibility	Large party	Left-leaning	−0.302	0.218	0.119
		Right-leaning	−0.401	−0.038	−0.157
	Small party	Left-leaning	−0.078	0.025	0.094
		Right-leaning	−0.007	−0.069	−0.087

[a] For the definition of a large and small party, see the footnote to Table 4.5.

is generated, as before, by summing the effects of a 1-unit increase in each economic indicator. The implications of these results are quite straightforward in the low-clarity countries. In these electoral contexts unemployment hurts all parties, yet it hurts the larger ones more than the smaller ones. In the case of inflation as well as economic growth, left-wing parties benefit, whereas right-wing parties are hurt. These effects also tend to be stronger for larger than for smaller parties.

How can these patterns for the low-clarity countries be understood? The interpretation that we consider most plausible is that voters in low-clarity contexts respond to the state of the economy in a prospective fashion. As argued in Chapter 3, in situations where it is not very clear who is responsible for the current state of the economy, it makes little sense to try to reward or punish parties for what they have done in the past. It makes more sense to look at what they are likely to do in the future. In times of high economic growth, and in times when public and private spending are relatively high (usually accompanied by somewhat higher inflation rates), the political programs of left-wing parties become more popular. Left-wing concerns such as environmental protection, equality of opportunity for different groups of citizens, and less restrictive asylum policies are more likely to be supported in times of economic prosperity than when the economy is in recession. This interpretation of our findings supports the luxury goods hypothesis put forward by Stevenson (2002).

The idea that voting in low-clarity elections is guided strongly by prospective expectations, rather than by retrospective evaluations, makes the finding for inflation and economic growth understandable in such elections. The results for unemployment are also interpretable in these terms. All parties lose from unemployment in these countries, but large right parties lose more than large left parties, which can only be understood in prospective terms along lines explained earlier. At the same time, the fact that virtually all parties do lose support in conditions of unemployment reminds us that even in low-clarity countries retrospective voting is still possible, in the sense of voting against the system as a whole. Differences in effects of economic conditions on parties of different types, however, have to be understood prospectively.

What of high-clarity countries? Table 4.7 shows effects that are somewhat similar to those in Table 4.6, but in this case in interaction with party size instead of government party. The comparison between Table 4.6 and Table 4.7 shows, however, that in high-clarity countries the results have more face validity when government–opposition status is taken into account rather than party size.

So, it seems that the puzzle of whether parties are held responsible on the basis of their size or on the basis of their government–opposition status may be largely resolved when we take account of the difference between high-clarity and low-clarity political contexts. In political contexts where credit and blame for economic conditions can straightforwardly be attributed to government parties, voters do indeed hold government parties responsible (though in ways tempered by ideological differences), as suggested by Powell and Whitten (1993) and Whitten and Palmer (1999). Effects of the state of the economy are to a large extent retrospective in these countries. On the other hand, in contexts where credit and blame for economic conditions cannot so easily be attributed to governments, voters choose on the basis of prospective considerations, basing their expectations of what parties will do if elected on the ideological leanings of these parties as well as on their size.[24]

---

[24] To evaluate this interpretation, we also conducted separate analyses of high-clarity and low-clarity countries. For the high-clarity countries we interacted economic

These findings both validate and clarify the findings that we reported, earlier in this chapter, from an analysis that distinguished parties on the basis of both government–opposition status and size but not on the basis of country types. There we found mixtures of prospective and retrospective behavior that we now see to be mainly characteristic of different types of political systems, with voters in low-clarity countries engaging mainly in prospective behavior, while voters in high-clarity countries are far more concerned with retrospective evaluations. Indeed, it seems clear that the best estimates of effects of economic conditions that will hold both in high- and in low-clarity countries will be estimates that do take account of both government–opposition status and the sizes of parties. Though we cannot show this to be the case because of our lack of degrees of freedom at the country level, it seems clear that Model I provides us with the best all-purpose approach to estimating the consequences of economic conditions across both high-clarity and low-clarity contexts.

Other Systemic Characteristics

In Chapter 3 we mentioned the possibility that clarity of responsibility might easily be confused with either or both of two other system characteristics that would predict weaker responses to economic conditions in certain countries. One of these was the consensual–majoritarian distinction suggested by Lijphart (1999), and the other was the distinction between liberal and other welfare states suggested by Esping-Andersen (1990, 1999). The idea that consensual decision making would make it hard to attribute credit and blame for economic conditions follows closely the logic we have employed in distinguishing between high- and low-clarity countries, but produces a slightly different list of countries from those picked out by Whitten and Palmer (1999). We derive

conditions with government–opposition status, and for the low-clarity countries we interacted economic conditions with party size. This research design (doing separate analyses for subsamples of countries) is similar to the one employed by Whitten and Palmer (1999). In the main text, we have presented the results based upon the full dataset, because we think that selecting cases is methodologically problematic. By selecting a subsample, one sometimes truncates the variance in the independent variables, thus making the findings less robust. However, the results of the separate analyses for the two groups of countries yield the same substantive results as those presented in the main text.

our list of countries with consensual decision-making practices from the first dimension in Lijphart's (1999) two-dimensional classification scheme (the parties–executives dimension), dichotomizing the variable according to whether countries obtained a positive or negative score on this dimension. Turning to Esping-Andersen's (1990, 1999) distinction, liberal welfare states are expected to motivate greater attention to economic conditions because in these countries citizens are least protected by the state against social insecurity in terms of unemployment and old age. In social democratic welfare states, citizens are most protected against these kinds of insecurities. Conservative welfare states fall somewhere in between. Most of the EU countries are conservative welfare states according to Esping-Andersen's definition. Three countries (Denmark, Finland, and Sweden) are social democratic welfare states, and two are liberal welfare states (Ireland and Britain).

In order to assess whether either or both of these classifications would change our findings based on distinguishing between systems of high and low clarity, we applied the following procedure. We first estimated Model I on the complete dataset (containing all forty-two contexts) and we saved the residuals. Then we selected a group of countries (for instance, the group of majoritarian systems) and reestimated Model I again on this selection of countries, but this time with the residuals of the full model as our dependent variable. If interactions with system characteristics prove to be significant, the variables should explain part of the unexplained variance in the full model. The analyses did not return very meaningful results, however. Within the majoritarian systems, the thirty-six variables of Model I combined explained 0.9 percent of the variance that was left unexplained by the original model. Within the countries Esping-Andersen classified as conservative, the variables explained only 0.4 percent.[25] Moreover, very few of the effects of variables measuring the state of the economy turned out to be significant (fewer than would have been expected on the basis of chance alone). Because these analyses did not yield much that was of substantive interest, we decided not to pursue this line of inquiry.

[25] The other groups distinguished by Esping-Andersen contained too few contexts to allow us to perform these analyses.

Conclusions

Theories of economic voting tell us that government parties are held responsible for economic conditions. Improvements in the economy are expected to benefit governing parties electorally and to hurt the opposition. In general, our findings support these theories. Well-specified models do indeed show that government parties are generally held more accountable than opposition parties for the condition of the economy. In Tables 4.3 and 4.5 government parties generally benefit from good economic times, with opposition parties sometimes being affected in the reverse direction, more frequently being affected in the same direction but less strongly. This pattern was not evident in models that failed to take account of party size and ideology, but once those factors were included the findings were clear.

Our findings reveal a complex pattern of voter reactions to economic conditions. The necessary inclusion of two additional party characteristics – party ideology and party size – reveals the fact that parties differing in these two respects are affected very differently by economic circumstances. Our finding that large left-leaning government parties lose support due to higher unemployment, while small left-learning parties often benefit, provides a much more nuanced view of the processes by which economic circumstances affect party support than we obtain from the previous literature, as does our finding that small right-learning parties are often particularly disadvantaged by economic growth. Our findings show asymmetries in voters' responses to economic developments that make sense only if we assume that voters respond not only retrospectively (punishing or rewarding parties for their past successes and failures) but also prospectively (taking account of the policies they expect parties to implement if those parties were to be members of a future government). Our findings thus suggest a type of prospective voting quite different from that previously suggested in the individual-level literature. The literature on subjective assessments of economic conditions (e.g., Lewis-Beck and Stegmaier 2000) refers to prospective voting in terms of anticipatory reactions by voters to expected future economic conditions, whereas what we seem to find is that voters' levels of support for different parties are affected by how they think those parties will influence future government economic policies. This behavior would be far more sophisticated and meaningful than was previously suggested, more in line with McKuen, Erikson, and Stimson's (1992) characterization of prospective voters whom they liken to bankers. We return to this theme in Chapter 7.

Our results considerably extend those of Powell and Whitten (1993) and of Whitten and Palmer (1999). We find economic conditions affecting the vote not only in high-clarity countries, but in low-clarity countries also. In high-clarity contexts, our analyses at the individual level yield results that are quite similar to the ones those authors found at the aggregate level: electoral support for left-leaning government parties is primarily hurt by rising unemployment, while electoral support for right-leaning government parties is primarily hurt by rising inflation. All government parties are hurt by low economic growth. However, because we distinguish between parties of different sizes, our findings are able to uncover a theme that was invisible to earlier researchers: evidence of prospective voting for small parties that sometimes gained from bad economic times (small left parties from inflation and small right parties from unemployment), as though voters felt that the ideological complexion of these parties particularly suited them to deal with the economic malaise from which the country was suffering.

In low-clarity countries, however, the picture is rather different, and our findings suggest that prospective voting is more widespread. When voting prospectively, it is not necessary for voters to know which parties are currently members of the government. Rather, the important question is what kinds of policies they will be better able to promote if they receive more electoral support. Hence, in low-clarity contexts, left-wing parties do well in times of economic prosperity, whereas right-wing parties benefit from recessions. Again, we have to assume that voters only hold certain parties responsible for economic conditions, but in low-clarity countries the parties held responsible are not government parties but large parties.

We must admit that these results as well as their interpretations – however plausible we consider them to be – are based upon a limited number of contexts, which inhibits us from simultaneously taking account, in one all-encompassing model, of all system and party characteristics that seem relevant. The analyses from this chapter, however, do allow us to formulate a new hypothesis that needs to be tested in future research. This hypothesis is: *in high-clarity contexts voters predominantly hold government parties retrospectively accountable for their management of the economy, whereas in low-clarity contexts voters predominantly react prospectively to the state of the economy, focusing their attention primarily on policies to be expected from the larger players among parties in their political systems.*

Anyone who has ever looked at changes in election results in multiparty systems will have noticed that in many cases the electoral fortunes of parties that were members of the same coalition government diverge widely. At election time the members of a coalition compete not only with opposition parties for votes, but also with each other, and in many cases some parties that are members of a cabinet gain votes at the expense of others. Our findings suggest that these sorts of differences in electoral success can be explained at least in part by the different ways in which voters' levels of support for different kinds of parties are affected by the economy. In Chapter 6 we will evaluate this insight by estimating the extent to which aggregate party support (and hence election outcomes) can be expected to change as a consequence of changing economic conditions.

The notion that left-wing parties are evaluated differently than right-wing parties is not new (e.g., Powell and Whitten 1993; Stevenson 2002), nor is the idea that party size matters (e.g., Anderson 1995). Nor even is the need to distinguish between low- and high-clarity contexts. So, our contribution in this chapter has been mainly to integrate the notions put forward by others in the context of a research design that would permit the implications of these ideas to become evident, and simultaneously to take account of all these variables in a single model. In the process, we have established that ideas about economic voting so far tested only in aggregate-level analyses do indeed have individual-level counterparts when tested on appropriate survey data.

We have found that effects of the economy on support for parties depend simultaneously on three party attributes: their size, their ideology, and whether they are in government or not. These findings provide a basis for our later investigation (in Chapter 6) of how votes shift from one party to another in the second stage of the two-stage process of electoral behavior that was set out in Chapter 1. We now know that any changes in actual votes, that occur as a consequence of changing levels of party support in the light of economic conditions will certainly depend on which particular parties, ideologically speaking, occupy which niches in the framework of party competition: which are large, which are small, which are government parties, and which are opposition parties. Exactly how parties in these different niches respond to economic conditions also depends on whether we are talking about high-clarity or low-clarity political contexts.

Because of data limitations, the analyses in subsequent chapters do not build on the models that take account of differences in system clarity. Early in this chapter, we developed a model (Model I) that appears to work quite satisfactorily in both high- and low-clarity systems. That model takes account of all three attributes of political parties that we have found to be important: their size, their government–opposition status, and their ideological complexion. This is the model we will generally employ in the chapters that follow.

So far in this book, we have only concerned ourselves with the first stage of the two-stage process described by Anthony Downs (1957). Preferences for parties are indeed formed much as anticipated in the economic voting literature. But how do preferences translate into votes? In Chapter 6 we will be taking the competitive situations of parties into account as we assess how the effects of economic conditions translate into votes. But first, we need to focus our attention on the individual voter. In this chapter we have been concerned primarily with how party characteristics condition the effects of economic conditions on party support, but parties gain or lose because voters prefer them or not. Ultimately, economic voting is about voters, not parties, and we need to consider what our findings imply for the behavior of voters before we move on to study election outcomes.

Our models in this chapter have taken account of individual-level characteristics, and we saw that taking account of these characteristics did not alter the effects of economic variables. But still there is the possibility that individual-level characteristics interact with economic conditions in ways that were not evident in this chapter. Evaluating this possibility is the subject of the next chapter.

5

The Economic Voter

The models of economic voting presented in Chapter 4 hardly paint a picture of *Homo economicus*. Effects of the economy are small compared to other effects on party support. Of course, small effects can have large consequences if they lead to a substantial segment of the electorate changing its party choice from one party to another. So, in order to assess the political consequences of changing economic conditions, we should know which groups of voters are affected by such changes. Much of the existing research has treated voters as homogeneous in the way they reach their decisions. However, some recent studies have suggested that voters are rather heterogeneous in the way they reach electoral decisions (Sniderman, Brody, and Tetlock 1991; Bartle 1997; Krause 1997; Pattie and Johnston 2001; Dorussen and Taylor 2002; Kroh 2003; Zaller 2005). One purpose of this chapter is to assess whether specific groups of voters are more responsive to changing economic conditions than others. We need this information in order to assess properly the consequences of changing economic conditions on election outcomes, which we turn to in the next chapter. Another purpose is to explore in more detail the effects of economic voting at the individual level and to evaluate those effects in the context of other effects on voters' party preferences. We will start by rehearsing the individual-level implications of our findings so far.

Effects of the Economy Compared to Other Effects

We mentioned in passing in Chapter 4 that effects of economic conditions on individual voters are rather modest. To illustrate this point,
Table 5.1 shows our full Model I (see also Table 4.5), but this time
with the effects of all control variables included.[1] Moreover, Table 5.1
adds standardized regression coefficients to the effects presented in
Chapter 4. For the purpose of comparing effects of the economy with
other effects, Table 5.1 also shows Model I without the effects of the
economy.

The first thing to notice, in comparing the two models in Table 5.1, is
that effects of the economy (in combination with their interactions with
other variables) add almost nothing (less than 1 percent) to the variance
explained. The second thing to notice is that effects of individual-level
variables are hardly changed by the addition of variables from the
party, election, and country levels. So, these contextual variables are
not at all collinear with individual-level variables.

Finally, we should note that the effects of economic conditions are
much less (judged on the basis of the standardized regression coefficients) than the effects of certain party and individual-level variables.
Among the latter, previous vote, ideological distance, and issue priorities exert the strongest effects. Even though standardized coefficients
are a crude criterion for comparing the impact of different effects, it
is clear that these latter variables contribute much more to determining the level of respondents' party support than do economic circumstances. Quite clearly, some of the effects of the economy are significant
only because of the enormously large dataset we employ in this study.
A dataset with the number of cases generally found in a typical election study (no more than 4,000) would find fewer significant effects of
economic conditions.[2]

The small magnitude of effects of the economy on party support has
a number of implications that deserve to be explored. The first is a clear

---

[1] Of course, the control variables were also included in the models presented in Chapter 4, just omitted from the tables, as mentioned in footnotes to those tables.
[2] Note, however, that a single election study would find no effects of the economy for a
more fundamental reason: at one point in time economic conditions are constant, and
an independent variable that does not vary cannot contribute to the variance explained
(see Chapter 1).

implication that past attempts to measure economic voting at the individual level have not been measuring what they purported to measure. The effects of subjective assessments of the economy measured in past research have been much too great (as argued by Wlezien, Franklin, and Twiggs 1997; Bartels 2002) to have been a reflection of economic conditions (even leaving aside the problem mentioned in Chapter 1 of understanding how economic conditions could be reflected in those assessments). The second implication arises as a corollary of the small effects of the economy in the formation of party support propensities: our findings hardly tell us anything new about how voters develop their preferences for parties.[3] A third implication is that the effects of other issues could in certain circumstances readily overwhelm any effects of the economy. Effects of issues (which relate, of course, to issues other than the economy) are shown in Table 5.1 to be substantially greater than effects of the economy. This implies that a salient issue of another type could easily nullify effects that would otherwise have been felt from economic conditions.

The most powerful effect on party support propensities is previous national vote. This is not a very exciting finding, as we do expect voters to generally vote the same way in successive elections. Apart from this, however, by far the most powerful influence is a strategic consideration: voters prefer parties that are large enough to have a good chance of putting their policies into effect. Party size can shift an individual's propensity to vote for a party by 3 points on a 10-point scale, these 3 points being the advantage a party controlling 50 percent of legislative seats has in comparison with a party that controls only 5 percent of legislative seats.[4] These findings thus confirm the old adage that "nothing succeeds like success."

The majority of the remaining effects on preference formation come from issues, including EU approval and left–right affinities (considered by many to be surrogates for unmeasured issues). Issues have most

---

[3] See the Coda to van der Eijk and Franklin (1996) for a detailed checklist of what was learned from the use of party support propensities in an investigation of the way people arrive at their evaluations of political parties across much the same universe of countries examined in this book.

[4] The 6-point effect shown in Table 5.1 would only apply to a comparison between parties controlling virtually no seats with parties controlling virtually all seats – something that does not happen in a competitive democracy.

TABLE 5.1. *Model I (cf. Table 4.5) with and without Interactions with the Economy*

	Without the Economy			With the Economy		
	B	SE	Beta	B	SE	Beta
Individual-Level Variables						
Previous national vote	0.764	0.009	0.402**	0.769	0.009	0.404**
Class	0.356	0.027	0.060**	0.355	0.026	0.060**
Religion	0.306	0.026	0.054**	0.306	0.025	0.055**
Left–right distance	−0.327	0.007	−0.241**	−0.322	0.007	−0.237**
Issues	0.471	0.020	0.113**	0.471	0.020	0.113**
EU approval	0.269	0.030	0.040**	0.272	0.030	0.041**
Left–right distance * perceptual agreement	−0.004	0.054	0.000	0.013	0.054	0.001
Issues * perceptual agreement	−1.198	0.174	−0.032**	−1.194	0.173	−0.032**
Party and System-Level Variables						
Government party * time since last election	0.003	0.002	0.009	−0.002	0.002	−0.006
Government party * time since last election squared	0.001	0.000	0.038**	0.001	0.000	0.041**
Government party	−0.154	0.055	−0.022*	−0.172	0.060	−0.025*
Party size	6.355	0.201	0.316**	6.347	0.208	0.315**
Government party * party size	−2.592	0.280	−0.091**	−2.217	0.308	−0.078**
Right party	−0.149	0.037	−0.023**	−0.153	0.037	−0.024**
Right party * government party	0.105	0.072	0.011	−0.074	0.076	−0.008
Right party * party size	0.872	0.292	0.029*	1.044	0.301	0.035**
Right party * government party * party size	0.130	0.416	0.003	0.266	0.440	0.007

Economic Conditions (and Their Interactions)

GDP	0.066	0.021	0.036*
Unemployment	0.137	0.025	0.044**
Inflation	−0.029	0.007	−0.028**
Government party * GDP	0.105	0.034	0.029*
Government party * unemployment	0.053	0.057	0.010
Government party * inflation	−0.070	0.013	−0.030**
Party size * GDP	−0.125	0.185	−0.011
Party size * unemployment	−0.258	0.187	−0.014
Gov. party * party size * GDP	−0.281	0.249	−0.018
Gov. party * party size * unemployment	−1.558	0.310	−0.062**
Right party * GDP	−0.119	0.028	−0.040**
Right party * unemployment	−0.202	0.041	−0.042**
Right party * inflation	−0.025	0.010	−0.016*
Right party * government party * GDP	−0.298	0.077	−0.057**
Right party * government party * unemployment	0.019	0.085	0.003
Right party * party size * GDP	0.252	0.237	0.016
Right party * party size * unemployment	−0.013	0.329	0.000
Right party * gov. party * party size * GDP	1.298	0.371	0.071**
Right party * gov. party * party size * unemployment	1.922	0.464	0.059**
N	27,505		27,505
Adjusted R^2	0.462		0.469

Note: Significant at * 0.01, ** 0.001.

effect, however, when there is lack of agreement on where parties stand in left–right terms.[5] Other research has shown that the effects of left–right affinities are positively affected by whether there is agreement as to where parties stand, but in this research that interaction is made redundant by the inclusion of past vote in the equation (see Chapter 4). One of the more interesting effects that we can estimate when we use party support as the dependent variable is the extent to which voters need to know where parties stand if they are to make use of left–right location as an aid to party choice. Lack of perceptual agreement about the political stances of parties can be seen to inject an element of uncertainty into the foundations of party support, forcing voters to rely more heavily on issues in order to compensate for the lack of shared meaning of ideological descriptors such as left and right.

Demographic effects on party support are much less than have been implied by the findings of some past research. Class and religion have much weaker effects than issues and left–right affinities. Nevertheless, even though demographic effects play only a marginal role in our findings, still the effects that we find on party preference formation are rather fixed. Parties occupy different niches in a political system, and it is hard for a party to change its policies or its ideological affinities over a short period of time. It is true that events (a scandal or a disaster) can change the salience of issues that favor one party or another, but the shifts in preferences that result tend to be rather short-lived and, except when an election occurs in the immediate wake of the event in question, such changes in issue salience seldom have long-term consequences for party preferences. A party can, of course, shift its ideological and issue positions, but not quickly. And even when a party has succeeded in making a shift in its ideological or issue stance, the effect will often be felt only by a few voters: those who take the party seriously as a contender for their votes.

It is for this reason that the economy is of so much interest as a possible source of political change. Because, unlike most other influences on vote choice, economic conditions can change radically from one election to the next, even effects as small as those of the economy that we measure in this book can have palpable consequences for election

---

[5] The negative effect of the interaction between issues and perceptual agreement reduces the effect of issues when perceptual agreement is high (see text).

outcomes if they change the rank order of party preferences (in terms of which party is preferred the most) of a substantial group of voters. The small effects of economic conditions are most likely to result in changes in election results if these affect all members of the electorate in the same way.[6] But is this in fact the case? Does the economy actually impact all voters the same way? This is the topic of the remainder of this chapter.

Relevant Distinctions among Voters

In order to be able to judge political parties by the state of the economy and to connect this to their ideologies, voters must have information about both the economy and the ideological positions of parties. Early studies of public opinion and voting behavior called into question whether the average citizen would have such information (Berelson, Lazarsfeld, and McPhee 1954; Campbell, Converse, Miller, and Stokes 1960; Converse 1964, 1970). Analyses of American National Election Study panel data from 1956, 1958, and 1960 revealed that about half of the respondents changed their opinions on policy issues as though they were answering at random. The implication drawn from these studies was that these people's policy attitudes, as expressed in opinion polls, were for the most part "nonattitudes" (Converse 1970). More recently, however, various scholars have proposed that, even though many citizens may not be very sophisticated, this does *not* mean that they are completely uninformed. With the aid of cognitive cues, they may still be able to evaluate candidates or parties in a meaningful way (Fiske and Linville 1980; Conover and Feldman 1982, 1984; Feldman and Conover 1983; Popkin 1991; Zaller 1992; Kinder 1993; Sniderman 1993). Moreover, it has been demonstrated that many people are quickly able to remedy their ignorance when they feel the need to because of urgent problems or changing issues and circumstances that affect them (Lupia and McCubbins 1998).

This view has the same implications as the notion of "information costs," which is central to rational choice perspectives on the electoral

---

[6] If different groups of voters are affected differently by the economy, losses of a party among one group could be compensated for by gains among another group. Under those circumstances, small effects of the economy are not so likely to result in significant changes in aggregate election results.

process (Downs 1957; Barry 1970; Enelow and Hinich 1984). In this perspective, the costs (in time and energy) of becoming informed about politics generally exceed the gains of doing so. To still behave rationally, voters need information-saving devices, that is, perceptual cues that help them to make informed judgments concerning the political world, including the policy positions of parties. According to Downs (1957), voters therefore make use of ideologies to evaluate parties, since ideologies summarize the differences among parties on the most salient issues at each point in time. Alternatively, it has been suggested that party identification provides cues even to those who are unaware of parties' ideologies (Campbell and Kahn 1952; Campbell, Converse, Miller, and Stokes 1960, 1966).

The extent to which a citizen makes use of economic conditions as a cue to decide which party to vote for equally depends upon his or her information. In order to vote on the basis of the economy, one should have information not only about the state of the economy, but also about which parties are in government. Moreover, when behaving retrospectively, one should want to reward government parties when the economy is doing well and punish them for economic recessions. When behaving prospectively, one needs information about parties' likely future policies. Different groups of voters may thus differ in their extent of economic voting for different reasons. Some voters may simply lack the necessary information about who is in government or about actual economic circumstances. At the other end of the spectrum, some voters may reach the conclusion that in a capitalist and global economy, a national government has only limited opportunities to affect economic developments. These voters may therefore decide that the government cannot be held responsible for the economy and hence may not take this information into account. In that case, we could again expect voters at intermediate levels of sophistication to be most affected by the state of the economy.

The kinds of considerations taken into account by different groups of voters when rating the support they give to political parties has important ramifications for our appraisal of electoral processes. Authors of classic studies of voting behavior have argued that citizens who decided the election outcomes were hardly aware of the issues at stake and of the positions of candidates on such issues (Berelson, Lazarfeld, and McPhee 1954). These arguments called into question the assumption that citizens cast meaningful votes in elections. The implication was that a large proportion of the (American) electorate was not able to vote on the basis of substantive considerations. These early findings led experimental researchers to distinguish between political "novices" and political "experts" when studying the effects of watching television news on evaluations of the president (Iyengar, Kinder, Peters, and Krosnick 1984). This American perspective has received little empirical support in European contexts (see Daudt 1961 for an analysis of British data and van der Eijk and Niemöller 1983 for the Netherlands). In the United States, too, this view has been heavily contested since the 1980s (for surveys of the relevant literature, see Dalton and Wattenberg 1992; Sniderman 1993). Zaller (1992) argues that a more nuanced distinction between levels of attentiveness is needed, because attitude change may be nonlinearly related to political attention. He expects citizens with intermediate levels of attentiveness to be the most affected by news stories. This argument is empirically supported by the study of Ansolabehere and Iyengar (1995: 189), who find that the effects of (negative as well as positive) political advertising are strongest among citizens with intermediate levels of information. New insights from a study by Zaller (2005) lead to a different appreciation of the electoral process. Zaller suggests that more sophisticated voters make their electoral decisions on the basis of ideology, whereas less sophisticated voters rely more on short-term factors, such as what happens to the economy.

These ideas suggest a number of ways in which electorates might fail to have homogeneous reactions to economic conditions. They can be checked by operationalizing suitable test variables to interact with the effects of economic conditions. In addition to the ideas already mentioned, various considerations pertaining to the personal circumstances of respondents need to be taken into account. To the extent that voters are motivated by self-interest, we might expect certain groups of voters to be more sensitive to economic developments than others. Dorussen and Taylor (2002) argue that this would be particularly relevant when estimating the effects of unemployment. Some citizens are not particularly vulnerable to unemployment, these authors argue, because their jobs are not at risk when unemployment increases, whereas others are more vulnerable to rising unemployment. If voters react differently depending on their personal circumstances, this will provide evidence of a form of pocketbook voting where voters bring concerns about their own situation to bear on their process of political preference formation.

We will check these notions by distinguishing two groups of citizens from the rest of the electorate.

From a pocketbook perspective, one would expect citizens who are themselves unemployed to be particularly sensitive to unemployment rates. This is because the unemployed have less chance of finding a job when unemployment increases, whereas their chance of finding work increases when unemployment goes down. In addition, such voters may be more sensitive to economic growth than other voters. When the economy slows down, governments usually cut their spending and the unemployed are often the first victims of such budget cuts, so a slowdown in economic growth might hit the unemployed harder than most groups. If we find this group reacting more strongly to changes in the economy, this will provide evidence of pocketbook voting.[7]

On the basis of similar logic, the group expected to be least sensitive to the unemployment rate consists of retired citizens, who (because they are not employed and are not seeking employment) do not have to concern themselves with the state of the job market. They may, on the other hand, be more sensitive to levels of inflation because at least some of them depend to a large extent on savings, which lose value as a consequence of inflation. Again, if we see more sensitivity to inflation by this group, it will be evidence of a form of pocketbook voting. Whether they are more or less sensitive to economic growth than other citizens remains to be seen.[8]

---

[7] We limit our discussion here to the consequences of being unemployed for party support. Other orientations and behaviors may also be affected by unemployment, such as withdrawal from politics, as found in some of the U.S. literature. We limit our discussion here to the consequences of being unemployed for party support propensities. It is evident that other political orientations and behaviors may also be affected by unemployment, such as withdrawal from politics, as has been suggested in some of the literature. As such effects do not impinge on the questions addressed here we will not pursue their presence or absence.

[8] In the typology of Dorussen and Taylor (2002), the least sensitive citizens are retirees and civil service employees. We did not use this typology because the extent to which civil servants are sensitive to job loss may well differ enormously among the different countries of the EU. Moreover, in many EU countries, various semipublic sectors exist in which employees have a status similar to that of persons who work in the public sector. In a cross-country comparison that focuses on fifteen countries, distinctions may then become arbitrary. Therefore, we decided to focus only on the two groups who can be most clearly distinguished from others and for whom the theoretical expectations are most clear: retirees as the least vulnerable group and the unemployed as the most vulnerable.

Although this has not previously been hypothesized, a final possible source of voter heterogeneity is ideological self-placement in left–right terms. In various analyses in Chapter 4, we noticed that the effects of economic conditions vary between parties of different ideological complexions. Support for large right-leaning government parties appears particularly sensitive to levels of growth, whereas support for left-leaning government parties appears particularly sensitive to unemployment levels. Similar differences may well exist among voters.[9] Left-leaning voters might be expected to give more weight to parties' performance in dealing with unemployment, whereas right-leaning voters may be more concerned with inflation. We will therefore distinguish between left-leaning and right-leaning voters and assess whether this distinction plays any role in the effects of economic conditions.

Defining the Effects

The discussions on voter heterogeneity focus on various concepts, such as political attentiveness, political knowledge, and political interest. The most general concept that most authors refer to is political sophistication. Luskin (1987) evaluates various measures of political sophistication and arrives at the conclusion that measures of factual knowledge produce the strongest effects. Other measures, such as education and interest, produce very similar but weaker effects. Unfortunately, our data do not contain measures of factual knowledge that can be compared across time and place, but they do contain measures of political interest and education. We will employ these measures in our analyses as proxies for political sophistication, because Luskin's analyses give no reason to suppose that patterns hypothesized as applying to knowledge would not equally apply to political interest or to education. Since the theory is still not entirely clear on whether we should expect linear interaction effects, we decided to distinguish a number of groups

---

[9] It might be thought that similar differences would have to be seen among voters, but this is not necessarily so. Voters could hold different types of party to account in different ways without themselves having different concerns. This would happen if they had different expectations for the behavior of different parties when in office – a prospective orientation that we have already documented in our findings (see Chapters 4 and 5).

of voters with different levels of interest and education. We have the advantage of a very large sample ($N = 32{,}950$), so we do not have to worry about losing two or three degrees of freedom if we explore these possible interaction effects in such detail.

Political interest was measured with a question that asks respondents how interested they are in politics. The response categories are "a great deal," "to some extent," "not much," and "not at all," enabling us to define dummy variables that distinguish between four levels of political interest.

Since the educational systems are different across various European countries, education is a difficult variable to operationalize in comparative studies. A common approach is to ask respondents how old they were when they completed their full-time education. Even though this provides only a very rough indication of how well people are educated, it does provide a measure that is comparable across countries. The categories that we distinguished for our study by means of dummy variables are low education (stayed in school only until age fourteen), medium low (graduated at age fifteen to eighteen), medium high (completed full-time education at age nineteen to twenty-one), and high (completed full-time education at age twenty-two or older).

In addition, we created two dummy variables to distinguish unemployed and retired citizens from the rest of the sample and several further dummy variables to distinguish between groups of citizens in terms of their positions on the left–right dimension. For all of these dummy variables, we sought to discover whether there were significant interactions between them and variables measuring the state of the economy.

Results

Our investigations in Chapter 4 led us to focus on a model (Model I in Tables 4.5 and Table 5.1) that seemed to us to encapsulate the considerations relevant to estimating the effects of economic voting. In this model (as in all the others we investigated), voters were assumed to react homogeneously to changes in economic conditions. If we are now to check that assumption, we evidently need to look for interactions between the effects estimated in that model and the different dummy variables defined for the purpose. This, however, would not enable us to evaluate the possibility that certain of our other models might also yield significant interactions. In particular, it is possible that our failure to find significant effects of changes in unemployment in the simple Model F (Table 4.2) was due to the fact that we did not distinguish there between left-wing and right-wing voters or between more or less sophisticated ones. Therefore, we decided to first check for significant interaction effects in the most basic Model F. This is the model that distinguishes parties only by their status as government or opposition parties, which is at the heart of most of the studies in economic voting. After checking for interactions in Model F, we checked for interaction effects in the fully specified Model I.

The common way to specify interaction effects is to define the necessary interaction variables and add them to the model. Doing so for Model I would imply, however, that we would have to create interaction terms for each of the thirty-six terms specified in Table 5.1 by interacting each of them with each of the eight test variables described earlier. Presenting the results of such analyses would be a Herculean task. We therefore decided upon a strategy already employed in Chapter 4 to study interactions with systemic characteristics. The procedure is as follows.

First, we estimated a Model (F or I) for the entire sample and saved the residuals from that analysis. We then selected a group of respondents distinguished by one of the dummy variables, such as the unemployed, and estimated Model I again for the selected group, but this time using the residuals as the dependent variable. These residuals represent the part of the variance in the dependent variable that was not explained by the Model (F or I) when it was tested over the entire sample. If any of the variables affect the selected group differently from the entire sample (i.e., if significant interaction effects exist), this would show up as significant coefficients of the independent variables on these residuals, corresponding to a significant interaction effect defined in the traditional way and included in a regression predicting the original dependent variable. Conversely, if no significant effects are found, then there is no significant interaction effect for the group in question and consequently no need to specify a traditional interaction term.

TABLE 5.2. *Significant Interaction Effects between Economic Condition and Individual Voter Characteristics, Using Model I from Chapter 4*

Characteristics of Respondents	Left–Right Distance	Right-Wing Party * Inflation
Unemployed		
Retired		
Education low	0.050**	
Education medium low	0.029*	
Education medium		
Political interest low	0.047*	
Political interest medium low		
Political interest medium		
Right-wing (position 8, 9 or 10)	−0.050**	−0.080**

Note: Significant at * 0.01, ** 0.001.

In this way, we explored Models F and I for the existence of interaction effects. Given the enormous sample, we have sufficient statistical power to detect quite small interactions. The tests largely failed to find such effects. We performed these tests for all three indicators of the economy (the main effects of unemployment, inflation, and economic growth), together with all the interactions of these variables estimated in Models F and I, using eight different dummy variables, thus checking for 200 interaction effects. Of these, only one turned out to be significantly different from zero at the 0.01 level of significance, and one was significant at the 0.001 level. Since one coefficient significant at the 0.01 level is rather less than what we could have expected to obtain by chance alone, our conclusion is that only a single significant interaction effect (significant at the 0.001 level) exists between the state of the economy as defined by Models F and I and various individual-level variables defined to test for heterogeneous effects of the economy as described earlier.

This finding is presented in Table 5.2, along with interactions with left–right distance, the only one of the individual-level variables to yield significant interaction effects. As is shown in the first column of Table 5.2, left–right distance affects party preferences of different groups of voters somewhat differently. The original main effect of left–right distance in Model I is a negative one: the smaller the ideological distance between a voter and a party, the higher the propensity to support that party. The negative interaction effect shown in Table 5.2 for right-wing voters in the first column thus indicates that the (negative) effect of left–right distance is stronger among these voters than among others. Similarly, the positive effects in that same column for citizens with low and medium-low education, and for those with low political interest, indicate that such voters are somewhat less driven by ideology than more sophisticated voters are, in line with past findings. It should nevertheless be pointed out that, although these effects are highly significant in this large sample, they are very weak effects that only slightly moderate the role of left–right distance. Given that assessing the effects of left–right distance is not a primary purpose of this study, we will not elaborate further on these findings here.

Our one clearly significant finding relating to economic conditions is that, among right-wing voters, right-wing parties are penalized even more as a result of higher inflation than among other voters (particularly left-wing voters). This amplifies, for these voters, the distinction already found between the effects of inflation on left and right parties. Because these voters prefer right-leaning parties more than left-leaning parties, preferences for the right-leaning parties are more strongly affected (for many such voters, their preferences for left parties will already be quite low, limiting the extent to which they could fall further as a consequence of poor economic conditions). Too much should not be made, however, of an interaction that, notwithstanding its high level of significance, still makes little difference to the import of our findings.

Much more interesting than the small number of significant interaction effects we found in our analyses of the effects of economic conditions is the large number we did not find. Out of 200 possibilities (twenty-five effects of economic conditions in Model F and Model I interacting with eight individual-level test variables), only one was significant at the 0.001 level.[10] Above all we find no evidence of pocketbook voting. Interactions with unemployed and retired status are nowhere significant. While we do find several instances where political interest and sophistication play an apparent role, these are no more than might have been expected by chance, and we should mention

---

[10] The other significant interactions in Table 5.2 are all interactions with left–right self-placement.

that even these effects (which we do not believe to be real and so have not included in Table 5.2) are restricted to assessments of economic growth. Unsophisticated voters react to inflation or unemployment no differently from those with more sophistication, quite in contrast to many research findings on this topic. How do we account for this?

We think the explanation lies in the failure of previous research to distinguish between the two stages in the two-stage process of party choice. We have shown that, in the first stage of this process, party preferences of all voters are about equally likely to be affected by the state of the economy. However, when it comes to the second stage, some voters may be more likely to switch their vote to a different party, *not* because they are more affected by the economy but because they are more cross-pressured (their highest support propensities are tied for two or more parties).

When preferences for two or more parties are tied (or nearly so) for first place in the minds of voters, even small changes in preference may lead to substantial numbers of changes in party choice. If the politically less interested and less educated citizens are more likely to be tied in their preferences for different parties, then they are more likely to change their votes – for whatever reason. This is the explanation that Zaller (2005: 194) gives for his finding that unsophisticated voters respond more to the economy: they are more often cross-pressured between two candidates. By giving this explanation, he implicitly admits that his findings could not answer the question of which groups of voters are more responsive to economic conditions. We have now answered this question: all groups are equally responsive in terms how their support for parties reflects economic conditions. Differences in behavioral consequences do not reflect differences in responsiveness, but rather differences in cross-pressures.

We will illustrate our point by focusing on the voters whose preferences for their two most preferred parties are tied and whose choices are therefore most liable to change. If the probability of being tied were distributed equally across all countries, within each country at different elections, and across all social groups within each country, we would obtain stable results when estimating the effects of economic conditions on party choice. However, when proportions of tied voters are distributed unevenly across countries and groups, a uniform effect of economic conditions on party preferences will have somewhat diverse

TABLE 5.3. *Proportions of Respondents Whose First Two Party Preferences Are Tied*

	Political Interest		Education		Retired		Unemployed	
EU average	Low	.23	Still studying	.23	Retired	.17	Unemployed	.23
	Medium	.20	Low	.19	Not retired	.22	Not unemployed	.21
	High	.18	Medium	.22				
			High	.21				

consequences for party choice for members of the different groups. Table 5.3 shows how the proportion of tied voters is distributed across various social groups in the EU as a whole in 1999.

We begin our discussion of this table with political interest. We can see that 23 percent of those with little political interest are tied, against 20 percent of those with medium political interest and 18 percent of those with high political interest. This is quite telling. We showed earlier that the effects of the economy on party support are uniform across these social groups. Suppose that we analyze a model of party choice on three subgroups of respondents selected by their political interest, and suppose that the economy has the *same* effect on the support propensities of each of these subgroups. If the dependent variable had been party choice, we would have nevertheless estimated a larger effect in the analysis of the least interested (almost a one-third larger effect than among those with high interest), *not* because the economy has a larger effect on these individuals, but because more of these voters change their party choice as a consequence of this uniform effect. Such a difference between the groups would have been highly significant, even with datasets of a more conventional size than ours, and would certainly lead analysts who focused on this dependent variable to conclude that effects of the economy were heterogeneous. Many of the same differences across subgroups are shown in Table 5.3 for the other social groups examined there: the retired, the unemployed, and those with various levels of education.

What makes matters worse is that the patterns of tied highest preferences are very different across countries, with much larger differences in certain countries than are seen across the EU on average. A table laid out in the same way as Table 5.3 but with rows for each of our fifteen countries is presented in Appendix B. There it can be seen that the least interested voters are most often tied in France, England, Ireland, Italy, Luxembourg, and Finland, and the median interested are most often tied in Flanders, Wallonia, Denmark, and Greece, whereas the most interested are most often tied in the Netherlands and Austria. Similar differences across countries are seen for the other social characteristics. It is no wonder, therefore, that leading scholars in the field of economic voting complain about inconsistencies in findings across different countries. When selecting a different group of countries in which to study change in party choice, one is bound to get different results, even if the underlying effects of the economy on party preferences are uniform across countries and social groups. This is exactly the mistake made in many studies of economic voting that do not take party competition into account (e.g., Dorussen and Taylor 2002; Zaller 2005).

It goes beyond the remit of this book to investigate *why* countries differ in terms of which social groups find more ties between parties in terms of support propensities. We can speculate, however, that it has to do with the different state of party competition in particular countries at different times. We will look at these differences in Chapter 6, though not with a view to elucidating this particular puzzle, whose exploration must wait on future research.

The Asymmetric Loss Curve

One of the inconsistencies observed in the literature pertains to the so-called asymmetric loss curve mentioned in Chapter 3. Economic recessions have sometimes been found, at least in aggregate-level studies (Bloom and Price 1975; Claggett 1986), to have a larger effect on the vote than economic gains of the same magnitude. This asymmetry has not been substantiated at the individual level, however (Kiewiet 1983; Lewis-Beck 1988; Nannestad and Paldam 1997). Though not, strictly speaking, a source of voter heterogeneity, this puzzle is one that we are able to address with our data in much the same way that we have addressed questions of heterogeneity among voters.

We have accounted for party support by means of a model that expects different reasons for party support to cumulate in a linear and additive fashion. Therefore, if the effects were not actually linear, but curvilinear instead, our model would be deficient in ways that would be

TABLE 5.4. *Correlations[a] between Economic Conditions and Residuals from Model I for Government and Opposition Parties (N = 27,505)*

	Government Parties	Opposition Parties
Economic growth	0.001 (p = .957)	0.003 (p = .580)
Inflation	−0.005 (p = .663)	−0.002 (p = .753)
Change in unemployment	−0.002 (p = .950)	−0.009 (p = .158)

[a] Cell entries are Pearson product moment correlations.

evident from the pattern of residuals from our predictions. If governing parties really lose support in an economic downturn at a higher rate than they gain support in an upturn, residuals from our analysis will correlate negatively with economic indicators when we run such an analysis only on government parties (and positively when we run such an analysis only on opposition parties). Table 5.4 shows the results of these two analyses: the left-hand panel contains correlations between saved residuals from Model I and the three measures of economic conditions for government parties, while the right-hand panel shows the same correlations for opposition parties.

Had the loss curve been asymmetric, as proposed by previous researchers, we should have found significant correlations between economic conditions and residuals from our analysis, but even with the enormous N available to us in these analyses, we find correlations so close to zero as to be very far from statistical significance. At least at the individual level, we fail to corroborate the aggregate-level asymmetry found in so many studies. In Chapter 6 we will see that our symmetric model of effects of economic conditions on party support does give rise to asymmetric effects in terms of choice, and thus to asymmetric gain and loss curves at the aggregate level of party vote shares, resolving the puzzle.

Conclusion

This chapter finds that the potential effects on party fortunes of economic conditions are small in comparison with the effects of some individual-level and party characteristics but that such effects are largely homogeneous. Only right-wing voters show a clearly significant deviation from homogeneous behavior (and only in respect to one feature of the economy), and that deviation merely serves to accentuate the general pattern found for all voters. Moreover, the effects are linear at the individual level. Our findings thus substantiate other individual-level analyses (Kiewiet 1983; Lewis-Beck 1988; Nannestad and Paldam 1997) that also failed to find asymmetric effects on government and opposition parties and give no support to H7 from Chapter 3.

Our failure in this chapter to find different effects of the economy on particular subgroups of the electorate speaks against the notion of pocketbook voting. There is no sign that either the unemployed or the retired react to economic conditions with their own circumstances in mind. Our results thus support findings beginning with those of Kinder and Kiewiet (1979), which show that, when deciding which party to support, voters respond to general economic conditions rather than to their personal situations. These findings run counter to the findings in some of the economic voting literature, however (e.g., Dorussen and Taylor 2002). This difference appears to be due to a failure in most of the literature to distinguish between voters' party support propensities on the one hand and their choices on the other. We have seen that less sophisticated voters are more likely to be tied in the competition between parties, and thus are more likely to react to anything that affects the strength of their support for each of those parties – but this does not mean that they are more strongly affected by the variable in question than other voters are.

More importantly, these largely negative findings reinforce the notion that effects of the economy are small but widespread, affecting all classes and conditions of voters almost equally. The homogeneity of responses somewhat mitigates the small magnitude of the effects of economic conditions. Because of this homogeneity, economic conditions do have the opportunity to influence election outcomes. So, the findings of this chapter do not undermine the notion that even small effects of economic conditions can have large consequences for election outcomes. On the basis of these findings, we can now move on to investigate the consequences of changes in individual preferences, resulting from changes in economic conditions, on election outcomes.

6

From Individual Preferences to Election Outcomes

So far, we have studied effects of economic conditions on the strength of voters' propensity to support each of the parties competing for their votes. In this chapter, we move on to the second stage in the Downsean calculus of voting and assess the consequences for party choice of these changes in party support.

Our findings so far indicate that economic conditions have significant though not especially powerful effects on support for particular political parties. But the fact that these effects are not very powerful does not mean that the impact of economic conditions on overall election outcomes is necessarily small. As pointed out in the previous chapter, most of the more powerful independent variables tend to be relatively stable over the short run. The alignments of parties with sociostructural variables such as class and religion have a character that is more or less given, especially in the short term. Political parties' ideological stances do change over time, but rather slowly. The same is true of their position on issues, particularly important issues. So, while these variables largely explain differences in the attractiveness of various parties as options to vote for, the same variables cannot explain short-term changes in party choice. Economic conditions, on the other hand, can (and occasionally do) change rapidly. An apparently booming economy may come to a grinding halt in a very few months, with immediate consequences for economic growth and often for unemployment as well, consequences that are widely and rapidly experienced.

So, whereas economic conditions (and changes in these conditions) are likely to be of little help in explaining which parties are attractive to which voters, they may be exceedingly important in explaining short-term fluctuations in the *relative* attractiveness of different parties. Such fluctuations would not matter much if most voters saw only a single party as a viable recipient of their vote, with all others so far behind that minor fluctuations in the propensity to support them were insufficient to bridge the difference (as we saw to be the case with Voter 1 in Figure 1.2). But for voters who consider their first and second most preferred parties almost equally attractive, a small change in the attractiveness of either one could tip the balance. Analyses of the same dependent variable that we employed in earlier chapters showed that most European voters do see two, sometimes three, parties as potential candidates for their vote (van der Eijk and Oppenhuis 1991; Kroh, van der Brug, and van der Eijk forthcoming). Such voters are subject to intense electoral competition, and the studies showed that there are large differences between the various EU countries at any particular election in the proportions of such voters.[1] Consequently, the same effect of the state of the economy on the strength of support for various parties could have very different consequences for actual party choice, and hence for aggregate election results, in one country than another and at one election than another. In this chapter, we will analyze the consequences of the effects of economic conditions for election outcomes in the fifteen countries that we study.

This chapter is intended primarily to address the last of the hypotheses that were listed in Chapter 3 by showing that responses to economic conditions in terms of actual party choice are indeed asymmetrical, with changes in the vote shares given to particular parties as a result of improving economic conditions failing in general to mirror the changes that result from declining economic conditions. At the same time, we will show how the asymmetric loss curve discussed in Chapter 5 is generated in practice, even though the strength of individual voters' support for each of the parties is not affected differently by improvements as opposed to declines in economic conditions. In the process, we

---

[1] Van der Eijk and Oppenhuis (1991) found for 1989 that the segment of voters whose highest preferences for parties are tied (or nearly so) ranges from a low of 10% in Spain to a high of 46% in France.

hope to make clear both how critical it is in analyses of this kind to distinguish between the two stages in Downs's two-stage model and also just how unstable and inconsistent the findings will be when researchers fail to make this critical distinction.

Estimating the Electoral Consequences of Economic Conditions

To evaluate the electoral consequences of changing economic conditions, we first assess the propensity of voters to support political parties under different economic conditions. We do this by calculating the expected value of this propensity using coefficients from Model I (Table 5.1). For all the independent variables we use the observed values from our dataset, except for the economic variables. For these we can use any values we choose and then obtain the resulting strength of support for each party. Making use of the observed regularity that almost all voters do choose to vote for the party for which they report the highest support (see Chapter 2, and particularly footnote 24 in that chapter concerning tactical voting), we also determine which party would – ceteris paribus – have been the one that received the vote from each of our respondents at an election held under the chosen economic conditions. Doing this for all voters and aggregating the results yields an estimated election outcome for the specified economic conditions. This, in turn, can be compared to the election result that would have occurred under a different set of economic conditions or to the result that occurred under the actual conditions that pertained at a certain moment in time.[2]

It might appear that we would wish to estimate the effects of changes in real-world economic conditions (e.g., from one election to the next in particular countries) in order to be able to compare these with changes

---

[2] The support for political parties and the resulting votes under the conditions actually pertaining at the time of our interviews need to be estimated in exactly the same way as for imaginary conditions. We cannot use the actually observed vote shares for political parties because we would then have prediction errors in one of the situations that we compare, and not in the other, which would make it impossible to tell to what extent any differences in party choice found between the two situations were due to differences in the stipulated economic conditions. By predicting the results under real-world conditions rather than using observed scores, we embed the same amount of error in both predictions, thus ensuring that the comparison we make reflects only the effects of differences in economic conditions.

in party support that occurred historically. That would require panel data with propensities to support each of the parties in a country at different moment in time. We do not have such data, as our observations for multiple elections in a single country are based on independent samples rather than on panels. Unfortunately, we can only estimate the effects of economic conditions for countries and occasions about which we have information regarding the propensity that voters had to support each party. Moreover, our models estimate effects on party support only of changes in economic conditions occurring in the year before each survey (see Chapter 3 for our operationalization of economic conditions). In practice, therefore, the only real-world comparisons that we can make are with party support in each country one year prior to each of our surveys. For most countries, this would be a random point in time of no particular interest as a benchmark. Commentators generally use the previous national election in each country as a benchmark against which to measure changes in party support, and only a few countries in our dataset held elections in the year prior to one of our surveys. Over the forty-two electoral contexts that we study, with elections every four years on average, one could expect to find about ten cases of elections occurring in the previous year. In practice we find seven cases, and, of course, there is no reason to suppose that these would constitute a random sample of all the elections conducted in the countries that we study.

Even if we had a complete set of countries for which to estimate the effects of changes in real economic conditions, this still would not enable us to address our primary research questions because changes in economic conditions would be idiosyncratic to each country. So, when we found differences in the effects on parties from country to country, it would not be clear to what extent these differences were due to differences in the competitive situation within the countries being compared or to differences in the economic stimuli that voters in those countries experienced. We can illustrate this problem by employing two real-world cases of changed economic conditions.

We start with the case of Greece in 1994 – a poster child for the fulfillment of conventional expectations regarding economic voting. Greece held a national election in 1993, so our data were collected one year after that election, precisely the lapse of time that our model uses for changes in economic conditions. In 1994 the economy was doing badly in Greece. Unemployment had risen 0.3 percent, inflation stood at 11.1 percent, and economic growth stood at only 1.5 percent. Bad though these conditions were, they actually constituted a huge improvement over the previous year, when unemployment had risen 1.2 percent, inflation stood at 14.4 percent, and economic growth stood at a mere 1.2 percent. So, the economy improved in Greece in 1994, and we find (working through the calculations outlined earlier – which will be described in greater detail later in this chapter) that voters indeed responded by rewarding the governing party with an additional 6.5 percent in terms of vote intentions. This increase in government support came entirely at the expense of opposition parties, all of which lost votes. These estimations, which we derived from our model, accord with expectations based on earlier models of economic voting. All such models would expect this sort of a boost for government parties (although this gain is an exceptionally large one) and a reduction in support for opposition parties in response to improving economic conditions.

But Greece is a high-clarity country. As a contrarian example, we will take Sweden in 1999. Again, this was one year after a national election, so our data are suited to modeling the changes in party support that were to be expected on the basis of changing economic conditions. Again, this is a country in which the economy had generally improved during the first year of a government's tenure in office, though not as unambiguously as in the case of Greece: unemployment had been getting better in 1998, declining by 1.5 percent, and continued to improve in 1999, though only by 0.9 percent; inflation had stood at 0.9 percent in 1998 and had been cut further to only 0.3 percent in 1999; and economic growth (which stood at 2.9 percent in 1998) improved markedly to 3.9 percent in 1999. This is a good economic performance, and conventional wisdom would expect the Swedish government to be rewarded for it. And in fact it was, but only marginally so. Working through the estimation of vote shares in the manner that will be explained later, we find that the minority Swedish governing party improved its position with voters in 1999 by 0.3 percent. Opposition parties in general lost votes, as expected, but there were large differences between opposition parties and one of them actually gained as much as the governing party did from the same change in economic conditions.

What do we make of the comparison between Greece and Sweden? In Greece a modest improvement in all the economic indicators appears to have led to a spectacular improvement in the standing of the government party relative to other parties. In Sweden a set of economic indicators, which generally would have been considered to represent a much better economic performance than in Greece, would only have produced a very small increase in vote share for the governing party – and an equally large increase for one of the opposition parties. Is the different outcome in Sweden due to the importance of inflation, which improved much less than in Greece, or is it due to something about the competitive situation of the parties in Sweden in 1999?

When there are multiple differences between countries, it is hard to determine which one is critical. If we knew that we were dealing with exactly the same changes in economic conditions in both countries, this would reduce the problem of understanding how changes in economic conditions translate into differences in party support. That is the approach we will take in the remainder of this chapter. We wish to investigate how party fortunes are affected by changes in economic conditions. In particular, we believe that there are asymmetries in the conversion of party support propensities into votes, depending on the relative strengths of parties in relation to their potential support (see Chapter 1). To address this question, we need to apply stylized changes in economic conditions, the same change for each country, and estimate the resulting changes in election outcomes. We will start by investigating the effects of each of the economic conditions (economic growth, inflation, and unemployment) separately and then focus on their combined effects.

Electoral Effects of Stylized Changes in Economic Growth

We look first at the effects of lower economic growth on election outcomes. Specifically, we estimate in each country the vote shares (in percentages) of the political parties when economic growth is given its real-world values (see footnote 2) and compare these against what their vote shares would have been had economic growth been one standard deviation lower (1.69 percent lower than the extent of economic growth actually registered in our data). In order to simplify our presentation, given the large number of results (one result for each of 295 parties divided over sixteen political systems and three moments in time), in Table 6.1 we present these results only for one of the years (1999), and only for the two largest government parties and two largest opposition parties. Appendix B contains the full table from which these results are taken (Table B.7). Later in the chapter, we will discuss the extent to which focusing on just the first two parties gives us a valid picture of our findings.

Table 6.1 summarizes the findings in terms of percentage change in vote shares. Positive values indicate that the party in question would obtain a higher share of the vote as a consequence of the stylized difference in economic conditions, while negative values indicate that it would obtain fewer votes. The table demonstrates, first of all, that the electoral consequences of small changes in individual-level propensities to support a political party, occasioned by changing economic conditions, can indeed be quite large. In Austria, Finland, Ireland, and France, the estimated effect in 1999 of one standard deviation deterioration in economic growth is for the largest government party to lose 2 percent or more of the valid votes – enough in many cases to result in a different coalition government taking office (see later). But effects of this magnitude are by no means ubiquitous. In Denmark, Greece, and Spain, the loss for the largest government party resulting from the same deterioration in economic conditions would have been less than half of 1 percent; and in Britain and Luxembourg, the largest party would actually have gained votes (by 1.7 percent in the case of Luxembourg) as a consequence of this deterioration in economic conditions. Among the largest opposition parties the variation is much less. In all but four countries, such parties increase their vote shares as a result of the decline in economic growth, as would be expected; and only in Denmark does the largest opposition party lose votes as a result of lower economic growth. The second largest opposition party loses very slightly in two countries, but the general situation is one of slight gains.

Before we present similar information for changes in terms of inflation and unemployment, we need to address the question of how the fortunes of different parties can be affected so very differently by an identical change in economic conditions. We will do so by looking at Luxembourg, where the electoral effects of a fall in economic growth are quite counterintuitive and quite contrary to the general pattern. In Luxembourg, instead of losing votes in response to declining economic growth, the largest government party is estimated to improve

The Economy and the Vote

TABLE 6.1. *Consequences of One Standard Deviation Less
Economic Growth (−1.69%) for the Election Results of the Two
Largest Government Parties and the Two Largest Opposition Parties
in 1999 (Baseline: Economic Conditions for 1999)*[a]

	Government Parties		Opposition Parties	
	Largest	Second	Largest	Second
Austria	−2.0	+1.7	+0.7	−0.2
Belgium: Flanders	−1.0	−1.0	0.0	+1.5
Belgium: Wallonia	−1.2	−2.3	+1.8	0.0
Britain	+0.4	inap	0.0	−0.1
Denmark	−0.3	0.0	−0.1	+0.1
Finland	−2.5	+1.5	+0.5	+0.3
France	−2.2	−0.3	+2.6	+0.5
Germany	−0.7	0.0	+1.0	−0.3
Greece	−0.2	inap	+0.2	0.0
Ireland	−2.2	−0.3	+1.8	+0.2
Italy	−1.2	−0.3	+2.4	+0.5
Luxembourg	+1.7	−1.5	0.0	0.0
The Netherlands	−1.0	+0.4	+0.9	0.0
Portugal	−0.7	inap	+0.8	0.0
Spain	−0.4	0.0	+0.4	0.0
Sweden	−1.8	inap	+1.8	0.0
Average (SD)	−1.0 (1.1)	−0.2 (1.1)	+0.9 (0.9)	+0.2 (0.4)

[a] *Note:* Parties in this table (in the rank-order government party 1, government
party 2, opposition party 1, opposition party 2) are:
Austria: SPO, OVP, FPO, LIB Forum
Belgium (Flanders): CVP, SP, VLD, Vlaams Blok
Belgium (Wallonia): PS, PSC, PRL, Ecolo
Britain: Labour (no second government party), Conservatives, Lib Dem
Denmark: Soc.Dem, Rad. Venstre, Venstre, Konserv
Finland: SDP, Kokoomus, Keskusta, SKL/Kristillisit
France: PS-PRG, PC, RPR, UDF
Germany: SPD, B90/Gruenen, CDU/CSU, FDP
Greece: PASOK (no second government party), ND, KKE
Ireland: FF, Progr Dem, FG, Labour
Italy: Dem di Sinistra, PPI, Forza It, All Nazionale
Luxemburg: CSV/PCS, LSAP/POSL, DP/PD, Dei Greng
Netherlands: PVDA, VVD, CDA, GR. Links
Portugal: PS (no second government party), PSD, CDS/PP
Spain: PP, CIU, PSOE, IU
Sweden: Soc.Dem. (no second government party), Vansterp., Miljop

its position by 1.7 percent of the total votes cast. Moreover, this effect of declining economic conditions is quite different for the second largest government party, whose vote share drops 1.5 percent. Using Luxembourg as an example for opening up the "black box" and investigating its workings has an additional advantage: the small size of the Luxembourg sample implies that many of these changes involve only small numbers of respondents. This makes it possible to report all relevant cases on an individual basis and still be able to discern the forest through the trees.

Understanding the Luxembourg Case

Table 6.1 showed that the consequence of a 1.69 percent decline in economic growth for Luxembourg in 1999 would have been that the largest government party there would gain 1.7 percent in vote share. Its partner in government, however, would have lost some 1.5 percent in vote share as a result of the same change in economic conditions.

These effects are spectacularly counterintuitive on the basis of conventional thinking about economic voting, first because the received wisdom is that government parties will be hurt by a deteriorating economy and second because all government parties are expected to be affected similarly. There is no provision in conventional accounts for one government party to improve its position at the expense of another. Even in the light of our own more elaborate model, finding that the largest government party gains votes due to a drop in the rate of economic growth could be quite surprising. In brief, it happens because the ideological complexions of the two government parties are different, while their sizes are rather similar. Working through the details of how these similarities and differences translate into changes in voters' party choices will help to clarify the workings of our model.

Table 6.2 uses a portion of Model I (Table 5.1) as a basis for estimating the consequences of a one standard deviation change in GDP growth for party preferences in Luxembourg. We need to include all parameters that concern GDP (notably its interactions with government parties, party ideology, and party size). The coefficients (b's) for many of these rows cannot be interpreted at face value for reasons that the reader will be familiar with from our exercises in interpreting similar effects in Chapter 4.

TABLE 6.2. *Effects of a One Standard Deviation (1.69%) Decline in GDP Growth on Party Preferences in Luxembourg (1999)* (Baseline: Economic Conditions for 1999)

	Model Parameter B	Change in GDP Growth	Party 1 CSV/PCS	Party 2 DP/PD	Party 3 LSAP/POS	Party 4 ADR	Party 5 DEI GRENG	Party 6 DEI LENK	Party 7 GAL
Size of party[a]			0.215	0.065	0.145	−0.055	−0.055	−0.135	−0.135
Government party			Yes	No	Yes	No	No	No	No
Left or right party			Right	Right	Left	Left	Left	Left	Left
Independent variables from Model I									
1. Growth in GDP	0.066	−1.69	−0.112[b]	−0.112[b]	−0.112[b]	−0.112[b]	−0.112[b]	−0.112[b]	−0.112[b]
2. Government party * GDP growth	0.105	−1.69	−0.177[b]		−0.177[b]				
3. Party size * GDP growth	−0.125	−1.69	0.045[c]	0.014[c]	0.031[c]	−0.012[c]	−0.012[c]	−0.029[c]	−0.029[c]
4. Gov. party * party size * GDP growth	−0.281	−1.69	0.102[c]		0.069[c]				
5. Right party * GDP growth	−0.119	−1.69	0.201[b]	0.201[b]					
6. Right party * gov. party * GDP growth	−0.298	−1.69	0.504[b]						
7. Right party * party size * GDP growth	0.252	−1.69	−0.091[c]	−0.028[c]					
8. Right party * govt. party * Party size * GDP growth	1.289	−1.69	−0.468[c]						
Effect of 1.69% drop in GDP growth on party support			0.004	0.075	−0.190	−0.124	−0.124	−0.141	−0.141

[a] The variable party size is centralized around its mean (of 0.135).

[b] The result of multiplying the entries in the first two columns (this is 0.066 * −1.69 for variable 1) for all parties.

[c] The result of multiplying the product of the first two columns by party size (top row) for all parties. This is −0.125 * −1.69 * 0.215 for variable 3, party 1.

The bottom row of Table 6.2 shows how the strength of the propensity to support each of the seven Luxembourg parties changes as a consequence of a 1.69 percent drop in GDP growth (the sum of the entries higher up each column). There we see that while assessments of the right-leaning government party (party 1: CSV/PCS) were hardly affected by the change in economic circumstances, assessments of the left-leaning government party (party 3: LSAP/POS) were reduced by almost one-fifth of a point (0.19) on the 10-point preference scale.[3] The reason is primarily that left-leaning parties gain more (in terms of party support propensities) from economic growth (and thus lose more from declining economic growth) than right-leaning parties do (see also Table 4.5). Government parties are more affected by economic growth than are opposition parties. This is why the left-wing government party is hurt more than the left-wing opposition parties (parties 4, 5, 6, and 7), while the right-wing opposition party (party 2) gains more than the right-wing government party. The result is that the smaller, more left-leaning government party was hurt the most by the lower rate of economic growth.

It remains to be shown how the changes in party preferences for all seven parties translated into the differences in party support that we saw in Table 6.1. This is easily done for Luxembourg because there are only 300 respondents in our sample for that country in 1999, and only 4 of them switched parties as a consequence of changes in their party support propensities resulting from changing economic conditions.[4] Working through the changes in party preferences and in predicted party choice for all 300 respondents would require too much space. We therefore present eight cases (labeled A to H in Table 6.3). These include all 4 of those whose choice of party actually changed as a consequence of the deterioration in economic conditions and, for illustrative purposes, another 4 respondents (picked at random from the

---

[3] The calculations conducted in Table 6.2 will reproduce the GDP components of Table 4.8 if the size used for the parties in Table 5.2 is replaced with the sizes of (1) large and (2) small parties, as defined in the note to Table 4.8.

[4] Our estimation procedure assumes that all of those affected by a given change in economic circumstances are affected equally by that change. Our analyses in Chapter 5 served to test this assumption, demonstrating that in terms of how party preferences are affected by economic conditions, the European electorates can indeed be seen as homogeneous.

remaining 296 cases) whose choices were not affected by the change in economic conditions.

Table 6.3 contains two rows for each of these eight individuals. The first row displays their propensity to support each of the seven parties in the 1999 economic situation, and the last column displays their party choice. The second row for each individual presents the same information for a rate of economic growth that is 1.69 percent lower, calculated from the change in party support propensity presented in the bottom row of Table 6.2. Since the effects of the economy are not interacted with individual-level characteristics, the predicted changes in party preference are the same for each individual. So, for example, all preferences for the Christian Democrats (CSV/PCS) increase by 0.004. In each row, the highest preference is indicated by an asterisk. The first four respondents (A, B, C, and D) are the ones whose party choice changed as a consequence of lower economic growth. The choices of the other four did not change, even though their support for each of the parties was affected in exactly the same way as for respondents A–D. As we can see, at the 1999 level of economic growth, each of the four respondents A–D has a lower propensity to support the CSV/PCS (Christian Democrats), the largest Luxembourg government party, compared with their most preferred alternatives (the LSAP/POS – Socialists – for three of these voters, the ADR for one of them). At the lower rate of economic growth, support for the LSAP/POS and for the ADR had dropped to a point below that for the CSV/PCS for these four voters, causing a change in actual choice (see for each voter the two choices in the last column). These changes in choice account for the 1.7 percent increase in vote share for the CSV/PCS. The corresponding loss of three supporters by the Socialists accounts for the drop in Socialist support of 1.5 percent shown in Table 6.1.[5]

If we now turn to the four respondents who did not change their party choice (chosen at random from all of the 296 Luxembourg respondents who did not change their party choice), we can see that, for three of them (respondents E, F, and G), their second highest propensity is so much lower than their highest one that their choice cannot be

---

[5] Because our procedure uses weighted data, the cases in Table 6.3 are not equally important in our analyses. This accounts for the discrepancy between four cases accounting for a 1.7% shift in vote shares, while three cases account for 1.5%.

TABLE 6.3. *Effects of Different Economic Conditions on the Propensity to Support Parties for Eight Luxembourg Voters*

Respondent	GDP Growth[a]	Party 1: CSV/PCS	Party 2: DP/PD	Party 3: LSAP/POS	Party 4: ADR	Party 5: DEI GRENG	Party 6: DEI LENK	Party 7: GAL	Predicted Vote
A	Higher growth	6.02	4.61	6.04[b]	Missing	4.32	1.90	3.68	LSAP/POS
	Lower growth	6.02[b]	4.68	5.85	Missing	4.19	1.76	3.54	CSV/PCS
B	Higher growth	4.33	3.24	4.40[b]	3.99	3.26	4.04	4.15	LSAP/POS
	Lower growth	4.34[b]	3.31	4.21	3.87	3.14	3.90	4.01	CSV/PCS
C	Higher growth	5.86	4.26	5.87[b]	Missing	Missing	1.59	2.49	LSAP/POS
	Lower growth	5.86[b]	4.34	5.68	Missing	Missing	1.45	2.35	CSV/PCS
D	Higher growth	6.58	3.97	3.98	6.59[b]	2.51	3.15	3.45	ADR
	Lower growth	6.58[b]	4.05	3.79	6.46	2.39	3.01	3.31	CSV/PCS
E	Higher growth	4.25	4.84	6.07	2.86	8.21[b]	4.08	3.97	Dei Greng
	Lower growth	4.25	4.92	5.88	2.73	8.09[b]	3.94	3.83	Dei Greng
F	Higher growth	4.43	7.89[b]	4.94	4.43	4.27	3.18	3.52	DP/PD
	Lower growth	4.43	7.97[b]	4.76	4.30	4.15	3.04	3.38	DP/PD
G	Higher growth	8.02[b]	3.83	4.97	3.32	4.50	2.49	2.76	CSV/PCS
	Lower growth	8.02[b]	3.90	4.78	3.19	4.38	2.35	2.62	CSV/PCS
H	Higher growth	4.98	5.00	5.76[b]	4.55	3.93	3.07	3.05	LSAP/POS
	Lower growth	4.98	5.08	5.57[b]	4.43	3.81	2.93	2.91	LSAP/POS

[a] Higher GDP growth refers to the real economic circumstances in 1999; lower GDP growth refers to the stylized situation with 1.69% less economic growth.

[b] Party yielding the highest utility.

affected by the small changes in their support for the various parties. For respondent F, the balance of support already favored the party whose support is increased. Respondent H, finally, supports many parties a little but none of them a lot. This voter is in one of those in a position to switch relatively easily as a consequence of events that affect the strength of their party support. However, in this specific case, the changes in party support propensities were not great enough to change the preference ordering for different parties.

Unemployment and Inflation

After having seen how individual changes in support for parties may lead to differences in parties' vote shares under different economic circumstances, we can return to our assessment of the electoral consequences of changes in economic conditions. In Table 6.1 we reported the aggregate effects of changes in economic growth. In Table 6.4 we present the same information for changes in inflation and unemployment, using the actual economic conditions in 1999 as our baseline. Once again, we see considerable differences between countries. A rise in unemployment or inflation by one standard deviation has mainly negative effects on vote shares of government parties and mainly positive effects on those of opposition parties. However, there are again substantial variations between countries, particularly in the effects of unemployment on government parties. Some large government parties would lose vote share as a consequence of higher unemployment (nearly 5 percent in Britain), while others would even gain (as much as 1.8 percent in Wallonia). These differences are less pronounced for inflation, where almost all government parties lose vote share when inflation worsens and where the range of electoral effects for government parties runs from +0.2 to −2.8.

In the case of increasing unemployment, there is nearly as much variation in the effects on opposition parties' vote shares as we saw for government parties. Some opposition parties gain and some lose, with a range of effects running from +3.7 to −5. This contrasts with what we see for GDP growth and inflation, where opposition parties gain support as a consequence of a deteriorating economy (with few and minor exceptions).

Nevertheless, despite much variation, overall effects of worsening unemployment on party fortunes are negative, in contrast to the overall positive effects that we found on party support in Chapter 4's Model F. Indeed, the consequences we see in Table 6.4 of (simulated) rising unemployment for party vote shares are closer to conventional expectations derived from the economic voting literature than are the effects shown in Chapter 4's Model F. Too much should not be made of the difference. In Model F we found a balance of effects that were mildly positive; in this chapter, we find a balance of consequences that are mildly negative. Neither chapter shows party fortunes unambiguously moving in accord with conventional expectations, since in both chapters we see large government parties losing ground but small government parties gaining ground as a consequence of worsening unemployment figures. Viewed in terms of vote shares, this can be easily demonstrated by correlating the gains and losses of the largest government party with the gains and losses of the second largest government party (for instance, the correlations between the first two columns in Table 6.1). These correlations are -0.49 for economic growth, -0.16 for unemployment, and -0.46 for inflation. The fact that all three correlations are negative suggests that the gain by one governing party often occurs at the expense of other governing parties.

The implications for discord within governing coalitions are the same whether we look at vote shares (as we do here) or at party support propensities (as we did in Chapter 4). Moreover, the different balance of outcomes we find in this chapter is easily explicable in terms of the different ideological balance of government parties in 1999 (the data used for Table 6.4) and overall (the data used in Chapter 4). Chapter 3's Table 3.2 shows that in 1999 there were almost four times as many left-leaning governments as right-leaning governments, in contrast to the roughly equal balance shown in the same table for all years taken together. So in 1999, a particularly large number of left-leaning governments were in a position to suffer the consequences of the simulated increases in unemployment used to generate Table 6.4. In practice, of course, during 1999 unemployment was declining virtually everywhere, as shown in Chapter 3's Table 3.1. So, the real situation will have been one in which left-leaning government parties generally benefited, at least in terms of their level of support, from the improving unemployment situation in that year. We will see later in this chapter that these increases in support may not have translated into higher vote shares, however.

TABLE 6.4. *Effects of One Standard Deviation Rises in Unemployment (1.02%) and Inflation (3.02%) (Baseline: Economic Conditions for 1999)*[a]

| | Unemployment | | | | Inflation | | | |
| | Government | | Opposition | | Government | | Opposition | |
	Largest	Second	Largest	Second	Largest	Second	Largest	Second
Austria	+1.5	−2.7	0.0	+1.0	−0.3	−1.2	+1.1	+0.2
Belgium: Flanders	−1.0	+0.5	0.0	0.0	−0.5	−0.5	0.0	0.0
Belgium: Wallonia	+1.8	+4.3	−5.0	+0.6	−0.6	−1.8	0.0	+1.8
Britain	−4.8	inap	+2.5	+0.6	−0.3	inap	+0.3	0.0
Denmark	−0.4	0.0	−0.2	+0.1	−0.3	0.0	0.0	0.0
Finland	−2.0	−0.3	−0.9	0.0	0.0	−0.9	+0.8	0.0
France	−6.0	+1.1	+3.0	+0.5	−2.8	0.0	2.0	+0.5
Germany	−1.7	+0.6	+1.0	+0.1	−0.8	0.0	+0.9	0.0
Greece	−2.7	inap	+1.6	+0.2	−1.1	inap	+0.9	0.0
Ireland	−0.7	+1.4	−0.7	0.0	−2.4	0.0	+1.7	+0.2
Italy	−3.6	+1.4	−1.2	0.0	−1.7	0.0	+0.7	+0.1
Luxembourg	+1.3	−1.3	0.0	0.0	−0.4	0.0	+0.5	0.0
The Netherlands	−0.4	0.0	−0.2	−0.1	+0.2	−0.4	+0.3	+0.1
Portugal	−3.9	inap	+3.7	0.0	−1.5	inap	+1.6	0.0
Spain	−0.4	0.0	+0.3	+0.1	−2.0	0.0	+1.8	+0.2
Sweden	−0.3	inap	+0.2	0.0	−2.1	inap	+2.0	0.0
Average (SD)	−1.5 (2.3)	+0.4 (1.7)	+0.3 (2.0)	+0.2 (0.3)	−1.0 (0.9)	−0.4 (0.6)	+0.9 (0.7)	+0.2 (0.4)

[a] The parties in this table are listed in the footnote to Table 6.1.

The Electoral Effects of Changes in All Indicators

The general impression that we get from evaluating the effects of worsening economic conditions is consistent with the picture presented in the economic voting literature (see Chapter 1). As we can see from the bottom rows of Tables 6.1 and 6.4 – which display averages across countries – in the case of each of the economic indicators, deteriorating economic conditions tend to benefit opposition parties and hurt government parties, particularly the largest ones. Small governing parties are generally less affected, and occasionally they even benefit from a deteriorating economy. But there are numerous and salient exceptions to this average picture that we will focus on later in the chapter. First, however, we need to take a broader look at the consequences of changing economic conditions. So far, we have looked only at economic downturns. What of economic upturns? The next two tables investigate both downturns and upturns in each political system. In order to keep the number of tables from getting out of hand, in these two tables we combine the effects of all three economic conditions, looking first at the effects of a downturn that takes the form of a one standard deviation shift in all three economic indicators: a situation that is simultaneously one standard deviation worse in terms of GDP growth, in terms of the evolution of unemployment, and in terms of inflation. Such a confluence of economic woes will not be very frequent, yet it is sufficiently common to be used as a point of reference. In view of the correlations between these three economic indicators, this combination of developments should occur about once every twenty elections, on average, or about twice in the forty-two elections we analyze in this book.[6]

Table 6.5 shows the effects on the two largest government and opposition parties in each country – expressed as change in their vote shares – of a downturn in economic conditions such as just described. Again, the full table for all parties is presented in Appendix B (Table B.7). There, each country's parties are listed in order of size and government parties are shaded, making it quite easy to differentiate the effects on government parties from those on opposition parties and to differentiate

---

[6] Economic growth and inflation are correlated −0.42; change in unemployment is not related to either of the other two variables.

between the effects on small and large parties. That table makes it clear that the effects on parties other than the largest two government and opposition parties are generally quite small, justifying our selection of parties for the tables in this chapter. By the time one gets to the third party, whether in government or in opposition, effects from changes in economic conditions are always less than 2 percent (gain or loss), and often they are trivial (particularly in view of the large changes in economic circumstances that provide the basis for our estimates).

Effects are more orderly than when we took the three types of economic conditions separately, as we did in Tables 6.1 and 6.4. In all countries, we see that the major government party would have been hurt by the stylized changes in economic conditions. In France and Portugal an election during such an economic downturn would almost certainly give rise to a change of government.[7] In Italy and Finland, this economic scenario would affect which party is the largest, with obvious (but not necessarily predictable) consequences for coalition composition. In Britain the electoral consequences of this kind of economic downturn would be substantial but not sufficient to bring down the government, given the overwhelming majority enjoyed in 1999 by the ruling Labour Party. We will return to the British case later in this chapter (see also Sanders 1999).

With all three measures of economic conditions working in concert, the effects on large parties in different countries are somewhat different than they were when we took the measures one at a time. Nevertheless, the same general findings hold: we see big variations between countries in the magnitude and even in the direction of effects for large parties as a consequence of changes in economic conditions. The governing French socialists (in 1999) would lose 8.4 percent of their vote share in the face of an economic downturn of this magnitude, while the Danish socialists would lose only 1.4 percent and the Luxembourg Christian Democrats

---

[7] How estimated election outcomes in terms of votes translate into parliamentary seats is, of course, contingent on a country's electoral system. Our samples are not designed, or large enough, to permit us to derive from the simulated election results a precise distribution of parliamentary seats. Nevertheless, if an incumbent government party received 50 percent or more (in practice, much less would often suffice) of the votes in a proportional representation system, or more than its major rival in a first-past-the-post system, it is likely that it would retain its hold on government power.

TABLE 6.5. *Change in 1999 Predicted Percentage Vote Share of Selected Parties Resulting from One Standard Deviation Deterioration in All Three Indicators of the State of the Economy (Baseline: Economic Conditions for 1999)*[a]

	Government Parties		Opposition Parties	
	Largest	Second Largest	Largest	Second Largest
France	−8.4	0.0	+5.8	+1.9
Portugal	−5.0	inap	+4.6	0.0
Greece	−2.9	inap	+1.8	+0.2
Spain	−3.5	0.0	+3.1	+0.4
Italy	−5.8	+0.9	+1.9	+0.2
Britain	−6.3	inap	+4.0	+0.5
Finland	−4.5	+1.7	+0.7	+0.5
Ireland	−4.5	+0.3	+2.8	+0.4
Germany	−3.6	0.0	+3.3	+0.1
Austria	−4.2	+1.8	+1.8	+0.6
Denmark	−1.4	0.0	−0.1	+0.3
The Netherlands	−2.6	+0.5	+1.9	+0.3
Belgium: Wallonia	−0.9	−1.9	+0.5	+1.6
Sweden	−3.6	inap	+3.4	0.0
Luxembourg	−0.2	−1.4	+1.2	0.0
Belgium: Flanders	−1.3	−0.5	0.0	+0.3

[a] The parties in this table are listed in the footnote to Table 6.1.

would hardly be affected. Table 6.5 also reinforces our earlier finding of no uniform effect on vote shares among government parties or among opposition parties. In only a few contexts are all the members of the same governing coalition hurt by the stylized change in economic circumstances (Wallonia, Luxembourg, and Flanders). More common is the observation that some government parties suffer electoral losses, while others are hardly affected (in Germany, Spain, and Denmark) or even benefit (in France, Italy, Finland, Ireland, Austria, and the Netherlands). These differences are due to the fact that government parties often compete with each other for votes (yielding the negative correlations we noted earlier in this chapter) and also to differences between opposition parties' ability to take advantage of the economic situation by siphoning off votes from particular government parties. Conventional models of economic voting that merge votes for (or support for) different government parties into one category "government party support" are thus necessarily mis-specified.

In contrast to government parties (where some members of the government gain while others lose), worsening economic conditions have more similar consequences for opposition parties. There is only one example of an opposition party that is predicted to lose votes when the economy deteriorates simultaneously in all three respects (the Danish liberals, Venstre). All other opposition parties gain or their election results are unaffected.

Some final remarks should be made about the contribution of our findings to observed electoral volatility. Changes in vote shares estimated in Table 6.5 are quite small – nowhere more than 8.4 percent and averaging just over 1 percent (see Table B.7 in Appendix B). To put this in perspective, in the Dutch national elections of 1998 the net change in party shares of the vote between April 1998 (in a panel interviewed a month before the elections) and May 1998 (in the same panel interviewed the day after the election) was only 2.3 percent,[8] an amount within the range of possible consequences of changing economic conditions (Table 6.5 shows the largest Dutch government parties in 1999 – one year later than the Dutch election study – losing on average nearly this amount in a major economic downturn). At the same time, it should be borne in mind that much else will have been going on at any real election apart from effects of the economy; indeed, in the Netherlands in 1998, the gross change in party support was more than four times as great, at 10.8 percent (van der Brug and van der Eijk 2000). The fact that gross electoral change is considerably larger than net electoral change is a commonly observed pattern (e.g., van der Eijk and Niemöller 1983). This indicates that movements of voters are largely self-canceling. However, effects of the economy on vote shares that we estimate in this chapter are

---

[8] Net change is computed as the total percentage of all losses (of the parties that lose votes). Gross change is the percentage of individual voters who changed their party choice. The two figures are equivalent only if voters switch from losing to winning parties. But if some voters switch from Party A to Party B, while others switch from Party B to Party A, the gross change is larger than the net change. The final two rows in Table B.6 (which provides the raw material for Table 6.5) give the total amount of predicted net change and gross change (in terms of Pedersen indices). In that table, the countries are ordered on the basis of the amount of predicted gross change in party choice as a consequence of economic conditions.

largely uniform, despite the countervailing flows that we highlighted earlier.[9]

How can we explain this discrepancy between real-world changes in the parties voted for (which are largely self-canceling) and the stylized changes that we estimate in this chapter (which are not)? In the first place, it should be pointed out that, in Table 6.5 (and in Table B.6, from which it is derived), we estimated the consequences of a decline in all three economic indicators. This reduces the likelihood of counter-vailing changes in party vote shares. Changes in economic conditions of this nature do occur in reality, but are exceptions rather than the rule. In the second place, we should note that, in estimating the effects of stylized changes in economic conditions, we take a ceteris paribus approach of holding all other effects constant. In the real world, of course, other effects would not be constant and there would be many additional movements, many of them presumably self-canceling. In our estimates in this chapter, we implicitly assume that those move-ments in party support are indeed totally self-canceling; but we have made the point (which we will repeat in the next chapter) that, in the real world, effects of economic conditions can easily be overridden by other effects. The net electoral changes that we estimate on the basis of actual (not stylized) changes in economic conditions in the sixteen systems that we study here were on average 4 percent, which is far less than the real electoral volatility, which was on average above 12 percent in Europe in the 1990s (Mair 2002a, 2002b). That this small portion of total volatility should contain few opposing flows is not surprising given our finding in Chapter 5 that economic conditions have largely homogeneous effects on voters. So, the conclusion that in Europe the economy matters for election outcomes is certainly supported by our findings, and its largely homogeneous effects result in vote shifts that are largely in the same direction from parties that lose votes to parties that gain. Equally certainly, election outcomes are not *just* a matter of "the economy, stupid," and other effects will certainly result in con-trary vote shifts that will increase total volatility and could relatively

---

[9] The two bottom rows in Table B.6 in Appendix B (the table that provides the raw material for Table 6.5) show surprisingly little difference between net change and gross change.

easily override the much smaller vote shifts due to changing economic conditions.

Asymmetries in the Effects of Improving and Deteriorating Economic Conditions

What about improvements in economic conditions? Do these mirror the effects of economic downturns? Analogous to the analyses giving rise to estimates reported in Table 6.5, we also examined the implications for election outcomes of a stylized situation in which all three economic conditions were simultaneously better than in 1999. Results for the two largest parties are shown in Table 6.6 (see Table B.8 in Appendix B for other parties), which is laid out using the same conventions as Table 6.5. The stylized economic conditions yield gains for most (but not all) of the largest government parties and losses for most (but not all) of the largest opposition parties. In general, the largest government party is seen to gain from the improved situation, while the largest opposition party loses, but there is one political system (Flanders) where the largest party sees no measurable improvement and one (Denmark) where the largest opposition party does make a small gain. Still, the general pattern of effects is the reverse of those of a worsening economy, as was to be expected.

Importantly, however, the gains that occur in specific countries as a consequence of good economic times often fail to mirror the losses that were seen in Table 6.5 for those same countries as a result of bad economic times. The correlation, country by country and party by party between vote change in the two tables, should, according to conventional wisdom, have approached a perfect -1.0. In fact, it is only -0.83 for the largest government parties, -0.72 for the next largest government parties, and a spectacularly low -0.38 for the second largest opposition parties. This finding (evident from a cell-by-cell visual inspection of the two tables), which would have surprised those who proposed the classic formulation of economic voting theory (see Chapter 1), comes as no surprise to us, given our stress on the moderating effects of the competitive situations in which parties find themselves. The asymmetries are caused by the degree to which a party has, at any given time, exhausted its electoral potential – the pool of voters

TABLE 6.6. *Change in Predicted Percentage Vote Share of Selected Parties Resulting from One Standard Deviation Improvement in All Three Indicators of the State of the Economy (Baseline: Economic Conditions for 1999)[a]*

	Government Parties		Opposition Parties	
	Largest	Second Largest	Largest	Second Largest
France	+9.5	−0.2	−5.7	−1.6
Portugal	+9.5	inap	−9.5	0.0
Greece	+3.2	inap	−2.6	−0.4
Spain	+4.5	0.0	−4.5	0.0
Italy	+5.6	−0.7	−2.1	−0.3
Britain	+4.0	inap	−1.6	−1.5
Finland	+3.5	−1.5	−1.4	0.0
Ireland	+0.9	+0.7	−0.4	−0.2
Germany	+3.1	−0.1	−2.6	−0.4
Austria	+2.9	−1.4	−1.1	−0.1
Denmark	+1.4	0.0	+0.2	−0.4
The Netherlands	+2.3	−0.7	−0.8	−0.6
Belgium: Wallonia	+1.4	+1.9	−1.5	−0.2
Sweden	+2.8	inap	−2.1	−0.2
Luxembourg	+0.5	+1.8	0.0	−1.0
Belgium: Flanders	0.0	0.0	0.0	+0.6

[a] The parties in this table are listed in the foonote to Table 6.1.

that conceivably might vote for it, as argued at various points earlier in this book. The conclusion is thus that opposite developments in the economy do not necessarily have opposite effects on parties' electoral fortunes, although they do have opposite effects on voters' propensity to support various parties, as we saw in Chapter 4.

Not only is there no strict symmetry between gains and losses of the same parties faced with opposite but equal changes in economic conditions. Just as interestingly, the same developments in economic conditions do not necessarily have the same electoral effect on any particular party at different points in time. The same stylized shifts in economic conditions as those applied in Tables 6.5 and 6.6 will not have identical consequences for the same parties in a different year because differences (even resulting from slow-moving changes) in other determinants of party support will have altered the competitive situations of different parties between the two points in time, both by shifting their electoral potentials (the maximum number of voters they could ever mobilize) and by altering the degree to which these potentials have been realized in practice as actual votes.

In order to illustrate this, we carried out the same estimates of consequences for parties' vote shares of stylized changes in economic conditions as those shown in Tables 6.5 and 6.6, but for a different election year, 1994. We present the results for only three exemplary countries: the one with the largest and the two with the smallest changes in election results in 1999: France on the one hand and Flanders and Denmark on the other. The results are shown in Table 6.7 (the results for all parties are given in Table B.9 in Appendix B).

From Tables 6.5 and 6.6 we know that that, in 1999, stylized changes in economic conditions in France had the largest consequences on election outcomes of those found in any country. Table 6.7 is based on the same model and on identical stylized changes in economic conditions. As a consequence, the effects of these changes on party support propensities are virtually identical in 1994 to those we found in 1999. However, in sharp contrast to 1999, we find in Table 6.7 that in 1994 those same changes in economic conditions have virtually no impact on the vote shares of French parties. Apparently, the number of voters whose support for their two most preferred parties is (almost) tied was much larger in 1999 than in 1994. Thus, the same changes in party support as those that gave rise to extensive changes in party choice in 1999 would have led to many fewer changes in party choice in 1994. The other two countries also show substantial differences compared to their situations in 1999. In 1999 Flanders and Denmark were the two countries for which we found the smallest estimated consequences of stylized changes in economic conditions (net changes in party votes below 2 percent). In 1994 net changes are above 2 percent in those countries, and in both countries the changes are greater than in France.

Implications for Model Specification

These estimates of the electoral consequences of changing economic conditions – consequences expressed in terms of parties' vote shares – go a long way towards clarifying why conventional approaches to the study of economic voting suffer from instabilities and inconsistencies

TABLE 6.7. *Change in 1994 in Predicted Vote Share of Parties (in Percentages) as a Result of Deterioration or Improvement in All Three Indicators of the State of the Economy (Three Exemplary Countries Only)*[a]

	France		Flanders		Denmark	
	Deteriorating Economy	Improving Economy	Deteriorating Economy	Improving Economy	Deteriorating Economy	Improving Economy
Gov. Party 1	−0.3	0.0	+0.6	−1.1	−2.0	+2.6
Gov. Party 2	−0.2	0.0	−1.9	+4.1	−0.3	+0.3
Opp. Party 1	+0.4	−0.1	−0.2	−1.0	+0.4	−0.4
Opp. Party 2	0.0	0.0	+0.3	0.0	+0.8	−1.1

[a] The parties in this table are listed in the footnote to Table 6.1.

in their findings (see also our discussion in Chapter 1). Conventional approaches focus on vote shares as dependent variables, often the vote share of all government parties combined. The received wisdom from these approaches is reflected in the average patterns of electoral consequences in Tables 6.1 and 6.4: governments are generally hurt electorally by poor economic conditions (and generally benefit from good ones). But the large number of exceptions to these general patterns (and the many cases of opposite electoral consequences for individual government parties) point to the source of the instabilities and inconsistencies that these choice-focused approaches suffer from – the same instabilities and inconsistencies that were lamented by their practitioners (Lewis-Beck and Paldam 2000: 114; Dorussen and Palmer 2002: 1). Our analyses demonstrate that these inconsistencies do not arise from great variability in the ways in which economic conditions impinge upon voters. To the contrary, they arise from the failure of earlier researchers to differentiate between the formation of propensities to support particular parties, on the one hand, and actual party choices on the other. The contradictions and inconsistencies are a direct consequence of failing to take account of complexities arising from the competitive situations in which parties find themselves, which are inevitably different from one party, one election (and one country) to the next.

Our findings show clearly that understanding the impact of economic conditions on individual vote choice requires a more elaborate approach than is conventionally employed, one that distinguishes party support from party choice and that investigates the effects of the economy on party support propensities before translating support for the parties in a political system into the choices made between them and, ultimately, into the vote shares that they would acquire in different economic conditions. Only on the basis of such an approach is it possible to detect the great stability and uniformity – across countries, across periods, across ideological inclinations of governments, and across most kinds of individuals – of the way in which economic conditions affect the electoral process. Only on the basis of such an approach is it possible to understand that what at first sight appear to be voter responses to economic conditions that are inconsistent and contradictory are in fact due only to differences in the competitive situations in which parties find themselves in different countries at different times.

Asymmetry in Loss/Gain Function

A widely observed fact in the economic voting literature is that economic recessions have more impact on the vote than economic prosperity. This has been explained by a psychological mechanism known as grievance asymmetry (e.g., Bloom and Price 1975; Price and Sanders 1994; Nannestad and Paldam 1997; 2002; Stevenson 2002). Yet, we showed in Chapter 5 that there was no such asymmetry in our findings regarding party support: party support propensities increase linearly with improving economic conditions and decline linearly with declining economic conditions.

Our explanation for the asymmetry in loss functions is thus a different one. Each party has a group of potential supporters (its electoral potential), which at a certain point in time consists of those voters who have a relatively high preference for that party. A party that has done relatively well in the most recent election – and has thus improved its chances of becoming a governing party – often will have achieved this result because it mobilized a large proportion of its potential supporters. As a consequence, governing parties are (on average) not in a very good position to win additional votes because they have already come closer to exhausting their potential than many other parties (with some of which they compete for votes). But, by the same token, they are very vulnerable to vote losses in bad economic times. The reverse is true for opposition parties, particularly large ones. In general, they will be closer to their bedrock of support than government parties, and in such circumstances they cannot lose much more when economic times are good. They do, however, stand to gain when the economy deteriorates.

We will illustrate this interpretation of the source of these asymmetries with two exemplary cases: the loss and gain of the two largest Irish parties, Fianna Fáil (FF) and Fine Gail (FG), in 1999 and similar patterns for the two largest British parties, Labour and the Conservatives, in 1999. We estimated the consequences of economic conditions on parties' vote shares for a large number of economic scenarios that vary gradually between a 2.5 standard deviation deterioration (compared to the actual economic conditions in 1999) in all three aspects of the economy simultaneously and a 2.5 standard deviation improvement in all three aspects of the economy simultaneously. We changed these scenarios in steps of 0.1 standard deviation, so that we estimated

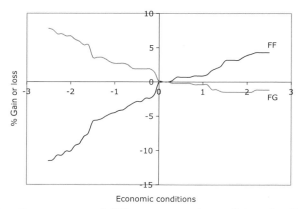

FIGURE 6.1. Consequences of different economic conditions for % votes for Fianna Fáil and Fine Gail in 1999.

the electoral consequences of fifty-one different scenarios. Figure 6.1 shows the results for the Irish case, and Figure 6.2 shows the results for Britain.

The loss/gain function of FF in 1999 runs from −11.5 percent (when the economy performs 2.5 standard deviations worse) to +4.3 percent (when the economy performs 2.5 standard deviations better). For FG these percentages are 7.8 percent and 1.2 percent. There can be no doubt that in 1999 Ireland was a clear example of a case where the loss/gain function was asymmetric, even though the underlying model is a linear one and generates linear changes in party support. These linear changes in party preferences do not only generate non-linear loss/gain functions, they also generate curves that are not smooth. There are some areas in which the economy may change without affecting the electoral fortunes of parties, but there are also inflection points where a small change in economic conditions generates large changes in parties' election results.

Turning to Britain, the loss/gain function of Labour runs from −18.3 percent to +14.0 percent, and for the Conservatives it runs from +10.2 percent to −2.4 percent. Clearly, in Britain the loss/gain function was asymmetric as well, albeit not as spectacularly so as in Ireland. Also, the curves presented in Figure 6.2 are smoother than those in Figure 6.1. An important finding is that a strongly improving economy would hardly lead to electoral damage for the Conservatives, the largest

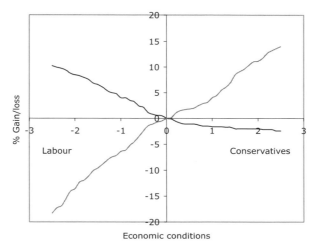

FIGURE 6.2. Consequences of different economic conditions for % votes for Labour and Conservatives in 1999.

British opposition party at that moment. In 1999 electoral support for the Conservatives was evidently composed mainly of true-blue loyalists who were unlikely to defect, no matter what. So, the Conservatives had very little to lose from an improving economy but much to gain from government economic discomfiture. Labour, on the other hand, had much to both gain and lose. It must be borne in mind that, even though it had won a landslide victory in 1997, Labour had done so on far less than 50 percent of the votes and evidently still had considerable potential for further gains, though these potential gains from an improving economy were nevertheless smaller than the potential losses Labour might have suffered because of a deteriorating economy.

How do these ideas work out in practice? Unfortunately, our data are not well adapted to testing the asymmetric loss hypothesis because they are not collected at the time of national elections, which is the time when mobilization of potential voters should be most complete for winning parties and most lacking for losing parties. Our data are collected at random points in time between elections, so that for many countries they will reflect poorly the structure of party competition that existed at the time of the previous national election, as much as 60 months previously. Nevertheless, if we focus on countries in which the 1999 government took office less than thirty months

TABLE 6.8. *Asymmetries in Estimated Gain/Loss for Government Parties in 1999*

| Country | Economic Conditions | | | Months Since Government Took Office |
	Decline	Improve	Gap	
Germany	−3.6	3.0	0.6	8
Italy	−4.4	4.6	−0.2	8
Sweden	−3.6	2.8	0.8	8
Netherlands	−2.3	1.7	0.6	10
Denmark	−1.4	1.4	0.0	15
France	−7.9	7.6	0.3	24
Ireland	−4.2	1.6	2.6	24
Britain	−6.3	4.0	2.3	25
Austria	−2.4	1.5	0.9	29
Greece	−2.9	3.2	−0.3	32
Spain	−3.5	4.5	−1.0	37
Portugal	−5.0	9.5	−4.5	44
Belgium: Flanders	−1.8	0.0	1.8	48
Belgium: Wallonia	−2.8	3.3	−0.5	48
Finland	−1.3	1.5	−0.2	50
Luxembourg	−1.6	2.3	−0.7	60
Overall	−3.4	3.3	0.2	
<30 months	−4.0	3.1	0.9	

previously, we do see the hypothesized asymmetry: government parties generally lose more votes in bad economic times than they gain votes in good economic times.

Table 6.8 shows loss of votes under conditions of economic decline compared with gains in votes under conditions of economic improvement, together with the gap between the (absolute) values of losses and gains. Asymmetries for opposition parties would evidently be identical, since vote losses must balance vote gains in percentage terms. Countries are ordered in terms of the number of months elapsed since the government took office (where there was a concurrent national election, the government is coded as having been in office for the full length of the previous parliamentary term). Over all countries, the expected asymmetry is not very evident, but in countries where the previous election occurred within the previous two-and-a-half years, the asymmetry between losses and gains is quite evident and shows up in terms of government parties losing one-third more votes in an economic downturn than they would gain in an economic upturn. The reverse will evidently have been true for opposition parties: they would have gained one-third more in a downturn than they would have lost in an upturn.

The fact that the asymmetry should be evident only in the two years following a national election is quite understandable. The passing of time makes it inevitable that changes will have occurred in the party support propensities that would have been evident at the time of the election and in the competitive structure of relations between parties shown by those vote propensities. When we use out-of-date propensities to estimate what the structure would have been at the time of a previous election, the results cannot be trusted. By contrast, we get better estimates from measurements of support propensities taken closer to the date of the election – precisely what is shown in Table 6.8.

Discussion

The findings in this chapter vindicate our insistence in this book on separating the analyses of party support propensities from the analyses of voting choice. The ways in which different support propensities translate into party preferences, and hence into the choices between parties and subsequently into party vote shares, is so largely affected by features of the competitive situation in which parties find themselves that there is no simple linkage between changes in support propensities and a party's vote share. Any factor that impinges on these propensities, such as economic conditions, will thus not necessarily show a clear relationship to changes in vote shares even if its effects on party support propensities are quite clear.

In this chapter, we have shown that a linear model of effects on party support can generate loss/gain curves that are highly nonlinear and that even follow quite irregular patterns. Moreover, the same linear model – which has the same effects on party support propensities in all countries at all times – may have very different consequences for parties' vote shares in different countries or at different moments in time. This means that any model that focuses on party choice or on vote shares as the dependent variable, but that does not incorporate the competitive situation pertaining at the time of each election, will run the risk of instabilities, inconsistencies, and even outright misleading results.

We have shown that once one does take account of the competitive situation between parties, the effects of changes in economic conditions on votes (and hence on election outcomes) make perfect sense. Party vote shares alter in a straightforward fashion as a direct result of the changes in party support propensities that evolving economic conditions bring about. Both of these functions are quite simple (the first is a linear estimation equation, the second a simple decision rule). It is only when analysts fail to differentiate between them that they find effects that appear unstable and asymmetric.

We should not leave the topic of election outcomes without revisiting one last time our story about effects of unemployment on support for European parties. We saw, earlier in this chapter, that governing parties overall lose votes as a result of increasing unemployment. We did not look separately at an improving unemployment situation, but we did see that such parties gain votes as a result of improvements in the general economic situation. However, we can assert on the basis of our findings in Chapter 4 that the gains and losses to government parties that result from changes in unemployment would not have been nearly as great had the parties in government at this time not happened to be overwhelmingly parties of the left (as shown in Table 3.2). Had governments been composed mainly of right-leaning parties, changes in vote shares as a consequence of changing unemployment levels would have been less, because we found that parties of the right are hardly held accountable for changes in unemployment.

In practice, we have said, unemployment declined throughout most of the EU in 1999 (as shown in Table 3.1), so the left-leaning government parties will have gained support. But the translation of this increased support into votes will not have benefited them much. Though we have not shown this for the specific case of unemployment, the implications of our findings about the asymmetric translation of support scores into votes is that, generally speaking, government parties do not stand to improve their situations very much. Equally, opposition parties will not have been much hurt by these decreases in unemployment.

Though again not specifically investigated in this chapter, the ambivalence that supporters of left parties apparently feel toward policies that, according to neo-liberal commentators, are needed to fight unemployment (see our discussion in Chapter 4) will not have been in evidence at a time of declining unemployment. At such a time, no new policies would presumably be called for to deal with unemployment, implying a second asymmetry applying particularly to unemployment, to complement the asymmetric loss/gain function that we did specifically investigate. Thinking through the implications of this chapter's findings for the fortunes of particular parties in the light of changes in particular economic conditions is a useful way of bringing home the manner that economic conditions affect the vote. The economy matters, but the specific ways in which it matters are mediated by the situation of particular parties at particular points in time. The fact that there were so many left governments in power in 1999 is one reason why the effects of changing economic conditions were so different in 1999 than they would have been in 1994. So, the effects of the economy are time-specific as well as party- and country-specific, a topic we will return to in our final chapter.

7

The Economy, Party Competition, and the Vote

In this book, we have made a point of separating the process by which party support propensities (and hence party preferences) are formed from the process of party choice. Our two-stage model, largely following Downs (1957), has allowed us to take account of different factors at each stage. With regard to the first stage, we were able to take account of independent variables that do not lend themselves to inclusion in conventional models of economic voting – models that focus on party choice as the dependent variable. In particular, separating the two stages enabled us to take account of party characteristics (such as their size and ideological complexion) at the first stage, when we modeled the formation of party preferences. In the second stage, when we modeled the choices that our respondents actually made, we were able to take into account the structure of electoral competition between parties – the aggregate-level counterparts of individual-level patterns of support propensities for the various parties.

In this final chapter, we will start by rehearsing our major objections to existing approaches that led to our adopting the two-stage model. We argued in Chapter 1 that the deficiencies that gave rise to our objections made it hard for past researchers to observe certain phenomena that we believed to be responsible for the instabilities and contradictions in extant research findings. In past chapters we have indeed observed these phenomena, and we will proceed to enumerate them by reiterating relevant findings from past chapters that make it clear how our research approach improves upon conventional approaches. We will then enumerate the major implications and novel insights that result from this approach.

Unpacking the Dependent Variable

Researchers responsible for past studies of economic voting have used a dependent variable that focused on the distinction between governing and opposition parties. Virtually all studies of economic voting employed this simplification, and some other studies as well. Its popularity was certainly due to the fact that it gave rise to a dependent variable that appeared to be a measure of the phenomenon of interest while also being comparable across countries and time periods. In any modern democratic country, political parties are either government parties or they are not, giving rise to a variable with considerable face validity for comparative research. The implicit assumption made by past researchers was that voters judge all government parties equally in terms of their responsibility for economic conditions. Effectively, these researchers also assumed that all opposition parties are also judged equally – presumably in complementary fashion – gaining when government parties lose and vice versa. Implicit in their approach was the notion that such variations in electoral fortunes as exist between government parties are random, at least in terms of economic conditions. These differences in electoral fortunes might, of course, have been systematically structured by other kinds of factors (such as the popularity of leaders, the support for a war, or major events like a nuclear accident), but these should not be related to economic factors. If this assumption held true, then combining government parties' vote shares should actually provide a better estimate of the effects of economic factors than separating out these vote shares among individual parties, as we have done, because the combined measure would tend to average out idiosyncratic deviations.

Whether or not this implicit assumption is tenable is an empirical matter, and we suspected that it was not. This suspicion might have been mistaken, and would have been shown to be mistaken if support for the different parties, when viewed separately, did not respond differently to changes in economic conditions. In that case, any heterogeneity that might have existed in the dependent variable, as a result of this conflation of different parties within the same category, would not have been relevant to economic voting.

But we were not wrong. Our findings demonstrate that (face validity notwithstanding) a variable that combines all opposition parties into one category and all government parties (if there are more than one) into another category incorporates substantial relevant heterogeneity: support for some opposition parties reacts in very different ways than support for other opposition parties to given changes in economic conditions (and the same for governing parties when these are members of a coalition government). Economic conditions were found to interact with parties' ideological complexions and their sizes in ways that are highly significant. We even demonstrated that, as a result of deteriorating economic conditions, some government parties could actually gain at the expense of other government parties. Thus, if sensible effects of economic voting are to be found, we have established that it is necessary to distinguish parties according to their sizes and ideological complexions, as well as (or, in many countries, instead of) their government–opposition status. This cannot be done if different parties are combined into a government–opposition dichotomy. Therefore, the procedure of combining the electoral results of government parties into a single outcome for "the government" is inappropriate. The resulting models are mis-specified and will not display the true effects of economic conditions on election outcomes.

Implicit in the aggregation of government and opposition parties into a simple dichotomy is a second simplification of the dependent variable to which we also objected. Along with virtually all other voting behavior researchers, scholars who have studied economic voting viewed data relating to voters' party choices as adequately revealing their electoral preferences. We suspected that this simplification would have two unfortunate consequences: it would prevent researchers from taking account of independent variables relating to the parties chosen (or not), and it would prevent them from taking account of party competition. Again, we might have been wrong. It might have turned out that independent variables relating to party characteristics had no explanatory power in accounting for party choice, and that the state of party competition had no influence either. But again, we were not wrong. As already mentioned, we found that party size and ideology have strong effects of fundamental importance to understanding the voting act, and the state of party competition does indeed account for considerable variations in election outcomes resulting from the same effects of economic conditions.

So, both simplifications of the dependent variable turned out to have adverse consequences for extant findings, helping to explain the instabilities and contradictions described in the Introduction to this volume, which Lewis-Beck and Paldham (2000: 114) referred to when they called for a "trick" that would make everything well.

Replications of Past Findings

Although we use a different dependent variable, our findings do replicate several of the most fundamental findings arising from past research. Government parties do generally gain votes as a result of good economic conditions and lose votes as a result of a worsening economy (the subject of our first hypothesis, H1), in line with the overwhelming majority of findings of past research, while for opposition parties the effects are generally less or oppositely signed (H2 – a hypothesis not explicitly formulated or tested in past research). Taking all countries together, and following past research practices in making no distinctions between government parties, we find that those parties do in general appear to be held retrospectively accountable for the state of the economy. However, the elaboration of these hypotheses that we derived from Powell and Whitten (1993) and from Whitten and Palmer (1999), that the effects would be stronger in countries with high clarity of government accountability (H6), was so thoroughly borne out as to make it clear that economic voting as traditionally formulated does not exist in low-clarity countries. Instead of government parties being held retrospectively accountable for the state of the economy, as was the case in high-clarity countries, in low-clarity countries we found quite different processes at work, which we will detail in the next section of this chapter.

Still focusing on high-clarity countries, we also replicated past findings in regard to ideology. In high-clarity countries, left government parties do indeed appear to be held particularly accountable for unemployment, while right government parties are held particularly accountable for inflation (H5), in line with previous research findings

(Hibbs 1977; Budge, Robertson, and Hearl 1987; Powell and Whitten 1993; Klingemann, Hofferbert, and Budge 1994; Whitten and Palmer 1999).

More importantly, we find these effects, even in high-clarity contexts, to be most true of large parties, in line with our fourth hypothesis (H4). Small parties often find themselves affected quite differently than large parties when faced with the same changes in economic conditions.

Some additional expectations found in existing studies, though having nothing specifically to do with the economy, were also replicated by our findings. We found that there is a cost of governing (H9a) that makes it hard for government parties to rule indefinitely, in line with theoretical expectations going back to Downs (1957). We also found a national electoral cycle (H9b) that replicates past findings from research that used the same data as we employ (surveys following elections to the European Parliament).

While we find different nuances, as will be detailed in the next section, the fact that our overall findings do replicate the thrust of past economic voting studies is encouraging. When we take high- and low-clarity contexts together, we do see more or less what past researchers have seen, and when we separate these contexts and focus on countries with high clarity of government responsibility, we do see what Powell and Whitten (1993) and Whitten and Palmer (1999) saw in those contexts. The nuances of difference (and our quite new findings for low-clarity contexts when those are distinguished) are made possible by the greater sensitivity of our dependent variable; but when we blunt that sensitivity in order to look at the world as past researchers have done, we do see pretty much what they saw.

Given that we criticize other studies for failing to deal with various contaminations, how is it that (in high-clarity contexts) those studies still produce findings recognizably similar to some of our findings? Such studies analyze choice for either a government or an opposition party. Their findings are dominated – particularly in high-clarity countries, where electoral systems tend to penalize small parties – by voters for large parties for the simple reason that these are the most numerous by definition. As a consequence, findings from such studies may tend to resemble what we find in our study as the effect of economic conditions on the support propensities for large government parties.

New Insights

The new insights made possible by our more sensitive dependent variable are of two kinds. One set of insights arises from the fact that this variable permits us to bring to bear effects of party characteristics on the formation of party preferences, while the other set arises from our ability to take account of the state of party competition when translating preferences into votes.

The first set of insights is most apparent in countries with low clarity of government responsibility (as defined by Whitten and Palmer 1999). Countries in which opposition parties play a role in policymaking, or that have a second coequal chamber or certain types of federal arrangements, are countries in which it is hard for voters to be sure which parties to hold responsible for economic management. In such countries, we find two large differences in the effects of economic conditions from those that we find in high-clarity countries. In the first place, in such countries, we find voters focusing their attention on large parties rather than government parties as the relevant policymaking actors, in line with our fourth hypothesis. In the second place, we find that in such countries voters focus not so much on holding these parties retrospectively accountable for past economic management (though this does happen to some extent), but rather taking a prospective view of the policies these parties can be expected to promote and support, in line with one aspect of our fifth hypothesis. Moreover, to the extent that small parties can be expected to have different (often more extreme) policies than large parties, we also find voters taking these differences into account.

This more nuanced view of the electoral consequences of economic conditions in both high- and low-clarity countries makes it possible to understand how the economy affects the competition for votes among different members of a governing coalition, benefiting some at the expense of others and helping to explain the fact that the electoral fortunes of different government parties are not generally observed to move in step.

Our unpacking of the dependent variable into two stages yielded results that went far beyond our ability to bring to bear party characteristics as independent variables. Our ability to take account of processes of party preference formation separately from the process of party choice enabled us to make the striking discovery that what seem to be patterns of heterogeneous behavior by voters in response to changes in economic conditions, hypothesized in past research and found in some past studies, are not the result of heterogeneous reactions by voters to economic conditions at all. Our seventh hypothesis, which proposed such heterogeneity in the reactions of less sophisticated voters and those with special economic interests, was unequivocally rejected. Support for political parties by different types of voters is actually affected very similarly by changes in economic conditions. Indeed, the heterogeneity hypothesized in past research and found in some past studies arises not at the point at which party preferences are formed or updated but rather at the point at which those preferences give rise to party choice. This is due to the fact that patterns of party competition differ between types of voters. In many countries, less sophisticated voters are more likely to have support propensities for different parties that are tied (or almost tied) for first place, as was also found to be the case for the retired and the unemployed. Because they are particularly likely to have more than a single party in a good position to receive their votes, the choices made by such individuals are more likely to be affected by anything that alters their relative preferences for different parties, including changes in economic conditions. On the other hand, voters whose party preferences clearly differentiate a most preferred party from all others are less likely to find their party choices affected by small changes in their party support propensities.

The same distinction between preferences and choice that enabled us to pin heterogeneous choices on the effects of party competition rather than on preference formation mechanisms enabled us to do the same for the seemingly asymmetric effects of economic conditions. A worsening economy does indeed (on average) have more marked effects on the fortunes of governing parties than an economic upturn of the same magnitude, as hypothesized in some past research, but these asymmetries arise not at the point at which preferences are made. Voters' support propensities do not react differently to economic downturns than to economic upturns, as previously hypothesized. Rather, the asymmetries arise at the point at which preferences are translated into votes (and hence into election outcomes). Government parties (which are more likely to stand high in popular esteem) find it hard to improve their support even when economic times are good, while the same improvement in the economy is relatively unlikely to hurt opposition parties (which are more likely to be close to the bedrock of their support). Economic downturns, by contrast, easily cost government parties a portion of their support and benefit opposition parties equivalently. Asymmetric loss is thus built into the competition for votes and requires no help from asymmetric cognitive evaluations of changing economic conditions. Indeed, we were able to rule out any such effect quite definitively by finding no significant negative correlation between appropriate residuals from our analyses of party support propensities.

Various embellishments to conventional ideas regarding economic voting – that governments would be held more accountable the longer they had been in office (H3), that what would matter about parties would be whether they controlled critical ministries (H4b), or that what would matter about political systems would not be their clarity so much as their decision-making rules or the nature of their welfare states (H6b and H6c) – all failed to receive support. Past research findings appear to have been correct as far as they went: government parties are indeed often punished for a worsening economy and rewarded for an improving one. But those findings did not go very far, partly because of the frequent anomalies that are amply documented in the literature and partly because past research did not have anything to say about low-clarity contexts. In all contexts, not only nuance and detail were missing, but more crucially, the causal mechanism linking economic conditions to party choice and election outcomes was fundamentally misconceived. A more appropriate conceptualization of the dependent variable allowed not only the replication of apparently correct insights from previous research, but also the rectification of past shortcomings.

Additional Insights

Apart from whether our hypotheses were supported or rejected, our analyses yielded the following additional insights:

- The consequences of economic conditions for party preferences and party choice are very different for economic growth, unemployment, and inflation. Conceivably, they may be different again for

other aspects of economic performance, such as national debt levels, currency exchange rates, or public sector sizes. In view of this, it
seems not very helpful to speak about the electoral effects of "the"
economy.

- Voters give their vote to the party that ranks highest in terms of
  their propensity to support it. Since many voters have support
  propensities that rank more than a single party first in their preference orderings – at least in the countries and time period that
  we study – relatively weak effects on party support propensities
  can affect the preference rankings of quite large numbers of voters.
  Therefore, even weak effects on preference formation can potentially result in large numbers of people switching their vote from
  one party to another.

- Effects of economic conditions on voters' propensity to support
  political parties are prime examples of just such weak effects. The
  strength of voters' preferences for political parties is predominantly
  explained by other factors, such as sociodemographic characteristics, ideological positions, and opinions regarding issues other than
  the economy. The reason changes in economic conditions can nevertheless affect election outcomes is that (1) these small effects are
  brought about by variables that can alter their values quite rapidly
  and (2) these small effects are largely homogeneous across all types
  and conditions of voters, and give rise to few countervailing flows
  of votes between one party and another (net effects on change in
  vote shares of political parties are not much less than gross effects).
  The economy is important only in explaining short-term electoral
  change, and it gains its ability to do so from the fact that other, more
  powerful influences tend to be stable in the short term.

- In high-clarity countries, voters distinguish parties according to their
  status as government or opposition parties, as hypothesized in previous research. In these situations, voters hold parties retrospectively
  responsible for their management of the economy. In low-clarity
  countries, voters are more inclined to take prospective considerations into account, which renders the identity of the current government less important (though causation might run the other way, with
  voters who can less readily discern which parties to hold responsible
  focusing instead on expectations regarding future party policies). As
  a result, in low-clarity countries, left-wing parties benefit from high

economic growth even if they are not part of the government. It appears in these countries as if voters' feel that they can "afford" the policies of left-wing parties only under conditions of higher economic growth. Right-wing parties benefit in low-clarity countries from economic downturns, irrespective of whether they are in government or opposition, which we interpret as the consequence of voters' belief that these parties will promote policies that will generate future growth. Small right-wing parties benefit particularly, apparently as a by-product of the fact that voters in low-clarity countries tend to blame large parties for bad economic times – a retrospective counterpart in low-clarity countries to the treatment of government parties in high-clarity countries.

These conclusions justify the proposition that economic conditions matter electorally. But the economy is not the only thing that matters. Other issues, taken together, are more important, as we saw in Chapter 5. So, there can be elections in which economic developments do not dominate the outcome, as was clearly illustrated in Britain in 1992 and 1997, in Ireland in 1997, and (for that matter) in the United States in 2000 and 2004.

Implications for Individual-Level Studies of Economic Voting

Our findings have important implications for our understanding of the role of subjective assessments of economic conditions. Much of the research about such assessments reports that they have very strong effects on electoral preferences, both in terms of effect coefficients and in terms of explanatory power (Kiewiet 1983; Lewis-Beck 1988; Nannestad and Paldam 1994). It has been pointed out that the strength of these effects might be due to endogeneity problems – the supposedly independent variables relating to the economy might well have been contaminated by party preferences. In other words, the supposed consequences of economic assessments might actually have caused them to take on the values they did (Wlezien, Franklin, and Twiggs 1997; Bartels 2002; van der Eijk 2002). As Kramer (1983) long ago pointed out, the only real test of effects of economic conditions on the vote is to see whether the actual economic context influences the behavior of voters. By relying exclusively on objective indicators of economic conditions we did just that, and were able to demonstrate – without any risk of contamination by other factors or by endogeneity – that the (real) economy matters. In the process, we also established that its effects are weak and contain little explanatory power. Consequently, a large part of the (much stronger) supposed effects of subjective assessments of the economy reported in past research must derive from these assessments being contaminated by other factors, most likely by the endogenous influence of electoral preferences themselves.

In a different set of analyses, based on a slightly different research design, we investigated the character of subjective assessments of the economy by relating them to objective economic conditions, and to political preferences.[1] We formulated a number of causal interpretations of the nature of these subjective assessments and tested them using structural models. One interpretation viewed subjective assessments of economic conditions as individual-level reflections of objective economic conditions – though overlaid with error and idiosyncratic factors. If this interpretation proved correct, subjective assessments could usefully be employed as mediating variables in studies of economic voting. A totally different interpretation viewed subjective assessments as entirely accounted for by endogenous political preferences such as party choice and government approval. If this interpretation proved correct, subjective assessments would have no sensible mediating role to play in the study of economic voting. Other possible interpretations entailed a mixture of mediating and endogenous effects. Comparisons of the fit, the parsimony, and the estimated coefficients of the models that represented these rivaling interpretations yielded very clear and unambiguous results:

subjective economic evaluations cannot be regarded as part of the causal mechanism by which "real" economic conditions translate themselves into approval for the government or votes for one of the incumbent parties. . . . [T]he causal mechanism by which real economic conditions affect voting for an incumbent party . . . is not a mechanism that involves subjective economic evaluations, but rather it is government approval that plays a role in transmitting the economic context to voting behavior. Not surprisingly, good economic times increase government popularity and a popular government is more likely to be re-elected. (van der Eijk et al. 2004: 17; cf. van Eijk et al. 2007)

---

[1] These analyses were based on the same 1999 data that we employ in this book.

These supplementary findings reinforce our earlier conclusion that studies estimating the effects of subjective economic evaluations cannot be taken seriously as proper estimates of the effects of economic conditions.

Implications for Aggregate-Level Studies of Economic Voting

We have already mentioned that, despite the deficiencies that our findings expose in conventional approaches to the study of economic voting, these new findings are consistent with the general pattern of findings from aggregate-level studies in the extant economic voting literature. In particular, we duplicate the findings of Whitten and Palmer (1999), who, building on the work of Powell and Whitten (1993), established that the widely hypothesized focus of economic voting, in terms of holding government parties accountable, occurs only in high-clarity countries. Our findings also replicate in large part the findings of those authors regarding the role of ideology in economic voting. We go beyond their findings mainly in establishing that economic voting also occurs in low-clarity countries, albeit with a focus on large parties rather than on government parties and (of necessity) a more prospective orientation. Since most Western democracies are low-clarity countries, and since no satisfactory explanations have previously been provided for the effects of economic conditions on elections in those countries, our ability to explain economic voting in low-clarity countries is an important step forward.

Our findings also have a bearing on the continuing debate in the economic voting literature regarding sociotropic versus egocentric motivations. As mentioned earlier, in relation to the implications of our findings for individual-level research, we have been able to discredit the often-touted suggestion of egocentric (pocketbook) voting by demonstrating that groups of voters who are particularly vulnerable to unemployment or to inflation are not more responsive to those specific economic conditions than other voters are. Interpreting these findings at the aggregate level, we can say that the unemployed and retired as aggregate categories of voters show no signs of reacting more strongly than other voters do to economic conditions that should be of particular relevance to them if they were motivated in their electoral behavior by pocketbook considerations. To the contrary, our findings strongly suggest that economic voting is invariably sociotropic. People consider how economic conditions impinge on the country as a whole. The heterogeneity found in past studies is real enough, but it is not heterogeneity in the impact of economic conditions on different categories of voters. Rather, it is heterogeneity in the way in which changes in party preferences are translated into changes in party choice (and hence, at the aggregate level, into changes in party vote shares), with certain categories of voters being more likely to switch their vote than others, even though their evaluations of political parties had been affected no more than the evaluations of other groups of voters by economic conditions.

The fact that we largely replicate the findings of Whitten and Palmer (1999) regarding high-clarity systems raises the question of whether our model is superior to theirs. Our model requires individual-level data, which are hard to obtain, whereas theirs does not. Our model, moreover, requires measures of party support propensities, which are rare even with individual-level data. If our model did not yield clear superiority in some important respect, researchers who limit themselves to high-clarity contexts would presumably wish to continue to use a model with less demanding data requirements.

Our findings make it clear that "business as usual" is not a viable option in future studies of economic voting. For reasons set out in Chapter 1, even a model that distinguished between different parties would still be unable to distinguish between the process of forming party support propensities, on the one hand, and the process of choosing a party on the other. As we have seen, this is a crucial distinction. Our research also makes it clear that studying election outcomes will yield findings that are very much contingent on the particular ideological complexion of parties in government at the time of the study, on the proportion of high-clarity countries included in the study, and so on. Studying party support propensities largely protects the findings from being contaminated by composition artifacts such as those we saw when discussing the effects of unemployment in Chapter 6.

In an Epilogue to the present volume, we briefly summarize a number of possible research designs for the study of economic voting that are less demanding in terms of data than the one we have employed in this book but that do take account of our main conclusions about the ways in which past research findings have been contaminated in various ways by the use of unjustified simplifications and shortcuts.

Political Implications of Our Study

There is a widely held belief among politicians, journalists, commentators, and political scientists that the reelection of political incumbents depends to a large extent upon their record in handling the economy. Clinton's famous words "it's the economy, stupid" provides a nice example of how deep-rooted this notion is. Early research on political business cycles (e.g., Nordhaus 1975; Tufte 1978)[2] suggested that this might even lead governments to increase spending in election years, presumably in order to stimulate the economy and hence secure reelection. Even though findings regarding business cycles are contested,[3] the notion that a growing economy helps the incumbent party or parties seems to be uncontested. An important implication of our study is that this notion is at best only partially correct.

Let us begin by focusing on the implications of our most general model, the model that disregards the distinction between low-clarity and high-clarity countries. On the basis of this model, we found that in fifteen of the sixteen political systems for which we investigate the effects of economic conditions in 1999, a very large improvement of the economy would indeed help the largest government party (see Table B.8 in Appendix B). However, this does not imply that *all* incumbents fare well under such conditions: in nine of the eleven countries with coalition governments, the second largest government party does not similarly gain votes as a consequence of favorable economic conditions. To the contrary, in all of these nine countries, the second largest government party's vote share either remains unchanged (in three cases) or declines (in six cases). Conversely, when the economy is not doing well, the largest government party usually loses votes, while, more often than not, the second largest government party gains votes (see Table B.7 in Appendix B). Because coalitions often consist of parties that are ideologically similar, coalition partners are among each other's strongest competitors for votes. Since the largest governing party receives most of

---

[2] Others have provided evidence for the existence of a business cycle in countries such as Germany (Galli and Rossi 2002), the Netherlands (van Dalen and Swank 1996), Russia (Treisman and Gimpelson 2001), and Canada (Blais and Nadeau 1992).

[3] It is beyond the purpose of this book to discuss the validity of this research and its interpretations, but for reviews of evidence of business cycles see, e.g., Golden and Poterba (1980), Berger and Woitek (1997), and Paldam (1997).

the blame when the economy goes bad and most of the credit when the economy does well, economic prosperity does not normally benefit the second largest governing party. If the largest party in a coalition were to propose increasing government spending in the run-up to an election – as it would be inclined to do according to the political business cycle theory – smaller governing parties would be well advised to oppose such an initiative. Indeed, it would behoove smaller government partners to demand control of the ministry of finance, as a condition for coalition membership, in order to be better placed to resist possible attempts by the leading party to make pump-priming public expenditures. Even if successful in generating additional votes for the leading party, such policies would generally be detrimental to the vote shares of smaller coalition partners.

Let us now focus on the model that does include the distinction between high- and low-clarity countries. Its findings strongly suggest that voting in low-clarity countries is to a large extent prospective, as we have already made clear. Voters in these countries do not much concern themselves with the identities of parties holding office, but instead focus on the policies that parties are likely to implement in response to economic conditions. Irrespective of whether they were in office or not, left-wing parties gain in low-clarity countries when the economy grows. Our explanation is that during times of prosperity, voters are more receptive to the political platforms of left-leaning parties (see also Stevenson 2002). This leads to the paradoxical situation that, if right-leaning government parties are successful in generating economic growth, they actually help the electoral prospects of left-wing opposition parties. If such a government were to increase spending in election years in order to promote growth and thus secure its own reelection, it might actually be shooting itself in the foot!

Since commentators are so used to thinking that governments are rewarded for a good economy and punished for a bad one, actual election results often appear puzzling. Why were governing parties not rewarded or punished? Are voters so irrational or do they not take the economy into account? Our findings may provide the key to solving such puzzles. Voters *are* rational, and they *do* take the economy into account. But in the absence of a clear view of who was responsible for what happened in the past, they direct their votes not toward punishment or reward but toward affecting the future course of public policy.

Rationality and Sophistication of the Economic Voter

One could think of economic voting as the simplest form of policy voting, for which voters need to have two pieces of information: who is responsible for managing the economy (which parties are in government, in high-clarity countries, or which parties are the players in low-clarity countries) and how well did these parties perform this task? Even the least sophisticated voters are surely able to pick up some news about changes in levels of unemployment, or about levels of economic growth or inflation. So, a retrospective vote on the basis of the state of the economy seems to require less from voters than some other forms of issue voting, many of which also require awareness of parties' policy positions. Mackuen, Erikson, and Stimson (1992) refer to voters who apply this simplest rule in deciding retrospectively which party to vote for as "peasants." They contrast these voters with those who vote prospectively, a group they call "bankers." MacKuen et al. find that prospective voters take account of more information than retrospective voters do.

Our findings for the EU countries that we studied support most of theirs for the United States, but our findings call for a refinement of their argument. In Chapter 5 we showed that voters respond very uniformly to objective economic conditions, which means that the same forward-looking or backward-looking behavior occurs for all voters, including the most and the least sophisticated. Any voter can apparently behave like a banker in appropriate circumstances, and any voter can behave like a peasant. Whether voters react prospectively or retrospectively depends on which party they are evaluating and which country they live in, not on what kind of voter they are. Indeed, the same voters can be both peasants and bankers at the same time in regard to different parties. Among forward-looking voters, there may well be some who take account of additional information as MacKuen et al. suggest. Our research does not rule this out. But we can say that, if there are such voters, either they do not vote differently because of the additional information, or they are not more sophisticated than other voters – at least over the countries and elections that we investigate.

The effects of economic performance at the individual level are subtle, strongly contingent on context. How these effects differ over a wider range of countries and over a longer time period should be high on the agenda for future research. Such investigations will require

survey data that permit the analyst to distinguish between party support propensities and party choice – preferably acquired in the aftermath of national elections worldwide. As we argue in the Epilogue
to this book, the data now becoming available under the auspices of
the Comparative Study of Electoral Systems show some promise of
permitting researchers to build on our findings.

Economic Voting in Real Elections

The data we have employed in this book come from interviews of
voters following elections to the European Parliament. We chose this
laboratory as a venue for our study to minimize the contamination
expected from the hype, scandals, and other idiosyncrasies that characterize "real" elections (see, for example, Wlezien and Erikson 2002).[4]
We have not explicitly addressed the question of whether, had our data
derived from real elections, our findings would have been different.
However, among the forty-two electoral contexts that we study, our
data do contain 6 instances of European elections being held concurrently with national parliamentary elections. This makes it possible for
us to test the effects of a dummy variable indicating that the election was
a real one. When the dummy variable is interacted with other party-
level and individual-level independent variables, none of these variables
yield significant effects (at the 0.01 level of significance), implying that
findings relating to individual-level and party-level variables would
have been no different had all of our analyses been conducted in the
context of real national elections.

Turning to effects of economic conditions, these provide insufficient
variance for detecting interactions with this dummy variable. What we
can perform with economic conditions is a (weaker) test in which we
omit all six contests where concurrent national elections were held.
The outcome of this test demonstrates that our findings would be no
different (at the 0.01 level) were they to arise uniquely from the cases
where real national elections were not held. Since we already know
from other studies (whose findings we largely replicate) that party

---

[4] We use quotation marks around "real" in this context to remind readers that we are
talking about a distinction made by those who study European Parliament elections
between national ("real") elections, where executive power is at stake, and other elections (often referred to as "second-order national elections") where executive power
is not at stake. From many perspectives, European Parliament elections are quite as
real as national elections, but not from the perspective adopted here.

support at the time of national elections is affected by economic conditions in accordance with economic voting theory, this finding enables us to conclude that the electoral contexts that did not contain national elections nevertheless see the same forces at work, thereby yielding the statistical power that makes our wider conclusions possible.

Still, our suspicion that real elections will see more "noise," through which it may be more difficult to discern the effects of economic conditions, may yet prove to be correct. To deal with data that contain more noise, we need better models and larger datasets than were available in the past. We believe that we have provided a better model and that our findings in this book confirm the superiority of this model. Larger datasets are already becoming available under the auspices of the Comparative Study of Electoral Systems project mentioned at the end of the previous section.

Discussion

Our findings might surprise some readers, but only because they came to our work with expectations about voter responses to economic conditions derived from past research that was based on (usually implicit) simplistic assumptions. Our research design has avoided a number of these assumptions. We did not assume that all government parties are equally affected by economic conditions. Nor did we assume that only government parties are affected and that opposition parties are unaffected by economic conditions (or that equal and opposite effects apply). And nor did we assume that improving economic conditions have effects on vote choices and election outcomes that are opposite to those found with worsening conditions.

We were able to avoid these naive assumptions because of the structure of our data, which does not in any way constrain voters' support propensities for different parties. Also, because voters were questioned separately about each party, without regard to its government or opposition status, we were able to avoid grouping all government parties (or all opposition parties) together. So, the question of whether all government parties were in fact affected similarly by economic conditions could be evaluated in our research, which it could not be in previous research. Our findings show that economic conditions do not have the same effects on all government parties (or, for that matter, on all opposition parties), as mentioned at the outset of this chapter.

Do economic conditions have political consequences? Our answer differs according to whether we consider party support propensities or election outcomes. There is indeed an effect of economic conditions on the strength of people's propensity to support different parties, whether they are in government or in opposition. This effect is essentially the same (to within sampling error) in all the countries that we study (after controlling for clarity of accountability, as explained earlier). It is also largely the same across all classes and conditions of voters within each country. Economic conditions appear to have "equal opportunity" effects on voters that do not depend upon their political sophistication or other characteristics. But more striking even than their homogeneity is the fact that these effects were small in comparison with other effects on party support. If the question is why certain people support one party while other people support a different party, then economic conditions play virtually no role, at least not in the countries and over the time period that we have studied.

Yet, when we consider effects of economic conditions on election outcomes, we do find consistent and palpable effects of economic conditions that, other things being equal (or, more to the point, other things canceling out, as they often do), can indeed affect election outcomes. But changes in economic conditions have effects on election outcomes that are strongly conditioned by political circumstances. We have found a natural asymmetry between popular government parties and unpopular opposition parties such that economic downturns are liable to reduce the gap between their vote shares, while an improving economy will do little to change the gap, other things being equal. The same asymmetries would exist with many other political developments, with adverse circumstances hurting the government only when it is popular and helping the opposition, while good news can do little to improve a popular government's standing.[5] All such developments will tend to swing the political pendulum back toward a situation in which parties are centrally located within the bounds of their competitive potential, having no more and no less than their fair share of the voters for whose

[5] There are, of course, notable cases where bad news fails to hurt a popular government, but this is unusual (except during "honeymoon" periods that closely follow a new government taking office, when one may well hear talk of a "Teflon president" and such).

support they compete with other parties. We thus see strong signs of a mechanism that virtually guarantees political swings and cycles, in that any deviation from the middle ground in terms of support for parties is naturally liable to be reversed, whatever the political direction that deviation takes.

Though our findings with respect to party support propensities hold true across all the countries that we study, we do need to be cautious in generalizing from these findings to economic or political circumstances much beyond the range of those we study. Our universe consists of developed European economies from the late 1980s through the end of the 1990s. In spite of all their differences, these countries in this period experienced real economic growth, relatively mild inflation, and unemployment that (while of political concern in most of these countries) was low in global perspective and accompanied by effective social safety nets. We cannot say with certainty what the political effects of changing economic conditions would be in quite different circumstances.

Our findings have clear implications for effects on party choice that go far beyond economic voting. If economic conditions are found to exert stable effects only when analyzed in the context of a two-stage model, the same will be true for other kinds of voting. So, the instability of vote functions in past studies of economic voting would apply equally to other sorts of voting – such as issue voting or personality voting – if those sorts of voting had been studied comparatively. The problem arose most obviously with economic voting only because this subfield is more advanced in rigorously testing its theories with comparative data. As other studies of comparative voting behavior proliferate in coming years, the same problems will certainly be encountered unless researchers distinguish, as we have in this book, between preferences and choice. Using party choice as a surrogate for party support propensities leaves too much indeterminacy (as explained in Chapter 2) for stable findings to emerge.

Toward a Revised Theory of Economic Voting

Our findings clearly demonstrate the need for a revision of basic economic voting theory, which holds that government parties are held accountable for economic conditions and rewarded or punished electorally for their performance in managing the economy. The additional elements that need to be incorporated into a more comprehensive view relate to (1) prospective voting, (2) the political weight of different parties in policymaking, and (3) the basis upon which voters identify which parties to vote for in light of economic conditions. These three aspects are linked in intricate ways.

In this book, we have not systematically distinguished between the second and third of these elements, using both as arguments for the importance of taking account of party size. Yet, theoretically and empirically, the two elements play out quite differently. If economic voting were fundamentally about crediting and blaming parties on the basis of their actual influence on economic policymaking, then one would have expected the length of time a party had been in government to play a role, at least in high-clarity countries. We do not find this happening. Instead, we find voters picking out large parties for particular attention. Large parties are, of course, generally parties that have held government office repeatedly over the years, but that does not appear to be why they are singled out for credit or blame. Rather, they appear to be singled out because they wield power (in low-clarity countries they do so even when not in government). Party size seems to be fundamental to economic voting, more so than holding government office, which plays a role only in high-clarity countries.

The importance of party size must be taken into account in conjunction with the importance of prospective voting, something else to which past studies have given short shrift. To the extent that voters focus on the policies that parties would like to promote, the role of party size is clearly that it discriminates between parties according to the likelihood of their ability to influence economic policymaking. Indeed, the ubiquitous division of our tables into government and opposition categories (because they are designed to test hypotheses derived from the existing literature) somewhat obscures what seems to be going on.

The most straightforward interpretation to place on our findings is that voters care about the economy and, when it is in bad shape, adapt their party preferences on the basis of expectations about what different parties would be willing and able to do about it,[6] supposing they

---

[6] This is not quite the same as the type of prospective voting referred to in much of the individual-level economic voting literature, in which prospective behavior is taken to refer to behavior in expectation of future economic conditions. Still, assessing likely

were given (greater) representation in the national parliament. These prospective orientations are somewhat tempered for large parties, especially large government parties in high-clarity countries, which are also generally held accountable for their past record of economic management. In low-clarity countries, by contrast, distinctions between parties on the basis of their government status are of questionable relevance (cf. Powell 2000), and we see all large parties being held equally accountable for economic conditions, effectively canceling out most effects of retrospective voting in low-clarity countries.

When we view the world as voters appear to do, rather than in terms of conventional scholarly ideas about economic voting, we see a world in which what counts is not so much the recent behavior of government parties, but rather parties' ideologies and general stance toward economic policy – as well as their likelihood of being able to influence actual policy decisions. Voters thus behave in a far more nuanced fashion than is often assumed. We should not really be surprised by this. Voters know what sort of a system they live in. They know whether parties can influence government policies even when not in government. They know which parties are players in the decision-making process. They also know what sorts of policies are likely to pursued by parties of different ideological types. And these very general insights are not restricted to better-educated or more politically interested voters but are widely shared. Without in any way wanting to overstate the amount of detailed knowledge that most voters possess, they "are not fools," as V. O. Key (1966) long ago observed. Their information base may be scant and largely dependent on general cues, but their assessments of credit and blame take into account whatever information they do have at their disposal, which amounts to more than just who is or is not in government (which information is, in any case, not very relevant in low-clarity contexts). We also see voters behaving in a far more public-spirited fashion than would be supposed from conventional scholarly ideas. Voters (at least in European countries) base their preferences on what they think would be best for the country, not on what would be best for themselves personally.[7]

---

future party policies is clearly a prospective orientation, and we thus employ the same word in regard to policies that past researchers have used in regard to expectations.

[7] The evidence that this also happens in the United States is very strong, with millions of voters in 2004 choosing an administration on the basis of its moral credentials even though the choice would manifestly hurt their pocketbooks.

This book does not formulate a new theory of economic voting. Indeed, its findings, though persuasive, are in need of confirmation over a larger universe and with different data. Nevertheless, its findings do provide a basis for future theorizing that should recognize the importance of prospective orientations and the sophistication of voters' reasoning – sophistication that far exceeds what many scholars have been willing to assume.

Epilogue

Where to Go from Here in the Study of Economic Voting?

In this book, we have demonstrated that some of the ways in which economic voting is traditionally investigated are inappropriate and bound to yield biased results, inconsistencies, instabilities, and anomalies. More specifically, we demonstrated that among the major sources of error are:

1. The use of subjective indicators of economic conditions, which are fraught with endogeneity problems and which customarily yield unrealistically high estimates of what are purported to be the effects of economic conditions. More importantly, as argued in Chapter 1, if we are interested in the extent to which voters hold governments accountable for economic conditions, then it is the real economy that is at issue, not a subjective reality that may help to determine vote choice but whose link to normative concerns, such as government accountability, is questionable.

2. The use of a dichotomy between government and opposition parties when (as is most often the case) there are more than two parties in a political system. This dichotomy is of little relevance for voters' reactions to economic conditions in so-called low-clarity countries. Moreover, it incorrectly forces the analyst to estimate a single effect for all government parties and assume an equal but opposite effect for all opposition parties. A final source of error arises from the following.

3. The use of an analysis design that does not distinguish between party choice, on the one hand, and propensities to support parties on the other. The absence of this distinction at the individual level makes it impossible either to take account of independent variables relating to parties or to take account of voters' cross-pressures; at the aggregate level, it prevents the analyst from taking account of the consequences of patterns of party competition. Moreover, the absence of this distinction – that is, the use of party choice as the dependent variable – imposes an unrealistic constraint on the estimated effects of changes in economic conditions such that, for a particular party, gains enjoyed as a result of improving economic conditions need to be identical (but oppositely signed) to the losses that would have been suffered from a deterioration of the same magnitude, a "finding" that is exceedingly unlikely under quite common circumstances.

In the wake of these findings, how should the field of economic voting studies move forward? We could, of course, list what we think are the prerequisites for a well-designed study of economic voting, but we have already done so in Chapter 1. To do so would appear as no more than an invocation to other scholars that they replicate our analyses with the same data that we used. This is because, to the best of our knowledge, there are no other data that permit the application of what we termed an ideal design. Yet, in the field of economic voting, there are too many questions that still need to be addressed for it to be reasonable for us to expect our colleagues to rechew our "cud" or to sit on their hands while waiting for more data of a similar kind to be collected (although we certainly would value their support in promoting the collection of such data over a wider variety of contexts). At the very least, it is imperative to collect additional data that would extend the range of countries beyond those that we studied in this book and to extend the range of economic conditions beyond what we observed in our data. Even without such developments, however, we think there are several other research opportunities in this field.

Aggregate-level studies are not encumbered by problems of subjective measures of economic conditions but are traditionally marred by the other two problems: using only a government–opposition dichotomy and focusing exclusively on party choice (in the form of vote shares). The first of these problems can be solved in a relative easy way. In particular, aggregate-level models can be constructed that distinguish individual political parties rather than dichotomizing them into government or opposition parties. Having stacked the data in much the same way as we have (but using party shares of the vote as the dependent variable rather than vote propensities), such models could characterize parties in terms of the same variables that we have employed: their government–opposition status, their ideological complexion, their size, their history of government activity, and so on. All of these could be used in conjunction with objective measures of economic conditions to explain parties' vote shares.

Such a model would, of course, still not be able to solve the problem that an exclusive focus on vote shares disregards parties' standing in terms of electoral competition. It would still be constrained to estimate effects of an improving economy that were the same (but opposite in direction) as those of a similarly deteriorating economy. The reason is that, even with a model that distinguishes between different parties, a focus on vote shares does not allow analysts to distinguish between the process of forming party support propensities, on the one hand, and the process of choosing a party on the other. As we have seen, this is a crucial distinction. Without it, we have to assume that the effects of the economy on voter behavior only manifest themselves in vote switching (or, in the aggregate, in changes in vote shares), and such assumptions would be just as incorrect in aggregate analyses as in individual-level ones Moreover, sundry factors that are unrelated to economic conditions will make the patterns of electoral competition vary from party to party and from election to election. Studies of a size (in terms of the number of countries and elections) that has been customary in past research would thus continue to yield unstable and contradictory results. In the long run, of course, over many replicatory analyses, the average predictions from all these mis-specified models may very well be correct, but that would offer little solace. In the meantime, all kinds of inconsistent results would have been published, confusing and distracting analysts in much the same way as has been the case in recent decades.

Still, it is possible to construct truly enormous party-level datasets in which it would not be implausible to assume that, on average, each party was centrally located within its potential variation in support. Of course, correct parameter estimates from such a dataset would only emerge as long as the causal processes involved and their parameters

remained unchanged over the period and across the countries concerned (so-called factorial invariance), an assumption that would need
to be tested. But we will suggest, later in this Epilogue, a way in which
that could be done. Still, it is an empirical question whether enough
cases could be obtained that did enjoy factorial invariance to permit
the construction of datasets of adequate size (see footnote 3).

Another possibility would be to build aggregate-level models that
did incorporate aggregate measures of each party's position vis-à-vis
its electoral competitors. In order to arrive at such measures, analysts
of economic voting would have to *"reculer pour mieux sauter"*: to
broaden their outlook and incorporate elements from the study of voting and elections that have no direct bearing on the question of economic voting other than that they provide information about parties'
competitive standing. These elements from mainstream electoral studies involve the notions of electoral potentials and normal vote shares.
A party's electoral potential is the share of the vote that it can conceivably attain under maximally favorable circumstances; in situations of
electoral competition, these potentials sum to more than 100 percent.[1]
The concept of a party's "normal" vote refers to the vote share a party
would obtain if all sorts of short-term factors, including economic factors, turned out to have a neutral effect on that party. These normal
vote shares are constrained to sum to 100 percent across parties, but
each party may at any given moment in time acquire more or fewer
votes than its normal share.[2]

These concepts have been elaborated during recent decades to be
applicable to multiparty systems. They are not without cost in terms of
data requirements and in terms of adding extra stages to data prepa-
ration that have to be accomplished before the impact of the economy on elections and voting can properly be assessed. But many of
the necessary data are easily available – at least in most developed
democracies – in the form of series of regularly conducted opinion poll
data. And existing approaches for estimating normal vote shares or
electoral potentials are sufficiently developed to allow "off-the-shelf"

---

[1] See, e.g., van der Eijk and Oppenhuis (1991) and Oppenhuis, van der Eijk, and Franklin (1996).

[2] For the origin of the concept of a normal vote, see particularly Converse (1966). A more recent elaboration that adequately avoids many of the original limitations of the normal vote approach has been formulated by Anker (1992).

applications, making it possible to characterize parties not only in terms of their existing vote share but also in terms of their normal vote share or their electoral potential. The combination of both kinds of information makes it possible to distinguish analytically parties that are approaching the rock bottom of their potential support (which are thus below their normal vote) from those that are approximately at par and from those that are performing better than normal (and that thus are approaching the ceiling of their potential). Including such distinctions in the analysis would undoubtedly demonstrate the same sort of asymmetry of effects of the economy on vote shares that we discussed in Chapters 6 and 7. But, more importantly, doing so would widen our understanding of the circumstances under which economic changes affect election outcomes.

A complicating factor in the analysis of individual parties' vote shares is that they violate the common regression assumption of independence of observations because vote shares sum to 100 percent. This problem is easily mitigated by not including some parties as cases in the data – usually a collection of parties for which little or no specific information is available and that are commonly lumped together as "other". If this is not sufficient to alleviate problems of nonindependence, jackknife methods provide adequate solutions.

The problem of nonindependence of observations can be circumvented entirely by characterizing each party by an average score that reflects the party preferences of a population. These scores can be derived from so-called thermometer scores or from proxies for propensity to vote measures, as will be discussed in the following paragraphs. However, the adequacy of the measure as a surrogate for vote propensity data is questionable and should be investigated in depth before the measures are used in this way. Still, in terms of analytic tractability, both types of measure can be analyzed without any problem by OLS. Such an approach links to the tradition in the economic voting literature of modeling popularity functions, whereas the analysis of vote shares in elections relates to the tradition of modeling vote functions.[3] Modeling

---

[3] Popularity functions can, of course, also be modeled on the basis of shares of intended votes that are observed in surveys outside election contexts. In that case, the problem of nonindependence of observations has to be addressed in the same fashion as mentioned in the text.

such averages of party preferences removes the need to include in the model measures of the extent to which parties have exhausted their electoral potential, while nevertheless allowing analysts to study the first stage of the two-stage model, which is the stage where independent variables (such as economic conditions) exert their influence. In particular, it would allow tests of the generalizability of our results.

Turning to individual-level studies of economic voting, few surveys have been conducted that include questions about propensities to support a country's various political parties. In addition to the European Election Studies that we used in this book, such questions have been included in various national election surveys in the Netherlands, Britain, Ireland, Germany, and several other European countries, but all in all, the number of contexts that can be studied with the use of these measures remains quite limited (probably no more than fifteen at the time of writing – not enough for adequate variation in economic conditions, as discussed in Chapter 1).

There are at least two ways, however, in which a relevant proxy can be obtained for the support propensity measures. Both require, as our recommendation for aggregate-level studies does, greater attention by those who study economic voting to insights from mainstream electoral studies. The first of these proxies can be obtained by classic analysis of party choice and political preferences – without any economic conditions entering the equation – in order to construct theory- and evidence-based measures of the likelihood that various kinds of voters would support each of the parties in a political system. The plausibility and usefulness of such measures would, of course, be dependent on the quality of the theory and data used to construct them. Constructing them in a manner that is comparable across surveys (necessary to obtain the required variation in economic conditions) would add an additional challenge. Yet, the accumulated empirical understanding of factors contributing to what we have referred to as support propensities should allow determined researchers to arrive at reasonable and plausible measures. From there on, researchers could employ the design we have used in the analyses conducted for this book.

The second and much more direct way to implement our two-stage analysis design is by using a different empirical measure of party support propensities: one that has been included in a much larger number of surveys. That measure is known by several names, including "sympathy scale" and "feeling thermometer." It originated in the American National Election Studies and consists of a series of questions – one for each party deemed sufficiently important to be included in the series of questions – that ask respondents to express their feelings of sympathy (or lack thereof) for each party in turn. Usually responses are provided in terms of a scale running from 0 (cold) to 100 (warm), in which the 50-mark is labeled as neutral. This question has most often been used in empirical tests of directional voting theories (cf. Rabinowitz and MacDonald 1989) and has been included in many national election studies. It is one of the questions that defines the comparative core of the Comparative Study of Electoral Systems (see http://www.cses.org). In spite of its similarity to our support propensity questions, it is nevertheless less well suited for use in the two-stage model of voter decision making that we advocate (see Chapter 2). The reason is that the linkage between the scores on this measure and the party that is actually chosen contains considerably more slippage than is found when using the propensity to support question. Kroh (2003) subjects both sets of questions to a comparative performance review, using one of the few datasets that contains both questions for the same set of parties (the Dutch Parliamentary Election Study of 1994; see Anker and Oppenhuis 1995). He observes that, whereas in 93 percent of the cases the party actually chosen is indeed the one that was given the highest score on the support propensity measure (see also our own Chapter 2), the corresponding success rate for sympathy or feeling thermometer scores was much lower at 72 percent. He also observes that sympathy scores are differently related to explanatory variables than support propensities, and he concludes that information from sympathy ratings for parties "is neither a necessary, nor a sufficient condition for vote choice" (Kroh 2003: 52). These findings imply that estimates of the effects of economic changes on election outcomes (see Chapter 6) are considerably less certain when based on feeling thermometer scores than when based on support propensities and are likely to be somewhat biased. Yet, in spite of these differences and their smaller suitability as elements in a two-stage model of voter choice, these measures provide infinitely more possibilities for adequate design of individual-level economic voting studies than an exclusive focus on party choice would offer. The fact that these questions constitute a central part of a comparative dataset comprising more than fifty countries (and comprising more than a single election for many of these countries) should provide numerous ways to advance the individual-level study of economic voting far beyond its current problem-ridden state.

Moreover, analyses based on thermometer scales might well be used to check assumptions of parameter invariance before proceeding to a party-level analysis of the kind discussed earlier. Though the parameters deriving from an analysis of thermometer scores might be incorrect, their stability should be a valuable indication of stability in effects of economic conditions that could be used as guidance in selecting countries and periods from which to construct a party-level dataset that contained enough replications of each type of party to ensure that, on average, each party was centrally located within its range of possible support. Considering the wide availability over a considerable period of thermometer scales in election studies, such a hybrid approach might appear quite attractive.[4]

---

[4] There is, of course, no guarantee that sufficient cases would be found that enjoyed parameter invariance. This is an empirical question that can only be answered by appropriate research using thermometer scores over a wide range of countries and time periods.

Appendix A

The Surveys Employed in This Book

The empirical data for most analyses in this book derive from the European Elections Studies (EESs) from 1989, 1994, and 1999. These were survey-based studies of the electorates of the member states of the (then) European Community (EC) in 1989 and of the European Union (EU) in 1994 and 1999. In all years, the surveys were conducted immediately following the June elections to the European Parliament. In 1989 and 1994 all twelve member states were surveyed, and all fifteen in 1999. The member states were (in 1989 and 1994) Belgium, Denmark, France, Germany, Greece, Ireland, Italy, Luxembourg, the Netherlands, Portugal, Spain, and Britain; and in 1999 additionally Austria, Finland, and Sweden. The questionnaires of the surveys focused in particular on the direct elections to the European Parliament, and contained a large number of items about political topics in the domestic and European political spheres.

The EESs were designed as stratified samples of the European population, in which each of the member states is a stratum. Although technical aspects of the sampling procedures varied somewhat between the various years and between the countries, all surveys were based on random samples from the electorates in each of the countries. Sample sizes varied likewise and are reported in Table A.1. Owing to missing data on the dependent variable (propensities to vote for parties), the number of cases included in the analyses is somewhat reduced, to 32,950 (in the weighted sample – about weighting, see later).

TABLE A.1. *Number of Interviews Conducted in Different Countries*

	1989	1994	1999
Austria[a]	inap	inap	501
Belgium	933	1,003	500
Denmark	948	1,000	1,001
Finland[a]	inap	inap	501
France	981	1,000	1,020
Germany[b]	1,170	1,082	1,000
Greece	940	1,002	500
Ireland	916	1,000	503
Italy	957	1,067	3,708
Luxembourg	289	502	301
The Netherlands	948	1,005	1,001
Portugal	956	1,000	500
Spain	916	1,000	1,000
Sweden[a]	inap	inap	505
Britain	902	1,078	977
Total	10,856	11,739	13,549

[a] Austria, Finland, and Sweden were not yet member states of the EU in 1989 and in 1994.
[b] Germany 1994: only West Germany.

Modes of interviewing differed between the three studies and occasionally between countries, ranging from face-to-face to telephone and telepanel approaches. Details are provided in brief characterizations of each of the three studies.

Though using the languages of each country, the questionnaires for each of the studies were otherwise identical in the various member states, apart from minor but unavoidable differences in the names of parties and other country-specific institutions. As a consequence, the surveys offer many opportunities for the comparative study of voters and elections. Between election years there are significant differences between the questionnaires, yet they share a large common core. The analyses in this book make use of this common core and are thus based on survey questions that were identical in all countries and in all three years.

The 1989 EES

The 1989 study consisted of three waves of interviews, the first two of which took place before the European elections in October–November

1988 and March–April 1989, respectively. The third wave was conducted immediately following the European elections in June 1989. All interviews were conducted face-to-face, in some countries by way of Computer Assisted Personal Interviewing (CAPI). In the first and second waves, the questions of the EES were added to regular Eurobarometer studies (EB30 and EB31); the questions of the third wave were added to a special postelection Eurobarometer (EB31a).

The questionnaires of the three waves of interviews partially overlapped, thus offering opportunities for longitudinal comparisons of voter behavior and orientations during the run-up to a European election. The three waves constitute a repeated cross-sectional study; that is, they were administered to three independently drawn random samples of the populations of the member states of the (then) EC. Consequently, comparisons between waves can only be made in terms of aggregates, not of individual respondents. In this book, we only analyze data that derive from the third (postelection) wave of this study.

The 1994 EES

The 1994 study consisted of a single wave of interviews, conducted immediately following the European elections of June 1994, with freshly drawn samples in all member states of the EU. As in 1989, the questions were added to a special postelection Eurobarometer (EB41.1). As in 1989, the questionnaires were identical in all member states (apart from unavoidable variations due to language and institutional differences), and a large number of the questions – including all those of central importance to the analyses reported in this volume – were identical to those used in the 1989 study. Interviews were conducted face-to-face, again with the use of CAPI in some countries. The area formerly known as East Germany was sampled separately. The data from this specific sample were not used in the analyses in this book.

The 1999 EES

The 1999 EES consisted of a single wave of interviews, conducted immediately following the European Parliament elections of June 1999, by Computer Assisted Telephonic Interviewing (CATI), except in Italy, where a telepanel was used. The surveys did not piggyback on the Eurobarometer, but drew on dedicated and freshly drawn samples.

Accessing the Data

The data of the 1989, 1994, and 1999 studies have been documented and archived and are publicly available without restrictions. They can be retrieved from www.europeanelectionstudies.net – the EES web site. This web site also contains detailed codebook information and auxiliary information about research teams involved, funding agencies, related studies of political elites and media, and publications that are based on these various data. Additionally, the EES voter studies can be obtained from academic data archives such as Steinmetz Archive (Amsterdam, the Netherlands), the ESRC Data Archive (Essex, UK), the Zentral Archive (Cologne, Germany), and the ICPSR (Ann Arbor, Michigan, USA).[1]

Weighting

Two kinds of weight variables are used in this book. The first one is a political weight variable, which is described in detail in van der Eijk and Franklin (1996: Appendix A). When applied, it generates distributions of turnout and party choice that are identical to the actual results of the European election in the respective years and countries. This variable was constructed in the same way for all three election years. Applying this weight leaves the effective number of cases unchanged from the raw data for each country. This variable was used for the country-specific analyses (e.g., some of the analyses in Chapters 5 and 6). Northern Irish cases were assigned a value of zero on this variable, which excludes them from the analysis, for all practical purposes. Too few interviews were conducted there for meaningful separate analysis, while, owing to its unique party system, Northern Ireland cannot be subsumed in the analysis for Britain.

[1] Note that the EES data available at the EES web site cited are not the same as those catalogued in the ICPSR catalog, since the latter is (for 1989 and 1994) simply the Eurobarometer study that accompanied and contained the questions of the EESs in those years. The Eurobarometer study contains data that have not been cleaned or rationalized in the same detail as the data available from the EES web site, and that have not been weighted in such a way as to permit replication of our findings.

The second weight variable is a transformation of the first one, which ensures that the effective number of cases is equal for each of the systems; this is accomplished by multiplying the weight of all cases of a specific survey by a specific constant. When this weight is applied to analyses that are conducted for each of the political systems separately, it produces results identical to those obtained when the political weight variable is used, except for the (effective) number of cases (and consequently for standard errors and tests of significance). This weighting was used in all pooled analyses in this volume in order to arrive at unbiased estimates of the effects of systemic (or contextual) factors, while at the same time ensuring that the sample distributions of turnout and party choice mirror the actual outcome of the European elections within each of the systems.

Organization and Funding

The EES of 1989, 1994, and 1999 were organized by an international group of researchers that came together for the first time in the corridors of the Joint Sessions of Workshops of the European Consortium for Political Research in Amsterdam in April 1987. Although not a formal member of the group, Karlheinz Reif (Commission of the European Communities and University of Mannheim) has to be regarded as its prime initiator and continuing supporter. The composition of the group has varied over the years but has comprised (at various times) the following people: Wouter van der Brug (University of Amsterdam), Pilar del Castillo (formerly CIS, Madrid, currently a member of the European Parliament), Bruno Cautres (University of Grenoble), Roland Cayrol (CEVIPOF, Paris), Cees van der Eijk (formerly at the University of Amsterdam, currently at the University of Nottingham), Mark Franklin (formerly at the University of Strathclyde, then at the University of Houston, then at Trinity College, Connecticut, currently at the European University Institute, Florence, Italy, Sören Holmberg (University of Gothenburg), Manfred Kuechler (formerly at Florida State University, currently at Hunter College, City University of New York), Renato Mannheimer (formerly at the University of Milan, currently at the University of Genoa), Michael Marsh (Trinity College Dublin), Pippa Norris (Harvard University), Erik Oppenhuis (University of Amsterdam), Hermann Schmitt (University of Mannheim), Holli Semetko (formerly at the University of Amsterdam, currently at Emory

University), Jacques Thomassen (University of Twente), Bernard Wessels (Free University of Berlin), and Colette Ysmal (CEVIPOF, Paris).

The studies could not have been conducted without generous support from a variety of sources. Data collection was made possible first of all by the Commission of the European Communities, which agreed in 1989 and 1994 to the use of the Eurobarometer as a vehicle on which to piggyback the EESs. The costs of the (large numbers of) questions added to the Eurobarometers for the EES89 were covered by a generous grant from the British Economic and Social Research Council (ESRC) and an additional grant from the Office of the French Prime Minister. Remaining costs were paid by selling prospective reports of analyses of the (yet to be collected) data to interested media and other institutions throughout Europe. The costs of the EES94 were covered by a large grant from the Deutsche Forschungs Gemeinschaft (DFG), a smaller grant from the Dutch National Science Foundation (NWO), and additional support from the European Parliament. EES99 was funded largely by grants from the University of Amsterdam and from the NWO, with additional support from CIS (Madrid), Trinity College (Hartford, Connecticut, the United States) and the University of Mannheim.

Nonfieldwork costs for the various studies, relating to data cleaning, data production, and documentation, were covered by NWO, the University of Amsterdam, the University of Mannheim, and the Steinmetz Archive (Amsterdam, the Netherlands).

Appendix B

Detailed Results Not Reported in the Main Text

For ease of presentation, some of the very large tables of results were not presented in the text or were presented in a condensed form. This appendix presents the full tables.

TABLE B.1. Adding Length of Time in Office to Model F (in Table 4.2)[a]

	Model B.1		Model B.2		Model B.3	
	B	SE	B	SE	B	SE
Months coalition was in office (0 for opposition parties)	−0.006	0.001**				
Months party was in office (0 for opposition parties)			−0.0004	0.000		
Government party * time since last election					−0.009	0.002**
Party size	5.843	0.108**	5.398	0.097**	5.638	0.107**
GDP	0.048	0.010**	0.047	0.010**	0.040	0.010**
Unemployment	0.068	0.017**	0.053	0.016*	0.053	0.017*
Inflation	−0.049	0.005**	−0.052	0.005**	−0.047	0.005**
Months coalition was in office * GDP	−0.000	0.000				
Months coalition was in office * unemployment	−0.001	0.001				
Months coalition was in office * inflation	−0.001	0.000**				
Months party was in office * GDP			−0.000	0.000		
Months party was in office * unemployment			−0.000	0.000*		
Months party was in office * inflation			−0.000	0.000		
Government party * time since last election * GDP					0.002	0.001
Government party * time since last election * unemployment					0.001	0.001
Government party * time since last election * inflation					−0.002	0.000**
Weighted N	27,505	27,505	27,505			
Adjusted R^2	0.462	0.462	0.462			

Note: Significant at *0.01, **0.001.
[a] The estimated model includes all control variables in Model F (see Table 4.2). Since the effects of the control variables are not relevant to the topic of this study, these effects are not presented here.

TABLE B.2. *Adding Party of the Prime Minister to Model F (in Table 4.2)[a].*

	Model B.4		Model B.5	
	B	SE	B	SE
Government party	−0.220	0.054**		
Party size	6.072	0.128**	6.101	0.127**
Party of the prime minister	−0.327	0.067**	−0.416	0.063**
GDP	0.035	0.011*	0.039	0.010**
Unemployment	0.072	0.018**	0.071	0.016**
Inflation	−0.041	0.005**	−0.045	0.005**
Government party * GDP	0.039	0.029		
Government party * unemployment	0.063	0.045		
Government party * inflation	−0.119	0.027**		
Party of the prime minister * GDP	0.076	0.035	0.100	0.027**
Party of the prime minister * unemployment	−0.120	0.056	−0.066	0.043
Party of the prime minister * inflation	0.049	0.029	−0.065	0.013**
Weighted N	27,505	27,505		
Adjusted R^2	0.464	0.464		

Note: Significant at *0.01, **0.001.

[a] The estimated model includes all control variables in Model F (see Table 4.2). Since the effects of the control variables are not relevant to the topic of this study, these effects are not presented here.

TABLE B.3. *Estimates of Model I (for Table 4.5)[a]*

	Model I	
	B	**SE**
Government party	−0.172	0.060*
Party size	6.347	0.208**
Government party * party size	−2.217	0.308**
Right party	−0.153	0.037**
Right party * government party	−0.074	0.076
Right party * party size	1.044	0.301**
Right party * government party * party size	0.266	0.440
GDP	0.066	0.021*
Unemployment	0.137	0.025**
Inflation	−0.029	0.007**
Government party * GDP	0.105	0.034*
Government party * unemployment	0.053	0.057
Government party * inflation	−0.070	0.013**
Party size * GDP	−0.125	0.180
Party size * unemployment	−0.258	0.187
Government party * party size * GDP	−0.281	0.249
Government party * party size * unemployment	−1.558	0.310**
Right party * GDP	−0.119	0.028**
Right party * unemployment	−0.202	0.041**
Right party * inflation	−0.026	0.010*
Right party * government party * GDP	−0.298	0.077**
Right party * government party * unemployment	0.019	0.085
Right party * party size * GDP	0.252	0.237
Right party * party size * unemployment	−0.013	0.329
Right party * government party * party size * GDP	1.298	0.371**
Right party * gov. party * party size * unemployment	1.922	0.464**
Weighted *N*	27,505	
Adjusted R^2	0.469	

Note: Significant at *0.01, **0.001.

[a] The estimated model includes all control variables in Model F (see Table 4.2). Since the effects of the control variables are not relevant to the topic of this study, these effects are not presented here.

TABLE B.4. *Interacting Economic Voting with System Clarity but Not with Party Size (Model K Is the Basis for Table 4.6)[a]*

	Model J		Model K	
	B	SE	B	SE
Government party	−0.342	0.057**	−0.486	0.074**
Right-leaning party			−0.519	0.059**
Government party * right party			0.377	0.096**
High system clarity	−0.321	0.040**	−0.484	0.051**
High system clarity * government party	−0.327	0.083	−0.329	0.108*
High system clarity * right party			0.423	0.085**
High system clarity * gov. party * right party			−0.143	0.145
GDP	0.029	0.014	0.012	0.015
Unemployment	−0.127	0.028**	−0.217	0.041**
Inflation	0.028	0.017	0.104	0.022**
Government party * GDP	0.076	0.014	0.105	0.030**
Government party * unemployment	0.283	0.051**	0.256	0.076**
Government party * inflation	−0.103	0.028**	−0.171	0.041**
Unemployment * right party			0.114	0.055
Inflation * right party			−0.198	0.034**
Government party * unemployment * right party			0.085	0.089
Government party * inflation * right party			0.232	0.058**
High clarity * GDP	−0.001	0.022	0.016	0.023
High clarity * unemployment	0.299	0.039**	0.440	0.049**
High clarity * inflation	−0.052	0.018*	−0.116	0.023*
High clarity * government party * GDP	0.103	0.048	0.075	0.049
High clarity * government party * unempl.	−0.525	0.071**	−0.615	0.102**
High clarity * government party * infl.	0.034	0.032	0.085	0.041
High clarity * unemployment * right party			−0.257	0.074**
High clarity * inflation * right party			0.168	0.032**
High clarity * gov. party * unemployment * right party			0.194	0.129
High clarity * gov. party * inflation * right party			−0.194	0.066*
Weighted N	27,505	27,505		
Adjusted R^2	0.468	0.470		

Note: Significant at *0.01, **0.001.

[a] The estimated model includes all control variables in Model F (see Table 4.2). Since the effects of the control variables are not relevant to the topic of this study, these effects are not presented here.

TABLE B.5. *Interacting Economic Voting with Party Size and System Clarity (for Table 4.7)[a]*

	Model L	
	B	SE
Government party	−0.297	0.047**
Party size	6.336	0.281**
Right-leaning party	−0.373	0.049**
Party size * right-leaning party	2.053	0.411**
High system clarity	−0.521	0.047**
High system clarity * party size	−1.032	0.335*
High system clarity * right-leaning party	0.450	0.078**
High system clarity * party size * right-leaning party	−2.051	0.505**
GDP	0.097	0.020**
Unemployment	−0.104	0.038*
Inflation	0.048	0.018*
Party size * GDP	0.082	0.176
Party size * unemployment	−0.748	0.310
Party size * inflation	0.641	0.145**
GDP * right-leaning party	−0.192	0.031**
Unemployment * right-leaning party	0.051	0.051
Inflation * right-leaning party	−0.109	0.028**
Party size * economic growth * right-leaning party	−0.316	0.229
Party size * unemployment * right-leaning party	−0.566	0.491
Party size * inflation * right-leaning party	−0.425	0.224
High clarity * GDP	−0.030	0.029
High clarity * unemployment	0.249	0.045**
High clarity * inflation	−0.074	0.019**
High clarity * party size * GDP	0.030	0.224
High clarity * party size * unemployment	−0.195	0.347
High clarity * party size * inflation	0.701	0.149**
High clarity * GDP * right-leaning party	0.080	0.049
High clarity * unemployment * right-leaning party	−0.244	0.074*
High clarity * inflation * right-leaning party	0.084	0.030*
High clarity * party size * GDP * right-leaning party	0.873	0.295*
High clarity * party size * unemployment * right-leaning party	1.827	0.550*
High clarity * party size * inflation * right-leaning party	0.469	0.231
Weighted N	27,505	
Adjusted R^2	0.470	

Note: Significant at *0.01, **0.001.

[a] The estimated model includes all control variables in Model F (see Table 4.2). Since the effects of the control variables are not relevant to the topic of this study, these effects are not presented here.

TABLE B.6. *Proportions of Respondents Whose First Two Party Preferences Are Tied (See Also Table 5.3)*

	Political Interest		Education		Retired		Employment	
Flanders	low	.21	still studying	.30	retired	.14	unemployed	.07
	medium	.22	low	.14	not retired	.21	not unemployed	.20
	high	.15	medium	.23				
			high	.15				
Wallonia	low	.21	still studying	.21	retired	.19	unemployed	.21
	medium	.23	low	.46	not retired	.21	not unemployed	.20
	high	.16	medium	.18				
			high	.17				
Denmark	low	.20	still studying	.22	retired	.20	unemployed	.29
	medium	.22	low	.12	not retired	.20	not unemployed	.20
	high	.18	medium	.23				
			high	.19				
France	low	.39	still studying	.45	retired	.28	unemployed	.33
	medium	.34	low	.25	not retired	.36	not unemployed	.34
	high	.26	medium	.31				
			high	.38				
Germany	low	.18	still studying	.15	retired	.11	unemployed	.20
	medium	.18	low	.16	not retired	.19	not unemployed	.16
	high	.14	medium	.18				
			high	.16				
Britain	low	.21	still studying	.19	retired	.12	unemployed	.23
	medium	.16	low	.18	not retired	.20	not unemployed	.19
	high	.20	medium	.19				
			high	.18				
Greece	low	.22	still studying	.16	retired	.12	unemployed	.42
	medium	.24	low	.19	not retired	.25	not unemployed	.21
	high	.20	medium	.30				
			high	.16				
Ireland	low	.35	still studying	.31	retired	.21	unemployed	.17
	medium	.20	low	.14	not retired	.25	not unemployed	.25
	high	.19	medium	.28				
			high	.26				

(continued)

Appendix B

TABLE B.6 *(continued)*

	Political Interest		Education		Retired		Employment	
Italy	low	.31	still studying	.38	retired	.30	unemployed	.28
	medium	.25	low	.26	not retired	.28	not unemployed	.28
	high	.26	medium	.26				
			high	.29				
Luxembourg	low	.19	still studying	.14	retired	.16	no unemployed	
	medium	.13	low	.22	not retired	.15	respondents	
	high	.16	medium	.16				
			high	.11				
The Netherlands	low	.21	still studying	.28	retired	.20	unemployed	.32
	medium	.21	low	.21	not retired	.21	not unemployed	.21
	high	.23	medium	.17				
			high	.26				
Portugal	low	.17	still studying	.22	retired	.13	unemployed	.24
	medium	.17	low	.13	not retired	.16	not unemployed	.16
	high	.12	medium	.22				
			high	.17				
Spain	low	.16	still studying	.18	retired	.15	unemployed	.16
	medium	.11	low	.15	not retired	.15	not unemployed	.15
	high	.16	medium	.17				
			high	.11				
Finland	low	.29	still studying	.24	retired	.14	unemployed	.11
	medium	.25	low	.33	not retired	.30	not unemployed	.27
	high	.20	medium	.21				
			high	.27				
Sweden	low	.23	still studying	.30	retired	.16	unemployed	.27
	medium	.24	low	.12	not retired	.23	not unemployed	.21
	high	.18	medium	.24				
			high	.20				
Austria	low	.21	still studying	.15	retired	.24	unemployed	.14
	medium	.15	low	.18	not retired	.18	not unemployed	.19
	high	.22	medium	.18				
			high	.24				
EU-wide	low	.23	still studying	.23	retired	.17	unemployed	.23
	medium	.20	low	.19	not retired	.22	not unemployed	.21
	high	.18	medium	.22				
			high	.21				

TABLE B.7. *Change in 1999 in Predicted Vote Share of Parties (in Percentages) as a Result of One Standard Deviation Deterioration in Each of the Three Indicators of the State of the Economy (for Table 6.5)*

	France	Britain	Italy	Finland	Portugal	Ireland	Austr.	Germ.	Sweden	Spain	Greece	Wallon	Neth.	Lux	Flanders	Denm
Party 1	−8.4	−6.3	−5.8	−4.5	−5.0	−4.5	−4.2	−3.6	+3.4	−3.5	−2.9	−0.9	−2.6	−0.2	−1.3	−1.4
Party 2	+5.7	+4.0	+1.9	+0.7	+4.6	+2.8	+1.8	+3.3	−3.6	+3.1	+1.8	+0.5	+0.5	−1.4	0.0	−0.1
Party 3	+1.9	+0.5	+0.2	+1.7	0.0	+0.4	+1.8	0.0	0.0	+0.4	+0.2	−1.9	+1.9	+1.2	−0.5	+0.3
Party 4	+0.0	0.0	+0.3	+1.3	+0.4	+0.3	+0.6	+0.1	+0.2	0.0	+0.5	+1.6	−0.2	0.0	+0.3	+0.1
Party 5	+0.2	+0.2	+1.6	−0.3	0.0	0.0	+0.1	+0.1	0.0	0.0	+0.5	+0.6	+0.3	+0.2	+1.4	+0.8
Party 6	+0.1	+1.1	+0.9	+0.5		+0.2	0.0	0.0	0.0	0.0	0.0		0.0	0.0	0.0	0.0
Party 7	+0.5	+0.6	+0.5	+0.5		+0.8			0.0		0.0		0.0	+0.2		+0.2
Party 8	0.0		+0.3	0.0									0.0			0.0
Party 9	0.0		+0.1										0.0			0.0
Party 10													0.0			0.0
Total net change	8.4	6.3	5.8	4.8	5.0	4.5	4.2	3.6	3.6	3.5	2.9	2.8	2.7	1.6	1.8	1.5
Total gross change	8.5	6.6	6.2	5.7	5.0	4.5	4.4	3.6	3.6	3.5	3.1	2.8	2.7	2.0	1.8	1.8

Government parties are in shaded cells. Parties in this table (in the rank-order party 1, party 2, etceteras) are:

Flanders: CVP, VLD, SP, VL Blok, Agalev, VU-ID21

Wallonia: PS, PRL, PSC, Ecolo, FN

Denmark: Soc.Dem, Venstre, Konserv, Soc FKPT, Dansk FKPT, Center.Dem, Rad. V, Rod-Gronne, Krist FKPT, Fremskr

France: PS-PRG, RPR, UDF, PC, LO-LCR, DL, Verts, FN/MN, RPF

Germany: SPD, CDU/CSU, B9o/Gruenen, FDP, PDS, Republikaner

Britain: Labour, Conservatives, Lib Dem, SNP, Plaid C., Green P., UKIP

Greece: Pasok ND KKE Synasp. Dikki Pol.Anixi Fileleytheri

Ireland: FF, FG, Labour, Progr Dem, SF, Green P, Dem Left

Italy: Dem Di Sinistra, Forza It, All Nazionale, Lega Nord, Rifond Comm, I Democratic, PPI, CCD/CDU, Lista Panella/Bonini

Luxemburg: CSV/PCS, LSAP/POSL, DP/PD, ADR, Dei Greng, Dei Lenk, GAL

Netherlands: PVDA, VVD, CDA, D66, GR. Links, SGP, SP, RPF, GPV, CD

Portugal: PS, PSD, CDS/PP, CDU, Bloco De Esquerda

Spain: PP, PSOE, IU, CIU, PNV, EH

Sweden: Vansterp., Soc.Dem., Miljop., Centerp., Folkp., Kristdem., Moderaterna

Finland: SDP, Keskusta, Kokoomus, Vasemm., SFP/RKP, Vihreat, SKL/Kristillisit, PS Perussuomalaiset

Austria: SPO, OVP, FPO, Gruene, Lib Forum, CSA

The standard deviations in economic conditions are 1.69% for GDP, 1.02% for unemployment, and 3.02% for inflation. To compute the consequences of economic conditions for the election results, the election results were predicted twice, once with the economic conditions as they were in reality and once with 1.69% less economic growth, 1.02% more unemployment, and 3.02% more inflation. Entries in the cells are the differences between the percentages of votes won by each party in both cases.

TABLE B.8. Change in 1999 in Predicted Vote Share of Parties (in Percentages) as a Result of One Standard Deviation Improvement in Each of the Three Indicators of the State of the Economy (for Table 6.6)

	France	Britain	Italy	Finland	Portugal	Ireland	Austr.	Germ.	Sweden	Spain	Greece	Wallon	Neth.	Lux	Flanders	Denm
Party 1	+9.8	+4.0	+5.6	+3.5	+9.5	+0.9	+2.9	+3.1	-2.1	+4.5	+3.2	+1.4	+2.3	+0.5	0.0	+1.4
Party 2	-5.7	-1.6	-2.1	-1.4	-9.5	-0.4	-1.4	-2.6	+2.8	-4.5	-2.6	-1.5	-0.7	+1.8	0.0	+0.2
Party 3	-1.6	-1.5	-0.3	-1.5	0.0	-0.2	-1.1	-0.1	-0.2	0.0	-0.4	+1.9	-0.8	0.0	0.0	-0.4
Party 4	-0.2	-0.6	-0.3	-0.3	0.0	+0.7	-0.1	-0.4	-0.2	0.0	0.0	-0.2	+0.1	-1.0	+0.6	-0.1
Party 5	-0.3	0.0	-1.2	-0.2	0.0	-0.5	-0.2	0.0	0.0	0.0	0.0	-1.6	-0.6	-0.9	0.0	-0.7
Party 6	0.0	-0.3	-0.7	0.0		0.0	0.0	0.0	0.0	0.0	-0.2		0.0	-0.4	-0.6	0.0
Party 7	-2.0	0.0	-0.7	0.0		-0.5			-0.3	0.0	0.0		-0.2	0.0		0.0
Party 8	0.0		-0.3	0.0									0.0			-0.4
Party 9	0.0		-0.3										0.0			0.0
Party 10			-0.1										0.0			0.0
Total net change	9.8	4.0	5.6	3.5	9.5	1.6	2.9	3.1	2.8	4.5	3.2	3.3	2.4	2.3	0.6	1.6
Total gross change	10.2	4.0	6.1	5.3	9.5	1.6	2.9	3.3	2.8	4.5	3.4	3.5	2.7	2.8	0.6	2.0

Government parties are in shaded cells. The parties in this table are listed in the note to Table B.7.

The standard deviations in economic conditions are 1.69% for GDP, 1.02% for the annual change in unemployment, and 3.02% for inflation. To compute the consequences of economic conditions for the election results, the election results were predicted twice, once with the economic conditions as they were in reality and once with 1.69% more economic growth, 1.02% less unemployment, and 3.02% less inflation. Entries in the cells are the differences between the percentages of votes won by each party in both cases.

TABLE B.9. *Change in 1994 in Predicted Vote Share of Parties (in Percentages) as a Result of Deterioration or Improvement in All Three Indicators of the State of the Economy (Three Exemplary Countries Only – for Table 6.7)*[a]

	France		Flanders		Denmark	
	Deteriorating Economy	Improving Economy	Deteriorating Economy	Improving Economy	Deteriorating Economy	Improving Economy
Party 1	0.0	0.0	−0.2	−1.0	−2.0	+2.6
Party 2	+0.4	−0.1	+0.6	−1.1	−0.3	+0.3
Party 3	0.0	0.0	−1.9	+4.1	+0.8	−1.1
Party 4	−0.3	0.0	+1.1	−1.9	+0.5	−0.5
Party 5	−0.2	0.0	+0.3	0.0	+0.4	−0.9
Party 6	0.0	0.0	+0.1	−0.1	0.0	0.0
Party 7	0.0	+0.2			+0.4	−0.4
Party 8	0.0	0.0			+0.3	0.0
Total net change	0.5	0.2	2.1	4.1	2.4	2.9

Government parties are in shaded cells. Parties in this table (in the rank-order party 1, party 2, etc.) are:
France: PC, PS-PRG, Mov Rad de G, UDF, RPR, FN, VERTS, Generation Ecol
Flanders: VLD, CVP, SP, AGALEV, VL Blok, VU-ID21
Denmark: Soc.Dem, Rad. V, Konserv, Center.DemM, Soc FKPT, Krist FKPT, Venstre, Fremskr
[a] For explanations of how changes in election outcomes were computed, see the notes to Table B.7 (for economic deterioration) and Table B.8 (for economic improvement).

References

Alvarez, R. M., and J. Nagler. 1998. "When Politics and Models Collide: Estimating Models of Multiparty Elections," *American Journal of Political Science* 42: 55–96.

Alvarez, R. M., and J. Nagler. 2000. "A New Approach for Modelling Strategic Voting in Multiparty Elections," *British Journal of Political Science* 30: 57–75.

Anderson, C. 1995. *Blaming the Government: Citizens and the Economy in Five European Democracies*. Armonk, NY: M. E. Sharpe.

Anker, H. 1992. *Normal Vote Analysis*. Amsterdam: Het Spinhuis.

Anker, H., and E. Oppenhuis. 1995. *Dutch Parliamentary Election Study 1994*. Amsterdam: Steinmetz Archive/SKON (the ICPSR version of this dataset was published in 1997, Study Nr. 6740).

Ansolabehere, S., and S. Iyengar. 1995. *Going Negative: How Political Advertisements Shrink and Polarize the Electorate*. New York: Free Press.

Ark, B. van, and J. de Haan. 2000. "The Delta-Model Revisited: Recent Trends in the Structural Performance of the Dutch Economy," *International Review of Applied Economics* 14: 307–21.

Barry, B. M. 1970. *Sociologists, Economists and Democracy*. London: Collier-Macmillan.

Bartels, L. M. 2002. "Beyond the Running Tally: Partisan Bias in Political Perceptions," *Political Behavior* 24: 117–50.

Bartle, J. 1997. "Political Awareness and Heterogeneity in Models of Voting: Some Evidence from the Recent British Election Studies," in *British Elections and Parties Review* 7, C. Pattie, D. Denver, J. Fisher, and S. Ludlam (eds.). London: Frank Cass, pp. 1–22.

Beck, N., and J. Katz. 1995. "What to Do (and Not to Do) with Time-Series-Cross-Section Data in Comparative Politics," *American Political Science Review* 89: 634–7.

Ben-Akiva, M., and S. R. Lerman. 1985. *Discrete Choice Analysis. Theory and Application to Travel Demand*. Cambridge: MIT Press.

Berelson, B., P. F. Lazarsfeld, and W. N. McPhee. 1954. *Voting. A Study of Opinion Formation in a Presidential Campaign*. Chicago: University of Chicago Press.

Berger, H., and U. Woitek. 1997. "Searching for Political Business Cycles in Germany," *Public Choice* 91: 179–97.

Blais, A., and R. Nadeau. 1992. "The Electoral Budget Cycle," *Public Choice* 74: 389–403.

Bloom, H., and D. Price. 1975. "Voter Response to Short-Run Economic Conditions: The Asymmetric Effect of Prosperity and Recession," *American Political Science Review* 69: 1240–54.

Bowler, S., and D. J. Lanoue. 1992. "The Sources of Tactical Voting in British Parliamentary Elections, 1983–1987," *Political Behavior* 14: 141–57.

Brug, W. van der, and C. van der Eijk. 2000. "De campagne deed er toe, mediagebruik niet," in *Tussen Beeld en Inhoud. Politiek en media in de verkiezingen van 1998*, P. van Praag, Jr., and K. Brants (eds.). Amsterdam: Het Spinhuis, pp. 214–43.

Brug, W. van der, and C. van der Eijk (eds.). Forthcoming. *European Elections and Domestic Politics. Lessons from the Past and Scenarios for the Future*. Notre Dame: University of Notre Dame Press.

Brug, W. van der, C. van der Eijk, and M. Franklin. 2002. "The Reasoning Public: Education, Interest and Political Choices." Paper presented at Joint Sessions of Workshops, ECPR, Turin, March.

Brug, W. van der, C. van der Eijk, and M. Franklin. Forthcoming. "EU Support and Party Choice," in *European Elections and Domestic Politics. Lessons from the Past and Scenarios for the Future*, W. van der Brug and C. van der Eijk (eds.). Notre Dame: University of Notre Dame Press, pp.

Brug, W. van der, M. Fennema, and J. Tillie 2000. "Anti-immigrant Parties in Europe: Ideological or Protest Vote." *European Journal of Political Research* 37: 77–102.

Budge, I., D. Robertson, and D. Hearl (eds.). 1987. *Ideology, Strategy, and Party Change*. Cambridge: Cambridge University Press.

Burden, B. C. 1997. "Deterministic and Probabilistic Voting Models," *American Journal of Political Science* 41: 1150–69.

Butler, D. E., and D. E. Stokes. 1974. *Political Change in Britain – the Evolution of Electoral Choice*, 2nd ed. London: Macmillan.

Campbell, A., P. E. Converse, W. E. Miller, and D. E. Stokes. 1960. *The American Voter*. New York: Wiley.

Campbell, A., P. E. Converse, W. E. Miller, and D. E. Stokes. 1966. *Elections and the Political Order*. New York: Wiley.

Campbell, J. E., and J. C. Garand. 2000. *Before the Vote. Forecasting American National Elections*. Thousand Oaks, CA: Sage.

Campbell, A., and R. L. Kahn. 1952. *The People Elect a President*. Ann Arbor, MI: Survey Research Center I.S.R.

Chrystal, K. A., and J. E. Alt. 1981. "Some Problems in Formulating and Testing a Politico-Economic Model of the United Kingdom," *The Economic Journal* 91: 730–6.

Claggett, W. 1986. "A Re-examination of the Asymmetry Hypothesis: Economic Expansions, Contractions and Congressional Elections," *Western Political Quarterly* 39: 623–33.

Clarke, H. D., and M. Stewart. 1995. "Economic Evaluations, Prime Ministerial Approval and Governing Party Support: Rival Models Considered," *British Journal of Political Science* 25: 15–70.

Clarke, H. D., M. Stewart, and P. Whiteley. 1998. "New Models for New Labour: The Political Economy of Labour Party Support, January 1992–April 1997," *American Political Science Review* 92: 559–75.

Clarke, H. D., and P. Whiteley. 1990. "Presidential Approval, Partisanship and the Economy: Evidence from the 1984 Continuous Monitoring Survey," *International Journal of Public Opinion Research* 2: 1–24.

Conover, P. J., and S. Feldman 1982. "Projection and Perceptions of Candidates' Issue Positions," *Western Political Quarterly* 35: 228–44.

Conover, P. J., and S. Feldman. 1984. "How People Organize the Political World: A Schematic Model," *American Journal of Political Science* 28: 95–126.

Converse, P. E. 1964. "The Nature of Belief Systems in Mass Publics," in *Ideology and Discontent*, D. Apter (eds.). Glencoe, IL: Free Press, pp. 219–41.

Converse, P. E. 1966. "The Concept of a Normal Vote," in *Elections and the Political Order*, A. Campbell, P. E. Converse, W. E. Miller, and D. E. Stokes (eds.). New York: Wiley, pp. 9–39.

Converse, P. E. 1970. "Attitudes and Non-attitudes: Continuation of a Dialogue," in *The Quantitative Analysis of Social Problems*, E. R. Tufte (ed.). Reading, MA: Addison-Wesley, pp. 168–89.

Dalen, H. P. van, and O. H. Swank. 1996. "Government Spending Cycles: Ideological or Opportunistic?" *Public Choice* 89: 183–200.

Dalton, R. J., and M. Wattenberg. 1993. "The Not So Simple Act of Voting," in *Political Science: The State of the Discipline II*, A. W. Finifter (eds.). Washington, DC: American Political Science Association, pp. 424–47.

Daudt, H. 1961. *Floating Voters and the Floating Vote*. Leiden: Stenfert Kroese.

Diez-Roux, A. V. 2000. "Multilevel Analysis in Public Health Research," *Annual Review of Public Health* 21: 171–92.

Dorussen, H., and M. Taylor (eds.). 2002. *Economic Voting*. London: Routledge.

Downs, A. 1957. *An Economic Theory of Democracy*. New York: Harper and Row.

Duch, R. M., and H. D. Palmer. 2002. "Heterogeneous Perceptions of Economic Conditions in Cross-National Perspective," in *Economic Voting*, H. Dorussen and M. Taylor (eds.). London: Routledge, pp. 139–72.

Duch, R. M., and R. Stevenson. 2003. "Re-evaluating Economic Voting." Paper presented at the Joint Sessions of Workshops, ECPR, Edinburgh.

Eijk, C. van der. 2001. "Measuring Agreement in Ordered Rating Scales," *Quality and Quantity* 35: 325–41.

Eijk, C. van der. 2002. "Design Issues in Electoral Research: Taking Care of (Core) Business," *Electoral Studies* 21: 189–206.

Eijk, C. van der, W. van der Brug, M. Kroh, and M. Franklin. 2006. "Rethinking the Dependent Variable in Voting Behavior – on the Measurement and Analysis of Electoral Utilities," *Electoral Studies* 25.

Eijk, C. van der, and M. Franklin. 1996. *Choosing Europe? The European Electorate and National Politics in the Face of Union.* Ann Arbor: University of Michigan Press.

Eijk, C. van der, M. Franklin, and W. van der Brug. 1999. "Policy Preferences and Party Choice," in *Political Representation and Legitimacy in the European Union*, H. Schmitt and J. Thomassen (eds.). Oxford: Oxford University Press, pp. 161–85.

Eijk, C. van der, and M. Franklin, with F. Demant and W. van der Brug. 2004. "The Endogenous Economy: 'Real' Economic Conditions and Subjective Economic Evaluations." Paper presented at the Workshop on "Perceptions, Preferences and Rationalization: Overcoming the Problem of Causal Inference in the Study of Voting," Nuffield College, Oxford.

Eijk, C. van der, and M. Franklin, F. Demant, W. van der Brug. 2007. "The Endogenous Economy: 'Real' Economic Conditions, Subjective Economic Evaluations and Government Support," *Acta Politica* 42(1).

Eijk, C. van der, M. Franklin, and M. Marsh. 1996. "What Voters Teach Us about Europe-wide Elections; What Europe-wide Elections Teach Us about Voters," *Electoral Studies* 15: 149–66.

Eijk, C. van der, M. Franklin, and E. Oppenhuis. 1996. "The Strategic Context: Party Choice," in *Choosing Europe? The European Electorate and National Politics in the Face of Union*, C. van der Eijk, M. Franklin, et al. (eds.). Ann Arbor: University of Michigan Press, pp. 332–65.

Eijk, C. van der, and B. Niemöller. 1983. *Electoral Change in the Netherlands. Empirical Research and Methods of Measurement.* Amsterdam: CT Press.

Eijk, C. van der, and B. Niemöller. 1984. "Het potentiële electoraat van de Nederlandse politieke partijen," *Beleid en Maatschappij* 11: 192–204.

Eijk, C. van der, and E. Oppenhuis. 1991. "European Parties' Performance in Electoral Competition," *European Journal of Political Research* 19: 55–80.

Enelow, J., and M. Hinich. 1984. "Probabilistic Voting and the Importance of Centrist Ideologies in Democratic Elections," *Journal of Politics* 46: 459–78.

Erikson, R. S. 1989. "Economic Conditions and the Presidential Vote," *American Political Science Review* 83: 567–73.

Erikson, R. S. 2002. "National Election Studies and Macro Analysis," *Electoral Studies* 21: 269–81.

Erikson, R. S., M. MacKuen, and J. A. Stimson. 2002. *The Macro Polity.* New York: Cambridge University Press.

Esping-Andersen, G. 1990. *Three Worlds of Welfare Capitalism.* Princeton: Princeton University Press.

Esping-Andersen, G. 1999. *Social Foundations of Post-industrial Economies.* Oxford: Oxford University Press.

Fair, R. 1988. "The Effect of Economic Events on the Vote for President: A 1984 Update," *Political Behavior* 10: 168–79.

Feldman, S., and P. J. Conover. 1983. "Candidates, Issues, and Voters: The Role of Inference in Political Perception," *Journal of Politics* 45: 812–39.

Fiorina, M. P. 1978. "Economic Retrospective Voting in American National Elections: A Micro-Analysis," *American Journal of Political Science* 22: 426–43.

Fiske, S. T., and P. W. Linville. 1980. "What Does the Schema Concept Buy Us?" *Personality and Social Psychology Bulletin* 6: 543–57.

Franklin, M., C. van der Eijk, and E. Oppenhuis. 1996. "The Institutional Context: Turnout," in *Choosing Europe? The European Electorate and National Politics in the Face of Union*, Cees van der Eijk and Mark Franklin (eds.). Ann Arbor: University of Michigan Press, pp. 306–31.

Franklin, M., and C. Hughes. 1999. "Dynamic Representation in Britain," in *A Critical Election? British Voters and Parties in Long-Term Perspective*, P. Norris, and G. Evans (eds.). Thousand Oaks, CA: Sage, pp. 240–58.

Franklin, M., T. Mackie, H. Valen, et al. 1992. *Electoral Change: Responses to Evolving Social and Attitudinal Structures in Western Countries.* Cambridge: Cambridge University Press.

Franklin, M., R. Niemi, and G. Whitten. 1994. "The Two Faces of Tactical Voting," *British Journal of Political Science* 24: 549–57.

Franklin, M., and C. Wlezien. 1997. "The Responsive Public: Issue Salience, Policy Change, and Preferences for European Unification," *Journal of Theoretical Politics* 9: 347–63.

Galli, E., and S. P. S. Rossi. 2002. "Political Budget Cycles: The Case of the Western German Länder," *Public Choice* 110: 283–303.

Golden, D. G., and J. M. Poterba. 1980. "The Price of Popularity: The Political Business Cycle Reexamined," *American Journal of Political Science* 24: 696–714.

Haverland, M. 2001. "Another Dutch Miracle? Explaining Dutch and German Pension Trajectories," *Journal of European Social Policy* 11: 308–23.

Heath, A., and G. Evans. 1994. "Tactical Voting: Concepts, Measurement and Findings," *British Journal of Political Science* 24: 557–61.

Hemerijck, A. 2003. "A Paradoxical Miracle: The Politics of Coalition Government and Social Concertation in Dutch Welfare Reform," in *Konzertierung, Verhandlungsdemokratie und Reformpolitik im Wohlfahrtsstaat*, S. Jochem and N. A. Siegel (eds.). Opladen: Leske and Budrich, pp. 232–70.

Hibbs, D. A. 1977. "Political Parties and Macroeconomic Policy," *American Political Science Review* 71: 1467–87.

Hibbs, D. A. 1982. "On Demand for Economic Outcomes: Macroeconomic Performance and Mass Political Support in the United States, Great Britain and Germany," *Journal of Politics* 44: 426–62.

Iyengar, S., D. R. Kinder, M. D. Peters, and J. A. Krosnick. 1984. "The Evening News and Presidential Evaluations," *Journal of Personality and Social Psychology* 46: 778–87.

Jacobson, G. C. 1983. *The Politics of Congressional Elections*. Boston: Little, Brown.

Kahneman, D., and A. Tversky. 1979. "Prospect Theory: An Analysis of Decision Under risk," *Econometrica* 47: 263–91.

Karp, J. A., J. Vowles, S. A. Banducci, and T. Donovan. 2002. "Strategic Voting, Party Activity, and Candidate Effects: Testing Explanations for Split Voting in New Zealand's New Mixed System," *Electoral Studies* 21: 1–22.

Key, V. O. Jr. 1966. *The Responsible Electorate: Rationality in Presidential Voting, 1936–1960*. Cambridge: Harvard University Press.

Kiewiet, D. R. 1983. *Macroeconomics and Micropolitics: The Electoral Effects of Economic Issues*. Chicago: University of Chicago Press.

Kinder, D. R. 1993. "Coming to Grips with the Holy Ghost," in *Experimental Foundations of Political Science*, D. R. Kinder, and T. R. Palfrey (eds.). Ann Arbor: University of Michigan Press, pp. 1–52.

Kinder, D. R., and D. R. Kiewiet. 1979. "Economic Discontent and Political Behavior: The Role of Personal Grievances and Collective Economic Judgments in Congressional Voting," *American Journal of Political Science* 23: 495–527.

Kinder, D. R., and D. R. Kiewiet. 1981. "Sociotropic Politics: The American Case," *British Journal of Political Science* 11: 129–61.

Klingemann, H.-D., R. Hofferbert, and I. Budge. 1994. *Parties, Policies and Democracy*. Boulder, CO: Sage.

Kramer, G. 1983. "The Ecological Fallacy Revisited: Aggregate- versus Individual-Level Findings on Economics and Elections, and Sociotropic Voting," *American Political Science Review* 77: 92–111.

Krause, G. A. 1997. "Voters, Information Heterogeneity, and the Dynamics of Aggregate Economic Expectations," *American Journal of Political Science* 41: 1170–1200.

Kroh, M. 2003. "Parties, Politicians and Policies. Orientations of Vote Choice across Voters and Contexts." PhD dissertation, University of Amsterdam.

Kroh, M., W. van der Brug, and C. van der Eijk. Forthcoming. "Prospects for Electoral Change," in *European Elections and Domestic Politics. Lessons from the Past and Scenarios for the Future*, W. van der Brug and C. van der Eijk (eds.). Notre Dame, IN: University of Notre Dame Press.

Lewis-Beck, M. S. 1988. *Economics and Elections: The Major Western Democracies*. Ann Arbor: University of Michigan Press.

Lewis-Beck, M. S., and M. Paldam. 2000. "Economic Voting: An Introduction," *Electoral Studies* 19: 113–22.

Lewis-Beck, M. S., and M. Stegmaier. 2000. "Economic Determinants of Electoral Outcomes," *Annual Review of Political Science* 3: 183–219.

Lijphart, A. 1999. *Patterns of Democracy*. New Haven, CT: Yale University Press.

Lupia, A., and M. D. McCubbins. 1998. *The Democratic Dilemma. Can Citizens Learn What They Need to Know?* New York: Cambridge University Press.

Luskin, R. C. 1987. "Measuring Political Sophistication," *American Journal of Political Science* 31: 856–99.

Maas, K., M. Steenbergen, and W. Saris. 1990. "Vote Probabilities," *Electoral Studies* 9: 91–107.

MacDonald, S. E., O. Listhaug, and G. Rabinowitz. 1991. "Issues and Party Support in Multiparty Systems," *American Political Science Review* 85: 1107–32.

Mackuen, M. B., R.S. Erikson, and J. A. Stimson. 1992. "Peasants or Bankers? The American Electorate and the U.S. Economy," *American Political Science Review* 86: 597–611.

Mair, P. 2002a. "De eigenaardigheden van de Nederlanders. De verkiezingen van 2002 in een vergelijkend perspectief," *B en M Tijdschrift voor Beleid, Politiek en Maatschappij* 29: 160–3.

Mair, P. 2002b. "In the Aggregate: Mass Electoral Behaviour in Western Europe, 1950–2000," in *Comparative Democratic Politics. A Guide to Contemporary Theory and Research*, H. Keman (ed.). London: Sage, pp. 122–40.

Markus, G. B. 1988. "The Impact of Personal and National Economic Conditions on the Presidential Vote: A Pooled Cross-Sectional Analysis," *American Journal of Political Science* 32: 137–54.

Markus, G. B. 1992. "The Impact of Personal and National Economic Conditions on Presidential Voting, 1956–1988 (an Update)," *American Journal of Political Science* 36: 829–34.

Marsh, M. 1998. "Testing the Second-Order Election Model After Four European Elections," *British Journal of Political Science* 28: 591–607.

Marsh, M., and M. Franklin. 1996. "The Foundations: Unanswered Questions from the Study of European Elections, 1979–1994," in *Choosing Europe? The European Electorate and National Politics in the Face of Union*, C. van der Eijk, M. Franklin, et al. (eds.). Ann Arbor: University of Michigan Press, pp. 332–65.

Nadeau, R., and M. S. Lewis-Beck. 2001. "National Economic Voting in U.S. Presidential Elections," *Journal of Politics* 63: 159–81.

Nannestad, P., and M. Paldam. 1994. "The VP-Function: A Survey of the Literature on Vote and Popularity Functions After 25 Years," *Public Choice* 79: 213–45.

Nannestad, P., and M. Paldam. 1997. "The Grievance Asymmetry Revisited: A Micro Study of Economic Voting in Denmark, 1986–1992," *European Journal of Political Economy* 13: 81–99.

Nannestad, P., and M. Paldam. 2002. "The Cost of Ruling: a Foundation Stone for Two Theories," in *Economic Voting*, H. Dorussen and M. Taylor (eds.). London: Routledge, pp. 17–44.

Nickell, S., and J. van Ours. 1999. "The Netherlands and the United Kingdom: A European Unemployment Miracle?" Paper presented in Frankfurt at the Economic Policy Panel Meeting, April 9, 1999, and in Ottawa at the CSLS Conference on the Structural Aspects of Unemployment in Canada, April 23, 1999.

Niemi, R. G., G. Whitten, and M. N. Franklin. 1992. "Constituency Characteristics, Individual Characteristics and Tactical Voting in the 1987 British General Election," *British Journal of Political Science* 22: 229–54.

Nordhaus, W. D. 1975. "The Political Business Cycle," *The Review of Economic Studies* 42: 169–90.

Norpoth, H. 1996. "The Economy," in *Comparing Democracies: Elections and Voting in Global Perspective*, L. LeDuc, R. G. Niemi, and P. Norris (eds.). Thousand Oaks, CA: Sage, pp. 299–318.

Oppenhuis, E. 1995. *Voting Behavior in Europe. A Comparative Analysis of Electoral Participation and Party Choice*. Amsterdam: Het Spinhuis.

Oppenhuis, E., C. van der Eijk, and M. Franklin. 1996. "The Party Context: Outcomes," in *Choosing Europe? The European Electorate and National Politics in the Face of Union*, Cees van der Eijk and Mark Franklin (eds.). Ann Arbor: University of Michigan Press, pp. 287–305.

Ordeshook, P. C., and L. Zeng. 1997. "Rational Voters and Strategic Voting: Evidence from the 1968, 1980, and 1992 Elections," *Journal of Theoretical Politics* 9: 167–87.

Paldam, M. 1991. "How Robust Is the Vote Function? A Study of 17 Countries Over Four Decades," in *Economics and Politics: The Calculus of Support*, H. Norpoth, M. S. Lewis-Beck, and J.-D. Lafay (eds.). Ann Arbor: University of Michigan Press, pp. 9–31.

Paldam, M. 1997. "Political Business Cycles," in *Perspectives on Public Choice: A Handbook*, ed. D. Mueller. Cambridge: Cambridge University Press, pp. 342–70.

Pattie, C. J., and R. J. Johnston. 2001. "Routes to Party Choice: Ideology, Economic Evaluations and Voting at the 1997 British General Election," *European Journal of Political Research* 39: 373–89.

Popkin, S. 1991. *The Reasoning Voter*. Chicago: University of Chicago Press.

Powell, G. B., Jr. 2000. *Elections as Instruments of Democracy*. New Haven, CT: Yale University Press.

Powell, G. B., Jr., and B. G. Whitten. 1993. "A Cross-National Analysis of Economic Voting: Taking Account of the Political Context," *American Journal of Political Science* 37: 391–414.

Price, S., and D. Sanders. 1993. "Modeling Government Popularity in Postwar Britain: A Methodological Example," *American Journal of Political Science* 37: 317–34.

Price, S., and D. Sanders. 1994. "Party Support and Economic Perceptions in the UK: A Two-Level Approach," in *British Elections and Parties Yearbook*, eds. D. Broughton et al. London: Frank Cass, pp. 46–72.

Przeworski, A., and H. Teune. 1970. *The Logic of Comparative Social Inquiry*. New York: Wiley.

Rabinowitz, G., and S. MacDonald. 1989. "A Directional Theory of Issue Voting," *American Political Science Review* 83: 93–121.

Reif, K. (ed.). 1984. *European Elections 1979/81 and 1984. Conclusion and Perspectives from Empirical Research*. Berlin: Quorum.

Reif, K., and H. Schmitt. 1980. "Nine Second-Order National Elections. A Conceptual Framework for the Analysis of European Election Results," *European Journal for Political Research* 8: 3–44.

Robinson, W. S. 1950. "Ecological Correlations and the Behavior of Individuals," *American Sociological Review* 15: 351–7.

Royed, T. J., K. M. Leyden, and S. A. Borrelli. 2000. "Is 'Clarity of Responsibility' Important for Economic Voting? Revisiting Powell and Whitten's Hypothesis," *British Journal of Political Science* 30: 669–98.

Sanders, D. 1996. "Economic Performance, Management Competence and the Outcome of the Next General Election," *Political Studies* 44: 203–31.

Sanders, D. 1999. "Conservative Incompetence, Labour Responsibility, and the Feelgood Factor: Why the Economy Failed to Save the Conservatives in 1997," *Electoral Studies* 18: 251–70.

Saris, W. E. (ed.). 1988. *Variation in Response Function: A Source of Measurement Error.* Amsterdam: SRF.

Sartori, G. 1976. *Parties and Party Systems. A Framework for Analysis.* Cambridge: Cambridge University Press.

Schmitt, H., and K. Reif. 2003. "Der Hauptwahlzyklus und die Ergebnisse von Nebenwahlen: Konzeptuelle und empirische Rekonstruktionen am Beispiel der Europawahlen in Wahlzyklus der Bundesrepublik," in *Politbarometer*, A. M. Wuest (ed.). Opladen: Leske und Budrich, pp. 239–54.

Schmitt, H., and J. Thomassen (eds.) 1999. *Political Representation and Legitimacy in the European Union.* Oxford: Oxford University Press.

Sniderman, P. M. 1993. "The New Look in Public Opinion Research," in *Political Science: The State of the Discipline II*, A. W. Finifter (ed.). Washington, DC: The American Political Science Association, pp. 219–45.

Sniderman, P. M., R. A.Brody, and P. E.Tetlock (eds.). 1991. *Reasoning and Choice: Explorations in Political Psychology.* New York: Cambridge University Press.

Snijders, T. A. B., and R. J. Bosker. 1999. *Multilevel Analysis. An Introduction to Basic and Advanced Multilevel Modeling.* London: Sage.

Steenbergen, M. R., and B. S. Jones. 2002. "Modeling Multilevel Data Structures," *American Journal of Political Science* 46: 218–37.

Stevenson, R. T. (2002). "The Economy as Context: Indirect Links Between the Economy and Voters," in *Economic Voting*, H. Dorussen and M. Taylor (eds.). London: Routledge, pp. 45–65.

Stimson, J. A. 1985. "Regression in Space and Time: A Statistical Essay," *American Journal of Political Science* 29: 914–47.

Stoker, L., and J. Bowers. 2002. "Designing Multi-Level Studies: Sampling Voters and Electoral Contexts," in *The Future of Election Studies*, M. Franklin and C. Wlezien (eds.). Amsterdam: Pergamon, pp. 77–110.

Thomassen, J. (ed.)., 2005. *The European Voter.* Oxford: Oxford University Press.

Tillie, J. 1995. *Party Utility and Voting Behavior.* Amsterdam: Het Spinhuis.

Train, K. E. 2003. *Discrete Choice Methods with Simulation.* Cambridge: Cambridge University Press.

Treisman, D., and V. Gimpelson. 2001. "Political Business Cycles and Russian Elections, or the Manipulations of 'Chudar,'" *British Journal of Political Science* 31: 225–46.

Tufte, E. 1978. *Political Control of the Economy*. Princeton: Princeton University Press.

Visser, J., and A. Hemerijck. 1997. *A Dutch Miracle: Job Growth, Welfare Reform and Corporatism in the Netherlands*. Amsterdam: Amsterdam University Press.

Whitten, G., and H. D. Palmer. 1999. "Cross-National Analyses of Economic Voting," *Electoral Studies* 18: 49–67.

Wilkin, S., B. Haller, and H. Norpoth. 1997. "From Argentina to Zambia – A World-Wide Test of Economic Voting," *Electoral Studies* 16: 301–16.

Wlezien, C. 1995. "The Public as Thermostat: Dynamics of Preferences for Spending," *American Journal of Political Science* 39: 981–1000.

Wlezien, C. 2004. "Patterns of Representation: Dynamics of Public Preferences and Policy," *The Journal of Politics* 66: 1–24.

Wlezien, C., and R.S. Erikson. 2002. "The Timeline of Presidential Election Campaigns," *The Journal of Politics* 64: 969–93.

Wlezien, C., M. Franklin, and D. Twiggs. 1997. "Economic Perceptions and Vote Choice: Disentangling the Endogeneity," *Political Behavior* 19: 7–17.

Zaller, J. R. 1992. *The Nature and Origins of Mass Opinion*. Cambridge: Cambridge University Press.

Zaller, J. R. 2002. "The Statistical Power of Election Studies to Detect Media Exposure Effects in Political Campaigns," *Electoral Studies* 21: 297–329.

Zaller, J. R. 2005. "Floating Voters in U.S. Presidential Elections 1948–2000," in *Studies in Public Opinion: Attitudes, Nonattitudes, Measurement Error, and Change*, W. E. Saris and P. M. Sniderman (eds.). Princeton: Princeton University Press, pp. 166–214.

Index